PATTI MAGUIR
ROXANE BEA

MW01088463

What Would
MONICA
Do?

Consolation, hope, and inspiration in the spirit
of St. Monica for those bearing the cross of
a loved one who is away from the Faith

ASCENSION
West Chester, PA

Excerpts from the English translation of the *Catechism of the Catholic
Church* for use in the United States of America © 1994 United States
Catholic Conference, Inc.–Libreria Editrice Vaticana. Used with
permission. English translation of the *Catechism of the Catholic Church:
Modifications from the Editio Typica* © 1997 United States Conference of
Catholic Bishops–Libreria Editrice Vaticana.

Unless otherwise noted, Scripture passages are from the Revised Standard
Version–Second Catholic Edition © 2006 by the Division of Christian
Education of the National Council of the Churches of Christ in the United
States of America. Used by permission. All rights reserved.

Ascension
PO Box 1990
West Chester, PA 19380

1-800-376-0520
ascensionpress.com

Cover art: *St. Monica, Tears of the Heart,* used with permission by
artist Jill Metz (Fort Wayne, Indiana)

Cover design: Rosemary Strohm

Printed in the United States of America
22 23 24 25 26 5 4 3 2 1

ISBN 978-1-954881-52-5 (paperback)
ISBN 978-1-954881-53-2 (e-book)

About the Cover Art

Depicting a saint who lived long before
photographic images existed is a unique challenge.

Jill Metz, the mixed media artist who created the cover art
St. Monica, Tears of the Heart, has been painting saintly icons
since she felt a call from God to do so shortly after she converted
to the Catholic Faith. Jill takes special care to discover an
accurate image of the saint, spending time in deep prayer prior
to composing sacred art. The image on the cover is how she
visualized St. Monica in prayer.

This rendition matches what the authors' research
revealed about what Monica may have looked like given
the characteristics of the Berber people of North Africa
in the fourth century.

For our husbands and children, each of whom has given our hearts an earthly place to call home. May the roots of our love and prayers grow deep within you and be an ongoing nourishment as we reach toward eternity in all our unique ways together.

CONTENTS

Introduction

With a pagan husband whose beliefs were far from the Catholic Faith, it was no surprise to Monica when her oldest son, Augustine, turned away from the Church. At college, this bright student had fallen for a "New Age"-like philosophy, and he would later return home accompanied by his girlfriend and their young son.

It is a story of yesterday ... and of today. Though the events of her life occurred sixteen centuries ago, the happy ending to St. Monica's story following many years of praying for her son has inspired countless parents over the years to plead for her intercession when their own children have left the Faith.

In the Church, the body of Christ, time and space converge. Though the modern and ancient worlds vary greatly in many ways, the hearts and souls of parents praying for their beloved children are the same yesterday, today, and tomorrow.

What Would Monica Do? brings past and present together as we journey through the story of St. Monica while going deeper into our own faith. Once a child no longer looks to us for answers or follows our suggestions, our best course of action becomes simply seeking to grow in our own holiness as we pray for them. From that vantage point, we can follow St. Monica's lead to join forces ever stronger with God and our faith.

We begin by introducing you to St. Monica, and to us, the authors. We never dreamed of writing such a book, but here we are. And here you are with us. So, too, is St. Monica. Ultimately, her prayers were answered beyond her own wildest dreams—though not quickly, and not in the way she had imagined. Still, God's grace bore fruit in his time, and we now have St. Monica to accompany us as we consider our own family situations amid the challenges in our Church and culture today.

We will then contemplate some of our own mistakes, moving into understanding and healing as we walk alongside our children as they tread paths we had not envisioned.

Finally, we will gain encouragement through stories, promises from Scripture, and devotions that take us deeper into divine consolation and spiritual empowerment.

Throughout, we will "drop in" on fourth-century Christendom, the era of Monica and Augustine, a time not so unlike our own, when sinners and saints mingled. Then, as now, despite worldly confusion and unrest, the God of life could be found in every corner—and in the heart of every worried parent open to his calling.

We will also get glimpses into the lives of several families, seeking to gain wisdom from their experiences. Though every family is unique, sharing our journeys can help us come closer to understanding, as well as find connection and consolation in knowing that we are not alone.

PART I

PART III

1

Survey Says … They Don't Even Care If God Exists

According to a 2021 survey conducted by Arizona Christian University, forty-one percent of millennials "don't know if God exists, don't care if God exists, or don't believe that God exists."[1] While that number surprised us, as mothers of millennials, we have experienced this sad reality within our own families. We suspected that we were not alone. But a particular comment posted online with this survey challenged our sensibilities: "It's the parents' fault!" *Ouch.*

It is easy to blame parents for the attitudes and practices of their children, both positive and negative, but such an overarching judgment is unfair. We personally know several holy priests whose parents did not even attempt to raise them in the Catholic Faith, as well as other individuals who have rejected God despite living in a faith-filled home and attending Catholic schools or being homeschooled.

Yet, as parents, it is hard to avoid the question, "Where did we go wrong?" All of us could benefit from a serious examination of conscience. We will undoubtedly discover things we could have done better, without needing to accept the harsh, smug judgments of others. Most of us thought that if we did all we could to hand on the Faith to our children, our efforts would be absorbed and bear fruit. And they did … in the lives of some. For others, not so much. To those who see the Catholic Faith as fundamental to achieving the goal of our earthly lives, this can be a hard truth to accept.

Why do some children reject the Faith while others thrive in it? No one-size-fits-all answer exists. Every child can be influenced by factors outside of the home, including our increasingly secular, materialistic culture, and each has free will. It is foolish to lay all the blame at the feet of parents. The Bible itself is filled with individuals who made bad choices: Adam and Eve, God's first children, disobeyed him; Peter denied even knowing Jesus; Judas betrayed him for thirty pieces of silver; and, during Jesus' passion, all of the apostles except John ran away and hid. So other influences are at work in our children's choices; it is not all due to parenting.

On day 98 of Ascension's *Bible in a Year* podcast, in discussing the story of the prophet Samuel, Fr. Mike Schmitz notes that "every generation has to choose [God] for themselves."[2] Though Samuel was a devout man and a prophet of the Lord, his own sons fell gravely short, shirking the righteous path of God despite having been raised in his truth. Likewise, our children can, independent of us, ultimately choose to accept or reject God. After all, many other influences in their lives can also sway them.

The same study mentioned earlier found the current generation of young adults, the millennials (born between 1984 and 2002), are less likely to consider themselves Christians—and even less likely to agree with the "Golden Rule" ("treat others as you would have them treat you")—than previous generations. They are also more likely to want to get even when they have been wronged.

Sociologist George Barna notes that due to these new "millennial-driven" attitudes, core institutions, including church and basic ways of life, are being radically redefined. Though the overall commitment to organized religion among young adults began diminishing in the late 1960s, "Millennials have clearly gone farther than any recent generation in cutting ties with traditional Christian views and normative biblical teaching."[3]

This phenomenon is something of a "reverse Exodus"—rather than an exodus to freedom in the Lord, it is an exodus of young adults away from God. As Barna notes, "The influence of the Christian church has diminished while the influence of arts, entertainment, and news media has exploded."[4] The Internet, particularly social media, seems to have more influence over our children these days than parents do. It is a mass cultural tide of faithlessness, or at least a departure from the faith of their roots. Millennials are "far more likely" than previous generations to define success in life as "happiness, personal freedom, or productivity without oppression," as well as consider abortion and premarital sex as morally acceptable.[5] Fewer are inclined to marry and raise children.[6] As we have seen, many of them either do not know if God exists, or simply do not care.

Given the prevalence of such modern, godless attitudes, a particular, possible consequence tugs daily on our hearts as parents: *Will our children make it to heaven?* We have much reason to hope. While sociological studies can reveal what ails a society, they cannot account for the hidden movements of God; they point out trends, but they cannot calculate the effects of prayer and the Holy Spirit on souls. The Lord remains at work in the lives of our children, even if they have wandered away from him. As Jesus himself says, "What man of you, having a hundred sheep, if he has lost one of them, does not leave the ninety-nine in the wilderness, and go after the one which is lost, until he finds it?" (Luke 15:4). Despite dire statistics, we should never lose hope.

In this book, we will introduce you to a mutual friend of ours—Monica—a mother, wife, and grandmother, who has given us hope and inspiration to lean upon. She has much to teach us on how to endure in the midst of our broken lives. We invite you to enter into this circle of friendship as we continue learning together and praying for one another.

As we embark on this journey, we reflect on another thought Fr. Mike shared regarding the Samuel story: "There's something so devastating when we don't see the faith in our kids. We need to pray for those with loved ones who've turned away," he said, adding a postscript from God, clarifying what often feels like rejection from our children: "They're not rejecting you. They're rejecting me." To this, he adds God's helpful suggestion: "Let *me* guide and guard."

Letting go and allowing God to take over can be the hardest step in finding freedom. We have discovered, however, that in clinging to his power and glory, we can make powerful leaps in our faith journey—and that this, more than anything, will benefit our children. Though we are not in control of the faith lives of our children, we can work on our own relationship with God. The more we align our prayers with the Lord and our intercessors in heaven, the more we can grow closer to his heart— and help draw others to him.

2

A Friendship That Started with Tea

It all began when both of us were mentioned in a Mother's Day article written by a mutual acquaintance, Donna Marie Cooper O'Boyle. Despite living on opposite sides of North Dakota, a family connection frequently brings us together several times a year. After discovering each other from Donna's article, we began meeting for either tea (Patti's preference) or coffee (Roxane's preference). But what began as a casual meeting in a tea shop progressed to us sharing our common professional interests and our family stories.

With a total of fifteen children between us, we found many connecting points as moms whose Catholic Faith frequently places us at odds with the culture. Not surprisingly, we began swapping prayer requests for our children's spiritual journeys. The Faith we diligently had tried to impart— the same Faith we had both slipped from in our own younger years but now embraced—has not held firm with all our children.

As our prayers and ponderings heightened, we welcomed a heavenly friend to our chats—St. Monica. "Walking" with her offers us communion with another anguished mother, but one whose story ended happily. Not only did Monica's wayward son Augustine experience a profound conversion, but he became a great saint and one of the most influential theologians in Christian history. For seventeen years, however, his rebellious life deeply grieved Monica, who had conscientiously tried to impart to him the joys of the Catholic Faith.

In many ways, St. Augustine's years of waywardness helped St. Monica reach heroic sanctity. Through our own disappointments and struggles, we too can increase in humility and holiness. By tapping into the lives of saints such as Monica, along with the stories of Scripture and other Catholic teachers, rather than give in to worry, we can enter a life of joy as we wait and pray for our children.

To be honest, this is not a book either of us sought to write. Though it had tugged at us for a while, we both resisted the inspiration. The topic of our children's struggles with their faith exposes some of our deepest vulnerabilities and most pressing sorrows. If given the choice, we would have gladly passed on carrying this cross. In the end, though, we decided to move forward, having discovered a gift in allowing our suffering to become a source of consolation for others. In these pages, we will map out a course of love, support, and conversion as we ask, "What would Monica do?"

Before we introduce you to this fascinating woman, let us share a little about who we are and why we are here.

PATTI'S STORY: CASTING A NET

Faith is a gift. But it is also a choice. How else can children who learned and loved the Catholic Faith slip away from it? In the end, faith is *personal*, so parents cannot force it on their children. *Darn.*

My husband, Mark, and I have been blessed with ten children. They were all raised Catholic, of course, and loved their faith, often going over and above anything we asked of them spiritually. All are now adults. While many still treasure the Faith of their childhood, others do not. So, same parents, mixed results. I had expected "one hundred percent faithfulness" among my children. I still pray and hope for it.

When people ask me how I am doing, I say, "Great!" And I mean it. God is good, all the time. I appreciate his many gifts, from having a television talk show and writing career—which I use to serve him and enjoy myself at the same time—to modern conveniences, a wonderful Catholic parish, and the blessing of a husband who shares my commitment to the Faith. So, in that respect, I am doing fantastic—except for the fact that some of my children are not living up to the promises they made at Confirmation. That part is *not* fantastic.

Mark and I met in the Marshall Islands, Micronesia, when we served in the Peace Corps. At the time, we were both "somewhat" Catholic. We had an ill-formed faith that simmered on the back burner, but life conspired to heighten our spiritual focus. When Mark lost his radio job in Montana while I was pregnant with our fourth child (with no insurance, by the way), we became inspired by good books, reacquainted with Our Lady of Fatima, learned about Our Lady of Guadalupe, and started praying the Rosary. Together, this set into motion a deepening of our Catholic faith.

Soon, a month before his unemployment compensation ran out, Mark received a job offer from a radio station in Bismarck, North Dakota. Interestingly, he had not even applied for the job; he received the offer through word of mouth when the station manager was looking for a radio newsman. God had answered our prayer to move to a good place to raise our family and grow spiritually. When we moved to Bismarck in 1990, it had many active Catholic parishes and has really blossomed as a diocese in the years since. From what my husband and I see in our travels, it is possible that a higher percentage of Catholics attend daily Mass in the Diocese of Bismarck than anywhere else in the country. Such Mass attendance has surely contributed to thriving vocations, many hours of Eucharistic Adoration, long lines for the sacrament of Reconciliation, and to the lively faith of our community.

Our fourth son was born four months after we arrived in Bismarck. His birthday is May 13, 1990 (the Feast of Our Lady of Fatima), which is also Mark's birthday. And they were both born on Mother's Day. *Happy Birthday, Mark, from God*. It was truly an answer to his prayers. You see, I was scheduled for a tubal ligation and backed out the day before surgery because I had a bad feeling. A few weeks later, I was pregnant.

As we strove to live the Catholic Faith, the blessings were many. For nineteen years, we homeschooled our children through middle school, then sent them to the local Catholic high school. Our eldest son attended public high school beginning in tenth grade before we had made the commitment and sacrifice for tuition to use the Catholic school. While they were in high school, I watched all the children practice their faith on their own. One child on the speech team told me after an event, "Mom, I told a friend of mine on the team that I always pray before competing.

He said, 'I do the same thing. Let's pray together.' So, we did." Of course, I loved hearing that!

Although all our children graduated from high school strong in the Catholic Faith, not all have gone the distance. After they left home, some began drifting away. Mark and I wondered, *What could we have done differently? Did we push too hard? Did we not push hard enough?*

One morning, while praying for my children after Mass, I perceived God saying, "Your prayers are casting a net. When they come back, they will not come back alone." It was a powerful thought that seemed to come to me from the Lord. Since then, I have stopped wondering *why* and just pray for my children. After all, God knows the situation; he wants them to be in union with him. As parents, we can now pray, fast, and offer sacrifices for God to give them the graces they need according to his timing.

ROXANE'S STORY: THE SHINING JEWEL

I received the jewel of the Catholic Faith from my parents at my baptism on September 12, 1968, in a small church in Lovell, Wyoming, where I was born. Of course, all I know of that day comes from photos of me in my baptismal gown, being held by my Aunt Anne, and the waters of sacramental grace and life being poured over my tiny head by the priest.

As a child, I would pore over those pictures, wondering what it was like to be a baby and who the priest was. One day, decades later, I was moved with emotion looking at them, understanding just how blessed I was on that day. I was filled with such gratitude that I sat down and wrote my parents a letter that began, "Thank you so much for raising me in the Catholic Faith!"

Leading up to that moment, though, there were times I questioned my faith. Though I came from a long line of faith-filled Catholics (my father was in the seminary for a while), my college years had brought queries from others that stumped me. It did not help that someone close and dear to me, whom I admired, decided to leave the Faith after her first year attending a Catholic university. Her departure confused me, but I would soon come up against some of the same roadblocks.

Looking back at my college years and beyond, I see how God stayed in pursuit of me, holding out this treasure of his Church. Deep inside, I knew that there was beauty to the Faith, but I did not understand enough what the Church was offering to fully embrace it. As I studied to be a journalist, I was unsure whether the world and the Catholic Faith I had grown up in could meld.

Thankfully, I heeded my father's final piece of advice as I walked out the door for college—to attend Mass at the campus Newman Center. The priest there turned out to be an incredible and faithful servant of Christ. His invigorating sermons, often focused on the Beatitudes, and vibrant preaching about the life of Jesus brought something alive in my soul. Though I remained somewhat fickle in my faith, I stayed connected to the Church.

My college sweetheart, who later became my husband, though, was not Catholic. So I didn't want to become "too Catholic" for fear I would lose him. I sometimes felt like a "spiritual boomerang," at one moment close to the Church, and suddenly flying away from it in confusion the next. Soon after we got married, however, realizing that I still had wounds that needed healing—and that my husband was not meant to fill that gap—I flung myself at the Lord's feet and committed myself to him and his Church.

I was determined then to learn everything possible about the Catholic Faith. I had come to see it as a brilliant jewel—one that had been given to me at Baptism, but which I had often shirked for seemingly more dazzling pursuits. Now, however, I could not get enough of the Church's exquisite teachings, starting with the just-released *Catechism of the Catholic Church*. Eventually, my newfound enthusiasm piqued the interest of my husband, and three years into our marriage, he entered the RCIA program and joined the Catholic Church nine months later.

Since I had come to know well my deficiencies and complete dependence on God, I came to see that the only way I could become a better wife and mother would be to stay near the Church. I did not want my children to experience the same devastating lack of catechesis I had. Recognizing now the jewel of the Catholic Faith, I anticipated how blessed our children would be to have this gift, too.

I did everything I could to keep my faith strong so that I could hand this precious gift down to my children in the best way possible. I thought that if I just read the right books, did the right things, and helped our children through their sacraments the right way, they would be on their way to a vibrant, lifelong faith, never to turn back. When I discovered that their path was their own—and that they might go through periods of struggle with their faith—it was, at first, devastating.

The brilliant jewel of the Catholic Faith is forever vibrant. If we let it, though, the world can cloak its brilliance with its many distractions. I do not have the ability to get inside my kids' heads and hearts to know if they are seeing and appreciating this precious jewel as they should, or from the same angle as I am. Perhaps they see tarnished edges that I do not; perhaps clouds from their vantage point have yet to lift. Ultimately, the intricacies of their souls are God's terrain alone.

God promises to bless those who turn to him. I know that he is good, merciful, and tender-hearted toward my family—and every family—and that he will never give up on them. After all, I know he has never given up on me, despite the many times I have faltered.

So, as I gaze upon this jewel, now near to my heart, I pray that someday it will draw those whom I love nearer to it. My prayer is that they see that its brilliance and beauty are meant for them too. Until then, I will do as God asks and love them and others the best I can, taking advice from the saints, like St. Pio of Pietrelcina (Padre Pio), who lovingly admonishes us to "pray, hope, and don't worry."

Indeed, the communion of saints stands ready, beckoning us on to the path ahead—not one promised to be smooth, but one marked by encouraging road signs held steady by our holy heroes assuring us that "with God all things are possible" (Matthew 19:26).

Among them, one saint beams particularly bright and hopeful: a mother named Monica. Let us meet this inspiringly tenacious, faith-filled woman and learn her secrets for a life well-lived.

3

Who Was St. Monica?

Due to the genetic influence of European invaders, clear blue eyes, a complexion lighter in tone than darker-skinned Africans without this genetic blend, and a slight but sturdy build are features that probably describe St. Monica, as these traits were common to the Berber people of North Africa in the fourth century. Of course, this is only conjecture based on historical genealogy.

A more telling snapshot of St. Monica can be seen in her clear eyes when they filled easily with tears for love of God and her family; in her frame, though slight, when it carried heavy burdens without bending; and in her sharp mind, her undeterred will, and her unfailing heart.

Most of what we know about Monica comes through the writings of her son Augustine, who is perhaps the most influential Christian theologian in history. His most referenced work, *Confessions*, was largely written as an outpouring of grief following his mother's death in AD 387 at the age of fifty-six. If not for this, Monica likely would have disappeared into the mists of history.

As St. Augustine writes in *Confessions*, "She was brought up to reverence you [God], schooled by the crook of your Christ, the shepherd's care of your only Son, in a faithful family that was a sound limb of your Church."[7] These are the very attributes that helped her tenaciously form her son, ultimately bringing his work to the far corners of the world and being named one of the thirty-six Doctors of the Church. Through Augustine, Monica has been made visible to us. By delving more deeply into her life, we can nurture a friendship with her and count her as an intercessor, abiding in heaven, who can guide us to the same eternal destiny.

MONICA IN SPIRIT

We might say that St. Monica is everything we want to be—a saint who prayed unfailingly for the conversion and salvation of her son. Though Augustine fell away from the Faith in spectacular fashion, he also returned in the grandest of ways. A brilliant, prolific writer, his most famous works, *City of God* and *Confessions*, are still in print more than fifteen hundred years later. He and his writings are revered by Catholics and Protestants alike.

But Augustine's remarkable story began with his mother's prayers.

Fr. Jacques Philippe, a retreat leader and author on prayer and Catholic spirituality whose books have sold more than a million copies in twenty-four languages, explains: "The life of prayer is the source of infinite riches. It transforms us within, sanctifies us, heals us, helps us to know and love God, makes us fervent and generous in love of neighbor. Provided they persevere, those who commit themselves to a life of prayer can be absolutely sure of receiving all this and more."[8] As we will see, St. Monica has much to teach us regarding steadfast prayer.

THE SAME THEN AS NOW

As the book of Ecclesiastes tells us, "There is nothing new under the sun" (Ecclesiastes 1:9). Though the particulars of life have changed throughout history, human nature—with all its flaws and fickleness—remains the same. The challenges of relationships—the challenge to love—remain the same.

While ancient times were different in many ways, Monica faced difficulties in her marriage, relationships, and parenting that mirror our lives today. She had plenty of reasons to become angry and bitter, but instead she forged a path of love that has been memorialized for the ages.

MORE OF HER STORY

Monica was born in the year AD 331 in Thagaste, Numidia (present-day Algeria), northern Africa. The area had been conquered by Rome in

146 BC, when Roman legions destroyed the city of Carthage. The Christian communities in North Africa were among the earliest, appearing in the first or early second century. According to tradition, the evangelist St. Mark brought Christianity from Jerusalem to Alexandria on the Egyptian coast.

In *St. Monica: The Power of a Mother's Love*, historian Fr. Giovanni Falbo writes that "Monica grew up in an atmosphere that had seen the fervor of the first generations of Christians in Africa, who with their blood spilled during the persecutions both sowed and watered the seeds of Christianity."[9] He notes that the first North African martyrs, in AD 180, "displayed their Numidian spirit in their combination of simplicity and unshakeable determination; after courageously professing their faith and refusing to sacrifice to the gods, they were decapitated."[10]

Memories of this persecution and martyrdom two decades before Monica's birth were still strong among the people of her town and in her family. She received instruction in the Catholic Faith from her family's maid, who was something of a taskmaster who strove to instill a hardy faith in her students through challenging exercises. For instance, to strengthen her self-control, Monica was forbidden to drink anything between meals. When the teenage Monica was caught sneaking cups of wine, the embarrassment not only stopped her sneaking, but going forward, Monica drank wine in great moderation.

Girls of the time married young through arrangement by their parents. Her husband, Patricius, was much older and a pagan. Though equipped with some redeeming features, such as being hardworking and civic-minded, he had a violent temper and a wandering eye. Early in her marriage, Monica also had to contend with her cantankerous mother-in-law and the family servants who did not always treat her kindly. But Monica's loving nature won everyone over. Her prayers and example eventually converted her husband and mother-in-law to Christianity. Patricius died in 371, a year after his baptism.

ST. MONICA'S CHILDREN

Monica and Patricius had three children who survived infancy—two sons, Augustine and Navigius, and a daughter, Perpetua, according to tradition (she is not named in Augustine's writings).

Monica instructed Augustine in the Christian religion and taught him how to pray. As a child, blessed salt was placed on his tongue. He thus formally became a catechumen, i.e., he was enrolled in the process of baptismal preparation. Once while still of school age, he became dangerously ill. He desired baptism and his mother prepared everything for the ceremony. Then suddenly he grew better, and his baptism was put off.

His baptism was deferred lest he should stain his baptismal innocence by falling into sin before reaching maturity (which is exactly what happened). This was an example of the practice of that era to defer baptism for fear that the recipient would fall into sin before coming fully to realize the great importance of the Sacrament. As a bishop in his later years, Augustine denounced this custom of deferring Baptism as being very ill advised. He preached strongly against it.[11]

As a young man, Augustine, by his own later admission, was lazy and wayward. He went off to study rhetoric in Carthage, but he returned home at seventeen upon his father's death. Monica was distressed to learn that Augustine had become a Manichaean while away at school. (Manichaeism was a heretical philosophy that combined elements of Iranian and Indian religion, along with Christianity, Buddhism, and Taoism.) He would be a follower of Manichaeism for the next eleven years.

When he returned home, Augustine was accompanied by his girlfriend, whose name is never mentioned, and their son. Understandably, this was a troubling situation for Monica on many fronts, as she had younger children in the household who did not need this kind of example. In her distress, she asked Augustine to leave. Later, though, Monica was inspired by what is believed to be a vision to reconcile with her son. So he returned home with his girlfriend, whom he was unable to marry due to social restrictions based on class differences, and his son, Adeodatus, which means "gift of God."

RENEWED HOPE

Monica, renewed with hope, continued her prayers and fasting for her son's return to the Catholic Faith as she kept close to him. She was able to keep her younger children on track, and she also instructed Augustine's girlfriend and son in Christianity.

In 383, at age twenty-nine, Augustine decided to go to Rome to teach rhetoric. Since her other children were now grown and out of the house, Monica planned on accompanying Augustine, but he deceived her, preferring to set out on his own, but not having the courage to tell her as much. He brought her to a chapel to pray and said he was going to say goodbye to a friend at the dock. Instead, he jumped on a ship bound for Rome with his girlfriend and young son. When Monica arrived at the dock and realized what had happened, she wailed aloud, heartbroken.

Monica eventually found her way to Rome. By the time she arrived there in 385, her son had left to teach in Milan. She managed to make it to Milan and moved in with Augustine. Given the difficulties in communication and travel at that time, Monica's success at tracking down her son is rather remarkable.

By this point, Augustine had become disillusioned with Manichaeism, but he was still searching. It was in Milan, at the church of St. John the Baptist, that Monica met the bishop of the city, St. Ambrose. They developed a quick rapport, and he became her spiritual director and an influence in Augustine's life. St. Ambrose had the answers—Catholic answers—that had eluded Augustine for so many years. As Augustine was drawn back, however, the issue of his girlfriend became an impediment since a social obstacle prevented him from marrying her. She returned to Africa, living out her life in a convent; Adeodatus, now a teenager, remained with Augustine. The parting was undoubtedly difficult for all.

Monica played an instrumental role in helping prepare Augustine and Adeodatus for Baptism, joining in their pre-sacramental philosophical discussions—even though her only education was a mind that had been sharpened through a well-formed faith in God. On Easter in the year 387, Augustine and his son were baptized by St. Ambrose. (About Adeodatus, Augustine writes that he had lived a life of such purity that no one needed to worry about his eternal salvation.)

MONICA'S TEARS

Monica's tears show up in a direct way in Augustine's *Confessions* when he relates how she brought her concerns for him to an unnamed bishop. "The bishop refused to speak to Augustine because he found him to be arrogant and proud, and unwilling to listen. That did not satisfy Monica so she continued to bug the bishop until in exasperation, he told her that a child of so many tears would not be lost. Perhaps he just wanted to get rid of her. But Monica took the bishop's words as a prophecy and continued with renewed strength in her hope that Augustine would come to the truth."[12]

JUSTIFIABLE TEARS

Monica's profusion of tears, now immortalized in those earlier days of mothering her young adult son, seem justifiable enough, and all too human. She had already been dealing with a feisty pagan husband and mother-in-law who often challenged her faith. Seeing her brilliant son also fall to the world's wooing was just too much.

Augustine would look back on his mother's tears and describe them as "rivers flowing down" from her eyes, "by which, before [God] and in my behalf, she daily watered the ground beneath her face." Given Augustine's eventual and fervent conversion, those tears now remind us that our pleas, when we cry out to God in sadness, do not fall upon deaf ears.

Through her life's mission, St. Monica and her tears invite us to let down our guard at times and bring our sorrows to the Lord. For not a drop of our tears is wasted. The tears we cry for our children are especially precious to God, for he gave us our children as gifts, and the tears we shed in their name reveal our love for them. God promises that if we wait in trust and fidelity, our tears will be replaced someday with joy. "You have turned my mourning into dancing; you have loosed my sackcloth and clothed me with gladness" (Psalm 30:11).

MONICA'S DEATH

Six months later, Monica joined Augustine and Adeodatus on a mission to spread the gospel to Africa, but she died at the port of Ostia, Italy, as they prepared to embark. While Adeodatus wept at her death, Augustine held back his own tears until he was alone. The journey to North Africa was postponed, and father and son spent a year together in Rome. Adeodatus then accompanied his father back to Tagaste, where Augustine began a lay Christian community. His early writings share some of the dialogues with his son, who was obviously as gifted intellectually as his father. In 390, Adeodatus died at the same age that Augustine had been at his birth—seventeen. Greatly saddened at his son's death, Augustine grew even deeper in his Catholic faith, eventually becoming a priest and, five years later, a bishop.

The rest, as they say, is history. Augustine became a highly regarded Catholic of his time, staunchly defending the Faith far and wide through his preaching and writings. He reached the heights of heroic sanctity, and he was canonized by popular acclaim soon after his death (this was centuries before the Church instituted an official canonization process). He was named a Doctor of the Church by Pope Boniface VIII in 1298. Undoubtedly, his mother's persistent prayers and witness played a significant role in his conversion and sanctification. Even Augustine's famous line, "You have made us for Yourself, and our heart is restless until it rests in You," reveals Monica's heart—the mother who would not rest until her son was united with God in the true Faith.[13] We can learn much from her example—and rely on her intercession in our own struggles with children who are away from the Church.

4

Feelings of Failure, Grief That Is Real

When children leave the Catholic Faith, a dream we as parents have been holding tenderly in our hearts seems to have died. Within this dream, we had a vision of a life of profound joy for our children in the love of Jesus and his Church. By living their faith, we saw their lives filled with meaning and fulfillment, even in times of suffering. When we realize this dream is not being fulfilled at present, strong emotions can follow—emotions we were not prepared to feel and do not want to face.

We now begin with one of several personal journeys we will see throughout this book. The following story is from Rose, one of the growing number of parents today whose expectations for her child did not play out as she had hoped. Later, we will discover that, despite such disappointments, new pathways can emerge, as we discover the stories of our children, buoyed by our prayers, are still unfolding.

ROSE'S STORY

When Rose and her husband were first married, she was still in college, and he was working. "We really had nothing," she recounts. Their first Labor Day together, they drove several hundred miles to visit a relative, and though they had enough money to get there, they ran short on cash for the return trip. "Thankfully, we had some pop bottles in the back of the car. At ten cents a bottle, we were able to sell them to recycling for $2.60—just enough to get us home."

And then there was the time her husband worked for a farmer who ended up giving the couple half a cow for Christmas. "Despite being poor, we ate like kings and queens every night, eating steaks," Rose says, delightedly. "We would go to dollar-movie night at the theater and on certain nights, eat free tacos at a little place near our home. Those times, hard as they were, built great memories."

She likes sharing these stories with her adult, married daughters, reminding them that through faith, suffering can bring a couple even closer together, because "at the end of that suffering, those times become something you have made it through together." But Rose says nothing could have prepared her for the deepest suffering she and her husband would experience: that of watching their oldest daughter leave the Church.

It is a heartache she does not feel comfortable sharing with many. "That suffering runs so deep, and mostly, is held within our hearts," Rose says. "It is not something you can really voice most of the time, so you stay silent, and, for the most part, just carry it with you."

Sometimes, Rose says she feels like a yo-yo because her daughter has returned to the Church several times for a spell, only to leave once again. "She has been so near, and then so far away, and I'm left standing still, wondering if the yo-yo will ever return permanently, as my mother-heart continually aches and breaks."

Her pain seems to echo that of another mother, Vicky, who describes her suffering related to her wandering child this way:

"Most days, I am OK. Life goes on despite our grief, right?" Vicky shares. "But there is a piece of my heart that is always broken. I continue to meet this grief, this sense of failure, over and over—and sometimes, when I least expect it, something will happen to trigger it. Maybe I will see someone at church that my child used to hang out with going up for Communion, and I again feel the loss. I have relatives and friends who seem to have intact families, with everyone still in the Church. I am happy for them, but I wonder what went wrong in my own family."

What happened? Every parent whose child has wandered away from Christ and his Church has asked this question, often without a clear answer coming back.

"We raised our kids in the Faith, and the girls would even come to daily Mass with me sometimes," Rose shares. "Both were very actively involved in the Church." She never dreamed either would walk away. "It seems like it should be straightforward. You just follow the rules, right? But their eyes can become set on different things, and they go about it their own way. Like any story of the soul, it can become complicated."

For a time after her marriage, Rose's oldest daughter even sang in the choir and seemed to be "on fire" for the Catholic Faith. She would assure her mom that her husband was going to convert. "We used to giggle about that," Rose says. "I would say, 'Well that means he's *convertible!*'"

However, that hopeful scenario has yet to play out. Rose senses he carries a wound of some kind, but she does not want to speculate too much and does not know for sure; the reason has never been verbalized or offered. Instead, it's become simply "part of the mystery" of the soul's journey, she says. But eventually, "rather than him drawing toward the Church, the two began attending a Protestant denomination, despite having baptized their four young kids Catholic."

Sometimes, memories enter in, and she tries putting the pieces together in her mind. One conversation Rose had with her daughter during one of her returns to the Catholic Faith continues to haunt her. "She told me about a dream she had surrounding the Eucharist, and it gripped me," Rose says, noting that the dream gave her hope. "I felt like what she was saying was that she had encountered Christ personally in the Eucharist in her dream, and I know God can use dreams like that to draw us closer." After hearing this, Rose says she remembers responding, "Do you know what's so exciting? There's no turning back!" But she will never forget her daughter's response. "She pulled back and looked at me with these big eyes, as if surprised by my words. I can only guess that maybe something was going on already at home—that she was already feeling like she might walk away."

ST. MONICA'S STORY

Sixteen centuries ago, Monica went through the same sense of disillusionment with Augustine. And it started with her dreams as a young mother that, for nearly two decades, seemed to have vanished altogether.

In his book *St. Monica: The Power of a Mother's Love*, Fr. Giovanni Falbo borrows an image from Augustine's own words from his *Confessions*, noting that "Augustine found his first catechist in [Monica]; from her he drew the name of Jesus Christ together with the milk that he sucked." Falbo imagines "the tenderness with which Monica, holding her baby on her lap, spoke to him of the things at the center of her life ... [the Christian faith] ... All of this came with a naturalness that imprinted the truth and beauty of a faith in a sweet and lasting way upon the heart of her son, molding him like clay."[14]

And yet, as he grew older, Augustine strayed, quite radically, from the exquisite molding Monica had tried to fashion and imbue in her son to make way for a life of deep contentment and holy living. Because of this, Monica grieved.

STAGES OF GRIEF

The grief experienced by parents of wandering children cuts to the center of our souls, often leaving us with an empty, hopeless feeling regarding our children's future. We can experience some of the traditional five "stages of grief" experienced by those who mourn the death of a loved one: Denial, anger, bargaining, depression, and acceptance. (Of course, we should never truly "accept" that our children are gone from the Faith for good; we simply need to accept that this is the current situation and continue praying that they return.) There is great pain and grief when we see our children no longer care about or participate in something we know to be so fundamentally important to their lives, both now and for eternity.

In addition to the typical stages of grief, parents of a wandering child might also experience feelings of failure and self-blame. This kind of grief can be like a pin that pricks us at the most inopportune moments and can even be accompanied by shame. Our children's departure is not just about them, but also points to us.

NO EMPTY PROMISES, BUT HOPE ALWAYS

But our sadness does not have to end in despair. Even if we cannot yet see the final result, we can hope in it with one another. By walking together through the hardships of this cross, we want to hold out a little light for you, and ourselves; one that can help us move along the path of hope, with Monica nearby offering her own light from her honored place in heaven. As Pope Francis has said,

> Faith is not a light which scatters all our darkness, but a lamp which guides our steps in the night and suffices for the journey. By contemplating Christ's union with the Father even at the height of his sufferings on the Cross, Christians learn to share in the same gaze of Jesus. Even death is illumined and can be experienced as the ultimate call to faith, the ultimate *Go forth from your land* (Gn. 12:1), the ultimate, 'Come!' spoken by the Father, to whom we abandon ourselves.[15]

By the end of this book, we hope to have equipped you with an eternal perspective that can help ease your worry and deepen your relationship with God. While there are no guarantees on how our own stories will end, the glorious ending of St. Monica's story gives us hope. As Falbo notes, the person of Christ to which Monica had introduced her son as an infant could not, despite all his wild wanderings, forget the picture she had helped paint in his soul: "He never forgot this name [of Jesus], even amid the darkest and stormiest moments of his life. When he was seemingly won over by the works of profane writers ... he never felt fully satisfied, because he did not find in them the name of Christ, which his mother's instruction had rooted deeply in his heart."[16]

Perhaps this is the first gleam of light we can shine on the path ahead. Like Monica, we have made an imprint on our children's hearts by presenting them a vision of the abundant life possible with Christ. In raising them up to God in Baptism, you gave them to God for anointing, not just for a day, but forever. Yes, they will have to make a choice and ascend to God fully on their own terms. But, dear parent, by doing what you could to give them this beautiful faith, even in your imperfections, you have planted seeds of life, and though still hidden in the soil, there they remain.

There is hope.

5

Unequally Yoked

Many Catholic families lack two parents who actively practice the Faith. Thus, the spouses can be said to be "unequally yoked"—one is Christian, the other is not. Handing down the Faith to our children becomes more difficult as they get older in the best of circumstances, but doing it alone makes the task all the more formidable.

Let's take a look at a few examples:

JACK'S STORY

Although he discerned a call to the priesthood while in high school, Jack decided to accept a scholarship and attend college first. He is now in his third year of seminary training. While he was still in high school, Jack's father left his mother. It was an ugly separation. His father became hostile to the Catholic Faith, and he has lived with several women over the past few years. His parents' divorce led Jack to spend many hours in Eucharistic Adoration, which undoubtedly helped foster his vocation.

Many of Jack's fellow seminarians are praying for his father's conversion. Jack's mother, Kim, remains a faithful Catholic, and she often spends time in Adoration seeking the Lord's comfort and help in forgiving her ex-husband. She hates what he has done to the family and the way he lives his life, but she prays for his conversion. It breaks Kim's heart that her children have had this brokenness forced upon them, but she turns to God with every fiber of her being, placing her family in his hands. She prays also that her other two children will remain in the Church and in thanksgiving for her son's powerful example.

SERVANT OF GOD ELISABETH LESEUR

Servant of God Elisabeth Leseur provides a beautiful example of how one might traverse a "chasm of faith" in a marriage, and the fruits of doing so. Born in Paris in 1866 to a wealthy family, she was a sickly child, and she would be plagued by illness for much of her life. Shortly before her marriage to Felix, a medical doctor, Elisabeth learned her fiancé was no longer practicing his Catholic faith. Soon, he became the editor of an anti-clerical, atheistic newspaper.

The natural tensions that arose from this spiritual divide inspired Elisabeth to go deeper into her faith. She diligently prayed for her husband's conversion and offered her sufferings up for this cause. Despite Felix's constant attacks on her faith, Elizabeth loved him, and she took her sadness directly to God in prayer. She drew the affections of many, who were influenced by her kindness in how she treated not only her husband, but others, always with charity, and focusing on redemptive suffering, as did Christ.

After her death at forty-seven, Felix discovered the diaries in which she had secretly recorded her conversations with God. So moved by her faith and love for him, Felix underwent a radical conversion, returned to the Church, and ended up becoming a Catholic priest, as detailed in the book *The Secret Diary of Elisabeth Leseur: The Woman Whose Goodness Changed Her Husband from Atheist to Priest*.

In *Thirty Days with Married Saints: A Catholic Couples' Devotional*, Kent and Caitlin Lasnoski look into the relationships of married saints who ranged from a union of two saintly couples to those of difficulty and even betrayal. "Not every married saint had the support of his or her spouse," they write. "In fact, even with the support and prayers of a saintly wife or husband, some married saints had spouses who never converted. In other cases, through God's grace and fervent prayer, some spouses did convert."[17] St. Monica was an example of a saintly spouse whose prayers and patience ultimately led to her husband's conversion.

Some couples were saints together, and some had only one saintly spouse in the union. They all faced weariness and trying times that come with every marriage. The goal, the authors explain, is seeking to attain holiness—our own and that of our spouse—as we also strive to encourage our children in this way.

They point out that some of those reading their marriage book might be reading it alone, lacking a supportive spouse. "Nevertheless, at some point, we are all guilty of neglecting to support our spouse and to prioritize his or her spiritual well-being," they write. "Even two believing spouses will disagree with one another about issues of faith, often in just simple ways."[18] They also noted that the differences can lead to loneliness and frustration and bitterness. Instead of despairing, they suggested praying for that spouse to receive whatever fruits the Holy Spirit wants to give them.

DIVERGING WORLDVIEWS

If Christian marriage involves a total communion of life, as the Church professes, how can a marriage with such differences survive? Could there be any doubt that such a marriage would inevitably bring some amount of confusion to the souls of its children? Monica and Patricius had widely diverging worldviews for much of their twenty years together. They were very much "unequally yoked."

Since Monica's parents were devout Christians, it is a mystery why they arranged a marriage with Patricius for her. He was much older and a pagan. On top of that, Patricius had a temper at times and was known as a womanizer. Monica put her faith in God. Patricius criticized Monica's faith, but she ignored it and turned to prayer and charity, loving others and serving the poor.

Over time, her love and example influenced Patricius. To her great joy, shortly before his death, Patricius was baptized into the Faith. St. Monica had prioritized the spiritual well-being of her spouse just as we are all called to do.

ONE IN CHRIST AS WE PRAY FOR OUR CHILDREN

A spouse who shares our faith and prays with us for our children is a blessing. Yet there are many single mothers and fathers due to divorce or the death of a spouse; marriages of mixed faith; and marriages where one spouse has no faith.

Regardless, we are all one in Christ as we pray for our children. We can all love our spouses or at least the parents of our children and pray for them—be they with us or not—imitating the example of St. Monica. That example was not lost on Monica's children. She practiced what she preached.

God sees all. He knows our needs. Though our spiritual journeys take different paths, let us keep following Monica's path of love for our families regardless of the brokenness.

6

When We Must "Go It Alone"

On Mother's Day in 2009, Marie learned the shattering news that her husband was in love with another woman. That day, her comfortable life as a stay-at-home mom and part-time parish youth minister came to a grinding, harrowing halt.

"Only a week later, my husband moved out. In the months that followed, I glimpsed the loveless-ness of hell for the first time, and my faith came crashing down around me," she continues. "I had believed all the feel-good slogans we hear, like 'The family that prays together stays together,' and I cried out to God in anger, desolation, and fear in what I perceived to be his betrayal."

Until then, she says, the family had done everything "right," attending church together each Sunday and praying before dinner every evening. "My husband and I even fell asleep holding hands at night," she says, wondering, "so why hadn't God made us the family that stayed together?"

She later would come to see this tragedy in a clearer light, enough to say, "It took being abandoned by my husband while pregnant with our fifth son to realize the true gift of my Catholic faith." But it didn't happen all at once.

At the time of her husband's abandonment of the family, Marie's oldest son, Jordan, who was eleven, had been reading Job in his catechism class.

He told his mom not to worry, saying that Job had lost everything but God ultimately restored him—and that their family would also be rebuilt stronger. "In so many ways, it has been," Marie says. "After nearly leaving the Faith, I have since become a devout Catholic, and Jordan, who is a young adult now, remains in the sacraments." At times, though, Marie worries that he is becoming a "cafeteria Catholic," picking and choosing which Church teachings he will follow.

Marie believes that the abandonment she and her children had experienced contributed to some of them becoming weaker in their faith. She worries that the faith she fought so hard to bring back into her life will not be what they turn to in times of need. Marie wonders how much their father's cheating and betrayal has stunted the children's faith development. If he had left when they were older, would their faith be stronger? She isn't sure.

A BREAKING HEART

Recently, Marie learned one of her adult sons had stopped attending Mass, telling her he believes in God but is not convinced that God cares what happens to us since we have too often disappointed him. "My heart broke when I heard this," she says, recalling a similar thought when her husband left. "My son still does not know how his thoughts echo my own from not that long ago."

Another son still attends Mass with her every week, but he is often distracted. He only reluctantly goes to confession with her. "Could he be another me?" she wonders, recalling the years when Mass meant little to her as well—which wasn't that long ago, she admits. At that time, Marie mainly saw Mass as a social hour to meet friends and admire how cute her boys were serving on the altar.

Marie remembers longingly when her oldest son was young. "He would laugh, run, and play. He would wrap his little arms around my neck and hug me so hard I thought I might break. He was always dirty and bruised," she says. "He was an amazing and wonderful bundle of curiosity and energy." When Marie's husband left, though, her eldest got put on the back burner while she worked two jobs to keep the family afloat. She says, "He needed me, and I was not there for him the way I wanted to be."

Recently, one of her sons moved out to live with his father. "Many nights, I go past the door of his room and put my hand out wishing him back to me. I stand next to his bed or even crawl into his top bunk wishing I could cuddle and squish him like I used to," Marie says. "He has been gone for months now, and I cry a few tears in secret, where no one else can see, almost every day, for him and for the time that we have lost that can never be given back. I pray and sing and fast for him and would do almost anything to let him know I am sorry, and wish I had been a better mom for him."

HOW JESUS MUST FEEL

If the experience has done anything, it has given her insight into how Jesus must feel when his children walk away. She says, "My heart longs to have my son near, and certainly, God feels this, too, when we abandon him."

It is her youngest, Marie says, the one with whom she was pregnant when her husband left, who always seems to restore her hope through his inquisitiveness about the Church and God. "He even surprised me recently by sharing that he prays a Hail Mary 'whenever something good happens.' He is the only one of the five who continues to willingly participate as an altar server."

Marie says she would like to believe this precious one will never have any straying moments from the Church, but history tells her things will probably take a turn for the worst at some point or another. "History also tells me God will not leave him there. After all, some saints overcame their own faulty backgrounds, so I can hope for this with each of my five sons."

A CHANCE TO IMPROVE

Marie says that she is still learning, and she sometimes doubts herself. But she does the best she can and tries to leave the rest with God.

Recently, one of her sons who had fallen away from the sacraments went up to receive the Eucharist during Mass when he was home, despite her quiet explanation of why he should refrain. When he later said he was only trying to be a good example to his younger brothers, she hesitated, then offered maternal correction. "I could not be content with this beloved child of mine receiving the Body and Blood of Christ to save his brothers at the expense of what the Eucharist is or at the expense of his soul," she says. "I told him I wanted him in heaven, too."

Marie says her suffering has allowed her to recognize some of her own imperfections. "My husband fell to adultery, pride, and material possessions," she says. "I crumbled to self-pity, feelings of worthlessness, and fear. But I was called by God and stood again. And, just as God pulled me from my scornful attitude, I believe the same will happen with my oldest prodigal."

Already, she has seen signs of hope. One day, while driving him back to college, she says, she happened upon a Catholic radio station. "It was around Halloween, and the host was talking about spirits and ghosts and other such things that have always fascinated my son. This opened a door to a meaningful conversation." Marie says she tried walking a careful line, not wanting to beat him over the head with what to her is so obvious. "Then, I quietly thanked the Lord for laying those few little steps toward faith."

PRAYER *IS* THE ONLY RECOURSE

Though she wishes she could demand her children embrace the Faith, Marie says she knows better and recognizes her only true recourse is prayer. "Through it, I am drawn close to certain saints, like Saints Monica, Augustine, and Ambrose. I pray for my prodigal child to not only embrace the Faith, but to become a priest, or at the very least, a great saint," she says, noting that she also recites the Rosary and St. Michael prayer almost daily for each of her sons, adding a Hail Mary for their future spouses.

"I have discovered that as much as I yearn for my prodigal to come back, God wants this even more," she says. "He wants all of my children back, just as he wanted me back when I was young and self-centered."

Recently, Marie has begun fasting more, not just in Lent, but in giving up coffee, ice cream, and cookie dough. "I know it sounds silly, but my boys have noticed," she says. "I also fast on the nights my boys are with me. They do not yet know why I have given up all this, but they know I am praying for something. I trust they will know in time, just as I trust God will bring them back to him in time, whether that is before my death or not."

Marie says that as she reflects on the mercy, love, and forgiving nature of God, she wants to instill in her sons that life—especially life in the Faith— is a celebration. "And like the party the Father threw for the Prodigal Son upon his return, I try to show my boys the joy of the Faith," she adds. "I must live in confidence and courage and love in the hopes of bringing them home. I must believe that in heaven, God will take away the intense sorrow I have had at missing out on my sons growing up. I must believe God will provide for all of us." She doesn't believe this to be a denial of the possibility of their spending eternity in loveless suffering. "It is in surrender and submission to God and his abilities, which far surpass my own," she says. "It is exactly what I am asking of my children. I can show no less of myself."

7

The Fatherhood Factor

While St. Augustine's father, Patricius, would have a conversion to the Christian faith at the end of his life, his pagan influences undoubtedly had a profound impact on his oldest son as he was growing up.

If a study were done in the year 355 regarding parental influence on the transmission of faith, we might discover that fathers of that time had a more significant influence on their children's faith than their mothers. As diligently as Monica tried to impart the Christian faith to her children, their young eyes could not help but absorb their father's behavior.

Though their mismatched union might confound us today, finding a husband for one's daughter was a primary concern during ancient times. A family with an unmarried daughter of a certain age would often feel shame and social stigma. As Falbo speculates, "Perhaps [Monica's parents] were thinking only of social stature, physical attributes, or other factors that escape the historian."[19] Some sources suggest that Patricius belonged to a family of "decayed nobility" and that he was probably a decade older than his new bride, perhaps thirty years old to her twenty.

Though Patricius ultimately left his pagan life behind, this did not come easily due to his apparent desire to continue indulging in pleasures not befitting a true Christian. Additionally, he went from "moments of tenderness and affection, in which he appeared entirely dedicated to his wife and children, to moments of uncontrollable rage."[20]

We know that Patricius was unfaithful to his wife, and that St. Augustine was influenced by this example. In his *Confessions*, he admits to not being in control of his sexual passions as a young man, conveying this common proclivity in his famous utterance, "Lord, make me chaste, but not yet." In this sense, the son was negatively influenced by the father.

A FATHER MATTERS

In an interview, Tyler Rowley, author of *Because of Our Fathers: Twenty-Three Catholics Tell How Their Fathers Led Them to Christ*, shares how he came to write about a father's influence on his children's faith. Inspiration for the book came from Fr. Gerald Murray, whom he heard speak of how his father's strong faith had rubbed off on him, beginning at age seven. At that time, the young Gerald Murray learned that his father left early every morning before work to attend Mass. When he asked him why, his father responded simply that he loved to be with Jesus every day, not just on Sunday.

Rowley recounts, "Fifty years later, he remembered this moment when the biggest and best guy in his life was doing something different than just going to a Sunday event with his family ... and there's a little seed there that starts to grow" in his son's soul. He realized how much impact a father's faith has on his children, recalling that this mirrored his own experience growing up. He began interviewing others with strong faiths and discovered that all had been heavily influenced by their fathers. "Everyone I talked to, all committed Catholics, all had the same response: 'I got my faith from my dad,'" Rowley said. "People take on the spiritual life of their fathers," he continued. "It's why we call priests 'Father.'"[21]

SEEKING HELP FROM GOD THE FATHER

Not everyone's father, though, has been grounded in the Catholic Faith—as we have seen with St. Augustine's father and as we see with many other fathers today. So what hope can be offered to such families?

Rowley says that while our fathers can lead us to Christ, if one does not have this witness, all is not hopeless. Above all, our Father in heaven, who created and us and loves us, is constantly at work drawing us to him and the Church.

In one of the essays, he notes what Fr. John Riccardo shared about the day of his father's funeral: "He and his brothers heard his mother walk up to the casket, bend down, and whisper, 'I know Christ because of you.' And that's the image right there—the children around the father, who has gone to his reward, and the mother who has been blessed with a great husband ... and she tells what the whole goal is of marriage—that they brought each other to Christ."

If Patricius had been alive when Monica died, he could have said the same: "I know Christ because of you." Jesus heard Monica's prayers, "filling in the gaps" in Augustine's upbringing left by a faulty fatherly role model. In the end, Augustine could bend down at his mother's casket and whisper words similar to those of Fr. Riccardo's mother.

We do not have to let our imperfect family situations keep us from believing God can heal our broken hearts and one another. We need only turn to him this day and trust.

8

St. Joseph to the Rescue!

"In my priesthood, I have discovered that the biggest hurt in the lives of many is the father wound," Msgr. John Esseff explained during an interview for an article on St. Joseph in the *National Catholic Register*. In his nearly seventy years of priesthood—particularly in his prison ministry—Msgr. Esseff has witnessed the deep suffering of those who lacked a strong father in their lives. He believes that devotion to St. Joseph can help heal this wound: "All of us are being called to look to St. Joseph as a father figure. We need an earthly father who will show us again what a real dad is like."[22]

As fatherhood has been maligned, downgraded, and even treated as non-essential, many men have failed to fulfill their grave responsibility as fathers—and society has suffered. Fathers are called to guide and protect their families. Without this guidance and protection, many children have suffered and gone astray. That epidemic of fatherlessness has contaminated our culture; the one that many of our children have gotten lost in.

During a radio interview about her book *Letters to Myself from the End of the World*, Emily Stimpson Chapman said that in our age, one of our greatest problems is that we lack courageous, faithful, loving leaders. "When fathers aren't being fathers, their children tend to run off in every direction."[23] In this "fatherless age," many kids need to grow up on their own and learn how to become "grown-ups in the Faith" without the guidance they should normally have.

Even when our children do have strong fatherly examples, few escape the influences of the culture. Or they may be among those who do not have a godly father in their own childhoods. For everyone, though, St. Joseph can be a refuge. We need his love and guidance to pour down on us and his protection to drive away evil.

NO WORDS, BUT A POWERFUL EXAMPLE

In Scripture, he spoke not a word, yet St. Joseph was chosen to head the Holy Family. The degree of his holiness is unimaginable yet measurable by the degree to which demons fear him, according to exorcists, who say that, after the Virgin Mary, the devil fears St. Joseph more than any other saint. In the Litany of St. Joseph, the earthly father of Jesus is invoked under a number of titles, including "terror of demons."

In a *National Catholic Register* article entitled "Fierce Defender: St. Joseph Is 'Terror of Demons,'" Msgr. Stephen Rossetti, associate professor at Catholic University of America and the president and founder of the St. Michael Center for Spiritual Renewal, writes, "God himself picked St. Joseph to defend the Son and his mother. They were the targets of great demonic assaults as well as human assaults, especially those of Herod. Next to Our Lady, he is the greatest of saints in defending against Satan, and we regularly invoke him in our exorcism sessions, with great benefit."

With devotion to St. Joseph surging, Msgr. Rossetti says, "I believe it is part of God's plan to assist us in these dark times ... St. Joseph will powerfully shepherd us, alongside the Virgin Mary, to safety. He is the model of human fatherhood."[24]

THE WONDERS OF OUR SPIRITUAL FATHER

As Fr. Donald Calloway, author of *Consecration to St. Joseph: The Wonders of Our Spiritual Father*, teaches, "With families under attack, marriages falling apart, people turning away from God, and so much anxiety and fear, we really need St. Joseph's protection."

According to Fr. Calloway, "When St. Joseph makes a petition to Jesus, it's a paternal petition," he said. "No one else can do that. The devil knows that, and it terrifies him. God doesn't obey angels, but Our Lady and St. Joseph are his mom and dad. The devil doesn't want us to tap into that."

The devil fears St. Joseph also because of his purity. In the words of Fr. Calloway, "That lily he's always shown holding is a spiritual lance. He has the most chaste heart. His virtue is only outdone by Our Lady, and that is a terror to the devil." He encourages all men to realize, by the example of St. Joseph, the power that fatherhood and purity have over the forces of darkness. "Men who are impure have no power," he said. "If men resemble St. Joseph, the kingdom of Satan will be destroyed. This terrifies them. The purity of St. Joseph is a weapon against the filth and perversions of the devil."

St. Joseph's quiet example of following God speaks loudly in today's world, according to Fr. Calloway. "He was always open to the will of God—and that's the terror of demons: people completely open to the will of God."[25]

In James 5:16, we read, "The prayer of a righteous person is powerful and effective." Prayers to St. Joseph must be *very* powerful and effective. The Catholic Church considers him to be the protector of the universal Church. He is also known as the patron of fathers and families and the "terror of demons," so we can place great trust in his intercession.

St. Joseph, pray for us!

9

The Power of Grandparents

Most children who leave the Catholic Church as young adults become parents who do not baptize their children—your grandchildren. When we raised our children as Catholic, we had the primary say in their upbringing. With grandchildren, our influence is less. We might be able to teach them some Catholic prayers and about the first Christmas—if their parents allow it. If not, this can stress our relationships, both with our children and with our grandchildren.

The great news is that grandparents are an unparalleled spiritual force, in part because they love their grandchildren so much and want what is best for them. How this plays out, of course, varies from family to family depending on circumstances.

We find in St. Monica not only a mother who sought after her son and his conversion, but a grandmother who took a vested interest in the faith of her grandson, Adeodatus, and his mother, Augustine's mistress. After Augustine's conversion, before his baptism, he realized that he could not continue living with his mistress. Their seventeen-year relationship ended with her returning to North Africa to live out her life in a convent. Augustine and his son were baptized by St. Ambrose in 387. Monica's other two children remained Catholic, so the entire family, including her husband and mother-in-law, ended up safe in the fold of the Church.

Several years ago, at an EWTN Family Celebration in Ohio, after several converts shared their dramatic conversion stories, they sat down together as a panel and fielded questions from the audience.

"None of you were raised Catholic, so what was the source of your conversions?" someone asked. Most responded that they had Catholic grandmothers praying for them, though their own parents did not practice the Faith. One of the speakers chuckled and said, "Never underestimate the power of a praying grandmother."

In Paul Darrow's conversion story of going from a same-sex-attracted supermodel living a hedonistic lifestyle, brushing shoulders with all "the beautiful people," to a devout and celibate Catholic, he mentions his Polish Catholic grandmother who prayed for him.

Ironically, his conversion was set in motion when he came across Mother Angelica while channel-surfing. Post-stroke, Mother Angelica was in full habit with a patch over one eye. Paul called his roommate into the room to see this ridiculous spectacle. He laughed and made fun of her. But he also listened. Soon Paul was hooked and secretly started tuning in to hear Mother speak truths that burned in his heart. He now dedicates his life to sharing the Good News, giving hope to others, and witnessing to the joy and freedom that comes from unity with Christ.

Catholic speaker and writer Jess Echeverry tells of being raised by divorced parents without religion. Wounds upon wounds were inflicted, including sexual and physical abuse, abortion, unwed motherhood, homelessness, a suicide attempt, and exploring the New Age. But Jess experienced a happy and Catholic ending that she believes came about through the prayers of her Catholic grandmother on her father's side.[26]

Another grandmother, Rose, whose story we read earlier, shared with us that the suffering she has experienced through her oldest daughter's departure from her beloved Catholic faith has been excruciating at times. "I'll admit, I've cried myself to sleep." But she has also received little signs of hope—most often through her grandchildren.

"Sometimes, when I let my mind linger on this loss, I will beg God for a glimmer that the reunion is coming," Rose recounted. "And in moments, he delivers it; like the time the kids came over and out of the blue, they started praying a Hail Mary! One of them said, 'We pray that (prayer) at nighttime before we go to bed.' I was able to thank God for that glimmer, knowing that those are my daughter's true roots."

When those stories seem fewer and farther in between, Rose says she often turns to saints like Monica for solace.

DEVOTION TO SAINTS JOACHIM AND ANNE

Saints Anne and Joachim are the parents of the Blessed Mother and grandparents of Jesus. Imagine the power of their intercession. This holy couple was handpicked by God to be the grandparents of his only begotten Son, Jesus Christ.

We learn of Saints Anne and Joachim from apocryphal literature (meaning that they are not part of the canon of Sacred Scripture), chiefly the *Protoevangelium of James*, which dates back to around the year 150.[27] From this, we are told that Anne, wife of Joachim, was advanced in years and that her prayers for a child had not been answered. As we read,

> Once as she prayed beneath a laurel tree near her home in Galilee, an angel appeared and said to her, 'Anne, the Lord hath heard thy prayer and thou shalt conceive and bring forth, and thy seed shall be spoken of in all the world.' Anne replied, 'As the Lord my God liveth, if I beget either male or female, I will bring it as a gift to the Lord my God; and it shall minister to Him in holy things all the days of its life.' And thus, Anne became the mother of the Blessed Virgin Mary.[28]

St. Anne bore the Immaculate Heart of Mary in her womb. Devotion to her, honored as the holy mother of Mary and grandmother of Jesus, found popularity among early Christians. In the year 450, a church to honor St. Anne was built in Jerusalem in an area marking the traditional site of the home of Jesus' maternal grandparents, Anne and Joachim, and the birthplace. Next to the church is the large excavation area of the Pools of Bethesda, where Christ healed a sick man (see John 5:2–9). It is the apocryphal Gospel of James that places the house of her parents, Anne and Joachim, close to the Temple area.

Churches and shrines to St. Anne are found throughout the world. One popular shrine, St. Anne de Beaupré, sits in the province of Quebec, where the first chapel was built in 1658. Today, nearly one million visitors come annually from all around the world, many claiming to receive miracles.

Grandparents wanting to increase their devotion to St. Anne can join the online group "The Grandchildren of St. Anne," formed to spread devotion to St. Anne as our grandmother and to obtain many graces. The creator of this site, Dr. Brian Kiczek, also authored the e-book *God's Grandmother: Saint Anne.* In it, he shares that he believes his daughter received healing through St. Anne's intercession. The book includes a reenactment of the life of St. Anne gleaned from historical writings, prayers and devotions, saints' quotes about her, reports of miracles attributed to her, and information about the Basilica of the Shrine of St. Anne de Beaupré.

Kiczek also draws on the visions of the mystic Blessed Ann Catherine Emmerich from her writings recorded in *The Life of the Virgin Mary.* Blessed Ann Catherine reported seeing a vision of an angel who appeared to St. Anne, who had prayed for a child after suffering many years of barrenness. "In the moment when the light of the angel had enveloped Anna in grace, I saw a radiance under her heart and recognized in her the chosen Mother, the illuminated vessel of the grace that was at hand. What I saw in her I can only describe by saying that I recognized in her the cradle and tabernacle of the holy child she was to conceive and preserve; a mother blessed indeed. I saw that by God's grace Anna was able to bear fruit."[29]

Although St. Anne and her husband St. Joachim must have lived seemingly uneventful lives, they are the grandparents of the Savior of the world and undoubtedly powerful intercessors for our own grandchildren. Their feast day is July 26.

Saints Joachim and Anne, pray for us!

10

Humility: Our Treasured Place

On the floor of the sanctuary of Saints Anne and Joachim Catholic Church in Fargo, North Dakota, are a line of artistic, symbolic floor tiles that lead up to the altar. Each represents one of the seven capital virtues, with the first, humility, depicted by a gray donkey with the word "HUMILITY" immediately below it—a powerful visual reminder that we can only come fully into the Lord's presence by being humble.

But our Faith teaches us to strive for humility. Before we enter the pew before every Mass, we make a gesture of humility by genuflecting to Jesus' Eucharistic presence in the tabernacle. The same is true when we bow or genuflect before receiving the Lord in Holy Communion, as well as when we present ourselves to receive God's mercy and forgiveness in the sacrament of Reconciliation. Humility, as the saints modeled so well, leads us to holiness ... but it requires a daily effort, with the help of the Lord's grace. True humility does not come easily.

Through our embrace of the various challenges the Lord allows in our lives, we find many opportunities to grow in humility. This is especially true in our journey with our children. But this can be "our treasured place," as Msgr. Thomas Richter of the Diocese of Bismarck calls it—the place we find ourselves when we have nowhere else to go, where all our human efforts have been exhausted so all we have left is God. We realize that we cannot expect God to follow our plan; rather, we must follow *his*.

"No one in the history of mankind ever asked God to become a man and come and save us," he noted. "We never would have thought of it. That was all God's activity."[30]

According to Msgr. Richter, we must focus on what God is doing in our life. "What God desires every minute of every day is to make [us] like Christ," he said. Quoting St. John of the Cross, he adds, "God acts for one purpose—to make our souls great." He advises us to pray, "God, I give you permission to do whatever you want with me, even if it makes me suffer. May your kingdom come; may your will be done." Such a prayer, he said, describes the Blessed Mother's prayer: "I am the handmaid of the Lord, let it be done unto me according to your word.'" In humility, though, we need to ask God to remove the obstacles that prevent us from desiring his will over our own.

Many of us, right now, are in a place not of our choosing; a place we did not expect to be. We have been humbled, but we can make humility our "treasured place."

ANN'S STORY

Ann and her husband, Paul, decided to homeschool their children to ensure that they would be taught the Catholic Faith. As Ann shares, "We could hand down the Faith without compromise and with the help of other homeschooling families. Our kids embraced the learning, activities, and friendships in their homeschool group, as well as their Catholic faith. Bible readings, saint stories, and daily Mass began every school day." Ann was often thankful for the many blessings that had come with their choice to homeschool, and the fruits were many.

Their children went from homeschooling to attending a Catholic high school. "In college, though, they began to fall away from the Faith," Anne explains. "They had a foot in two worlds—faith and secular. The secular eventually won out." Their three oldest boys have stopped being practicing Catholics.

Ann admits, "We thought we had more control over things than we actually had. Now, our eyes have been opened to how prideful and sure of ourselves we had been. We see some families at Mass surrounded by their adult children and grandchildren, and the painful hole in our own family seems to grow deeper. All we can do now is to keep putting our children in God's hands, through his Blessed Mother and all the angels and saints, and to keep praying."

JENNIFER'S STORY

Jennifer, the mother of a large family, admits to once having judged harshly another family whose two daughters had cut off contact with their mother. "I thought, 'Well, she must have done something to cause that. After all, I had a child who was an atheist and three who just didn't think they had to go to church, and others still in the Church, but we all got along.'" Regardless of their faith—or lack of faith—none of her children ever questioned their parents' unconditional love for them. So she assumed there must be good reason a child would cease contact.

She continues, "Then, two families who I knew to be kind and loving parents with very liberal older daughters were eventually cut off by them. And then, unbelievably, it ended up happening to us. Our oldest son no longer speaks to us."

Jennifer reports that her son believes she and her husband are "dangerous to society" and does not want them to influence his children. Although they do not challenge him about his faith or political views, he says that their beliefs hurt others—such as being against giving children puberty blockers to change their gender, not supporting same-sex marriage, and opposing adoption for same-sex couples.

While this has grieved her and her husband, Jennifer says that it has also humbled her. "Not until I experienced the rejection of my son did I realize that I was still hanging on to some of my pride. It is not for me to judge other families or decide who is at fault. I know we are simply called to pray for others and not to judge them."

THE CORE OF OUR HOLINESS

The more we empty ourselves of our pride, the more room we have for God. Humility lies at the very core of holiness; it is the "power" behind our spiritual strength. It is through humility and thus obedience to God that the devil is defeated. St. John Vianney, patron saint of parish priests, was often harassed by the devil. But his humility and faithful perseverance, unabated by these attacks, created an impenetrable shield of protection.

> For about thirty-five years (1824-1858), the devil tried in vain to discourage the Curé from his work for souls. But the devil fought a losing battle. As the wind fans the flame to burn more brightly, so those diabolical manifestations, far from snuffing out the Curé's efforts for souls, served rather to enkindle zeal.

... Soon the *grappin* [what he called the devil] became a kind of messenger of big sinners. When the devil suspected ahead of time that a big sinner was returning to confession, in his jealousy, he would take out his vengeance on the Curé of Ars. Once, after a night of hellish hubbub, the Curé mentioned to a villager, "No doubt at this moment there are some sinners on the road to Ars."

The devil could not win; and coward that he is, gradually he gave up his nightly visits. Hell was more pleasant than defeat; fire burns less than broken pride. So the devil returned to hell and the Curé went on saving souls.[31]

Humility does not mean beating ourselves up for our failures. Rather, it means simply acknowledging our weakness and woundedness so that we can allow God to fill us with his grace. Jesus calls us to love our neighbor as ourselves (see Mark 12:31), but this means first that we must love ourselves as God loves us—and humbly go from there.

When we feel that we have messed up, we are in good company—with the likes of St. Peter, who denied Jesus, and all of the other apostles (except John), who abandoned Jesus during his passion. We are not perfect. But that is why Jesus died for us—and why, through his Church, he has given us the sacrament of Reconciliation.

As we have seen, St. Ambrose advised Monica to stop talking so much to her son about God and talk more to God about her son. She humbled herself by surrendering her own human abilities, realizing she had failed to convince her son of anything, and turned everything over to God. That took humility. It also led to her own holiness—and that of her son.

11

When Anger Gets in the Way

Anger can ignite in an instant and keep burning for a lifetime. It can also build up until it is ready to explode. This is why anger is one of the seven deadly sins, along with pride, lust, gluttony, greed, sloth, and envy, all of which can be fatal to the spiritual life.

At first glance, anger might not even seem like a "choice." And if it is not a choice, how can it be sinful? After all, isn't anger stirred up by the actions of others or circumstances? In many cases, yes. We might even be justified in feeling angry. But what we *do* with our anger *is* a choice. We can choose to express our anger morally or immorally; we can choose to bring it to prayer and cool down or act out on it and hurt others and ourselves.

If we grew up in a family where anger was given free rein, we have probably been wounded by it and need healing. We may have brought it into our relationship with our children, who might now be struggling in their relationship with God. We can pray for healing and the grace of self-control.

THE BROKEN WINDOW

ROXANE: I have no recollection of what prompted me to pick up the plastic lotion bottle and fling it at my bedroom window that fall afternoon when I was fourteen. It probably had something to do with a hurtful comment my father had made. He could be hard on me at times, and his refusal, or inability, to really take time to listen to what I was going through had taken a toll over time.

On that long-ago day, so foggy in memory of detail, but not emotion, I only knew the fury I felt at being so severely misunderstood—again. So I grabbed whatever was near and thrust it at the glass.

Crash! The moment I heard the sound, I regretted it, for the force of it on the pane was so strong, it broke through and left a large, gaping hole.

Over time, I became haunted by that broken window. Each glance at it called to mind my inability to act with restraint in times of deep frustration, reminding me, I suppose, that I was broken, too, maybe even unfixable. Because it was a very tall, double-paned window on an old home, and the outside pane remained intact, Dad never did get around to fixing it. Maybe that was on purpose. Maybe he wanted me to be reminded, every day, of my wild emotions, and the damage they could cause if left unchecked. If so, it worked. I lived with that moment of uncontained emotion every day until leaving for college.

Eventually, I came to understand a bit more about that frustrated girl, and why I had reacted so strongly. My life had a lot of missing pieces, especially concerning my father's drinking. I loved Dad dearly, but over time, he abandoned our adventures together, when we would spend hours fishing for walleye, trout, or catfish in the nearby rivers of our home, or picking buffalo berries to make jam. In my high school years, he began spending more and more time drinking beer, and less and less with me. My sister, more the indoor type, content to hang out at home, loved doing crossword puzzles with him. I did not share that enjoyment and soon felt left behind.

This interior disquiet—an aching void—began to manifest in occasional outbursts. In truth, they came from a deeply sad heart; one that even led me to contemplate, and attempt, suicide on at least one occasion. Somehow, even then, I sensed a quiet voice, pulling me back into life, and never had the courage to go through with it.

Years later, I would sort through this dotted history of frustration, one my husband seemed to share. Together, we were quite the pair, passionate, yes, but often overly so. And in those earlier years of our marriage, young and unhealed, we often let our anger take hold. Because we did not always plan when this would occur, sometimes our children were within earshot—a regret I carry to this day.

As I sought healing, a counselor explained how our brains work in times of extreme emotion. "It's like a bucking bronco," she said. "You are not thinking rationally at all. You are just reacting. It's as if the part of your brain that is rational is uncovered—that is where the term 'flipping your lid' comes from. You are not in control."

Because neither my husband nor I were created with meek personalities, it makes sense that our children have inherited some of these qualities, too. Our firstborn has an intense personality, and most of his siblings share that spirited nature, which, while delightful in moments, can be a great challenge as well.

Not only did their strong personalities challenge me, but they tapped back into my own wounds. In raising them, as much as I adored motherhood and relished those tender years, at times, I also revisited some of those moments in my own childhood when anger would rise up unexpectedly. Sometimes, I would raise my voice more than necessary and not react as tenderly as I would want. On those days, I always felt utterly defeated as a parent.

FRUITS OF THE SPIRIT

Though the fury with which I had hurled that lotion bottle was real, and a reminder of how weak we can be, God's grace is real, too. Thankfully, he has shown me his favor. Each time I have advanced toward him, despite setbacks, he has blessed me, encouraging me in my ascent. Knowing how very weak I am, and how anger could have destroyed our marriage, I am ever grateful for the patience he has helped grow in me every day.

Recently, in reading Galatians, I realized something important about anger. In chapter 5, verses 19–21, we read about the works of the flesh, and anger is included among them. To offset that, however, we also read, in verses 22–23, about the opposite. "But the fruit of the Spirit is love, joy, peace, patience, kindness, goodness, faithfulness, gentleness, self-control; against such there is no law."

During a *lectio divina* session, I realized that by combating the works of the flesh, such as anger, we can literally let in more of the fruits of the

Spirit. Do I want more love, peace, patience, and kindness in my life? Yes! To have that, I need to work on subduing those fleshly works so that the good fruits can permeate my soul, becoming a conduit of grace in my interactions with others—including my husband and children.

Knowing this now, I work at it daily. But our children still have, along with seeds of grace, the seeds of this frustration and contempt that have colored their own histories, either through our unfortunate examples, their own concupiscence, or the generational sin that has been passed down. I know that my husband's and my weaknesses, which we still battle occasionally, also affect our relationships with them, and possibly even how they see God.

Thankfully, I am not the person I was at age fourteen, nor even twenty-four. I have grown and flourished, all glory to God, and have much more to offer now. But I have had time to work through those wounds. Our children are just beginning to process their own insufficiencies and hurts. I can only hope that as they do, they will also process the many things that have gone right, with us and in their own souls, and the gift of faith we tried to offer them, which, as I have experienced, can be transforming.

I have been able to peel away the layers of my past, forgive the weaknesses of my parents, and draw on my faith to help me heal. As I learned new techniques for responding to my husband, he, too, has learned a new way to relate.

Our home is much more peaceful now than in the earlier years of our relationship, when we still had so much to learn about ourselves and how our past wounds were driving us, thanks be to God.

ST. MONICA AND ANGER

St. Monica had a gentle spirit, despite the failings of her husband and son. Every discovery of her husband's adultery surely hurt, but she did not resort to outbursts of anger. Instead, it was her husband, Patricius, who displayed fits of rage, sometimes resorting to physical and verbal abuse. Her wild son's pursuit of pleasure and defense of Manichaeism frustrated and concerned her, but she did not address it with anger. It was her love and gentleness that won over her loved ones.

Monica held her tongue during these bouts—choosing not to engage at that time—waiting until he had cooled down to address a situation. As Falbo notes, when Patricius lashed out in anger against his wife, she did not respond in kind: "Gradually his anger blew over and he calmed down. After the episode had passed, Monica would then approach her husband and calmly present her thoughts and opinions ... She knew the art of choosing the right moment. She did not allow herself to be provoked by a situation, ruining everything by acting in the heat of emotion."[32]

But neither did she reject confrontation nor passively accept injustice, which might have led her husband to think he was always right. "She was a competent strategist," Falbo says, "gradually leading Patricius toward truth and goodness by means of a certain innate psychology, but above all through her patience and virtue."[33]

It must have taken a great deal of grace and discipline for Monica to rise above the bad behavior of her husband and son. We know her source of strength was God. Striving to focus on the things we can control, and surrender those we cannot, can become a way of living that works toward undoing bad habits such as losing one's temper.

A NEW APPROACH

PATTI: Since anger can be an opening for the devil, we can see how family arguments harm relationships. I wish I had had a better understanding of that in earlier years. I regret times that I acted in anger in the past and offer up that regret to God and pray for healing for any of the ways it caused harm.

Years ago, when a friend shared about a deep hurt caused by one of her children, it hit me that she could take the hurt and give it back to that child as a spiritual gift of love and forgiveness, completely contradicting what the devil intended. Otherwise, if we lose our temper over someone's bad behavior, the devil can kill two birds with one stone, so to speak.

That insight has carried into my own life. Whenever I am tempted to anger now, I consider the spiritual danger. I stop and pray, giving the negative emotions to God, asking him to transform them as an offering of love to the person who caused them. I step away from the feeling of anger and meditate on loving the person who is the source. If they are a loved one, I focus on the previous relationship and not the irritation. Whoever it is, I muster a feeling of love, which sometimes means considering them from God's point of view as a child of God. It is not always easy, but it is always a choice.

What the devil intended for harm, we can turn into a gift, praying for healing and holiness. On two recent occasions where someone behaved unkindly toward me, rather than react angrily, I prayed and offered up the hurt. In both cases, the offending person apologized a short time later, renewing our relationship. There are also long-term hurts, for which I have done the same. I cannot control bad behavior or animosity from others, but I can choose to love and forgive and reject anger.

OVERCOMING SINFUL ANGER

In the book *Overcoming Sinful Anger*, Fr. Thomas Morrow explains that the feeling of anger happens without our choice, but what we do with that feeling *is* our choice. As he notes, St. Paul mentions outbursts of anger along with several other sins, saying: "I warn you as I warned you before, that those who do such things shall not inherit the kingdom of God" (Galatians 5:21). We need to remember Christ's words in the Sermon on the Mount: "I say to you that every one who is angry with his brother shall be liable to judgment; whoever insults his brother shall be liable to the council, and whoever says, 'You fool!' shall be liable to the fire of hell" (Matthew 5:22). Later, he tells his disciples to "love your enemies and pray for those who persecute you" (Matthew 5:44).

According to Fr. Morrow, we are "wired" to get angry, but giving in to anger is not the solution. There are different ways we can choose to deal with it. Some negative options for dealing with anger include desiring revenge against those we feel have wronged us, punishing someone with the silent treatment, or suppressing anger into the subconscious, where it will simmer until it explodes. Instead, we can choose to do something constructive with our anger.

Fr. Morrow recommends that a person with a temper could benefit by meditating on these words from Ephesians: "Let all bitterness and wrath and anger and clamor and slander be put away from you, with all malice, and be kind to one another, tenderhearted, forgiving one another, as God in Christ forgave you" (Ephesians 4:31–32).

"Even more motivating," he says, "should be the words of the apostle John: 'He who does not love remains in death. Any one who hates his brother is a murderer, and you know that no murderer has eternal life abiding in him'" (1 John 3:14–15).

12

Don't Be Trapped in Unforgiveness

Unforgiveness is a trap. The bait is always an offense against us. Jesus tells us repeatedly in Scripture that we are to forgive one another—and that we are not even to approach the altar if we have a grudge against someone. As Jesus tells us, "Leave your gift there before the altar and go; first be reconciled to your brother, and then come and offer your gift" (Matthew 5:24).

In his book *The Devil Is Afraid of Me*, former Vatican exorcist Fr. Gabriel Amorth (1925–2016) explains that in order to free someone from an evil spell, forgiveness is necessary:

> Heartfelt forgiveness toward the one who did this evil is the basic requirement. At times I am made to understand that the exorcisms on a particular person are not having any effect, and I ask this person: "Have you forgiven the one who did this evil to you?" "No." And then enough with the exorcisms. One must at least make an effort to pardon the one who has done evil to us. Forgiveness also occurs through the action of the Holy Spirit—that that is through the love of God, who alone can cure hearts. Therefore, one should invoke the Holy Spirit.[34]

One of the problems in our culture is that people misunderstand what it means to forgive. It does not mean that abusers should not answer for their crimes and go to prison or that we should have warm feelings toward our abusers. Forgiveness is simply letting go of resentment and anger and asking God to bless the person who has offended us. In the end, forgiveness is an *act of the will*, not a feeling.

RESIST THE TEMPTATION

Having our children leave the Faith means that disagreements and misunderstandings can tempt us to unforgiveness. Even if it is not our children, everyone has someone they need to forgive. Or maybe our children are the ones not forgiving us for something.

It is human nature that we are going to disagree and sometimes offend or be offended. Recall that Augustine tricked his mother by leaving her behind while he set sail for Rome. Monica was packed and ready to go, but Augustine had convinced her to go to church to pray while they waited for departure. He wrote in *Confessions* that she was so grief-stricken when she realized what he had done to her that she stood at the docks and wailed aloud.

Travel and communication were extremely difficult back then. Would she ever see her son or her grandson again? How could he have been so callous? We know Monica was deeply saddened, but was she angry? Monica's strong prayer life led her to work everything out with God. She was already doing that with her grief over Augustine's radical departure from the Faith. She grieved and she prayed.

As we work through our own feelings of disappointment regarding our children's wanderings, we might come up against realities of the past that require us to seek forgiveness. We can all find things that we did right— and should take time to consider that—but there is a time to consider the things for which we should apologize. It is not a sign of weakness, but of strength. "For when I am weak, then I am strong" (2 Corinthians 12:10).

HEALING THE HEART THROUGH FORGIVENESS

In an interview on EWTN's *Women Made New* with Crystalina Evert, Fr. John Burns explains that forgiveness allows bonds of charity in our relationships to be established or even reestablished.

Fr. Burns offers the following thoughts for helping us think through forgiveness, and why we should prioritize it:

- **Choosing the way of Christ:** When we have been hurt, we can either strike back and plot our revenge or choose the way of Christ; the way of forgiveness and mercy. "It's easier to punch back when we're hurt, but it never really satisfies us."

- **An atrophied heart:** The heart, when living in unforgiveness, is closed, and when trapped inside that self-defense, our hearts atrophy. "We become impervious to [the Lord's] mercy and let the bitterness take lordship and authority over our lives." If pain sits and simmers, it can be difficult to be docile and sensitive to the movement of the Holy Spirit. "Unforgiveness callouses up our hearts, and we begin to despair. We begin living on our own terms, and we're always going to be lost on that road."

- **To move forward:** We need to uncover anger and resentment in our human relationships to move forward. Dr. Robert Enright, of the International Forgiveness Institute, a mentor, suggests looking at Christ on the Cross and then meditating on how he looks at his persecutors. "He has the power to strike them down, but he chooses to look the other way, and hopes for heaven for them," Fr. Burns said. "It's beautiful to see Jesus in his strength, in being merciful." He encouraged us to try to emulate this. "Forgiveness is actually connected to all the other parts of healing, and if forgiveness is not addressed, we can become stuck and unable to advance in the spiritual life and in our relationship with others."

- **Emotions are not generic:** Emotions are caused by events, objects, people, and memories. By bringing moments that cause duress in our minds back to the Lord, we can ask him if we might approach that moment differently. "We surrender to our pain and seek to look at finding out what pain our loved ones are carrying," Fr. Burns said. Then we start looking at the core of the other's pain by asking, "Is there a way to take on Christ's heart in this?"

- **Forgiveness is mercy:** Noting that the Latin word for mercy is *misericordia*, which contains the words "misery" and "heart," Fr. Burns explained that forgiveness is just mercy toward those who have hurt us, and Jesus teaches us that kind of love. We can ask the Lord to show us how he sees us and for help to forgive to reestablish the relationship, even if repentance is not sought by them.

- ***Distrust of God:*** "If those [false] beliefs aren't confronted, we can carry within us a distrust in God and of others, and a set of conclusions that are not representative of truth," Fr. Burns said. "We're trapped in a false sense of self, and of God," rather than "letting God cleanse and purify our hearts, and redeem us in his mercy, then lead us to the most satisfying path—the path to heaven."

- ***Healing the heart:*** Healing work involves healing of the heart, he explained, so we come out of hiding, leaving behind our old ways of self-reliance and discovering freedom. "And in the end, we all want to be free," he said, suggesting we ask the Holy Spirit to "put a light on our hearts for the places where he wants to bring grace." When the Lord calls us to himself, he said, it's always to restore our hearts first. "Only then can love be born once again in our hearts."

- ***There is time:*** "Where there is wounding and layering of pain, that leads to distrust," Fr. Burns said, noting that it can take time to heal. "You don't have to solve that problem tonight. You only have to welcome God to show you that pathway to freedom," he explained. "He wants to come into your heart ... to convert you, to turn you back to him and show him how much he loves you, that he's safe, that he's strong, and that he wants to provide and protect."[35]

What would have happened if Monica had not forgiven Augustine for his transgressions? She would not have followed him to Milan, and both would have missed out on her loving influence in his life. They ended up as close as any mother and son could be and united in the Faith. Forgiveness had opened up the path.

13

Regret and Second-Guessing

Dr. David Anders, host of *Called to Communion* on EWTN, regularly fields calls from concerned moms and dads whose children have left the Faith. One show stands out because of the fatherly focus it seemed to take.[36]

One father who called in described himself as a cradle Catholic who eventually wandered away from the Church. Regrettably, he said, in the process, he had led the rest of his family away, too. Later, after coming to recognize the Catholic Faith as a gift, he returned, but now grieves as he walks alone, feeling the weight of having led his family in another direction. "Do you have any idea of what I might do to get [my daughter] back in the Catholic Faith?" he asked Dr. Anders.

After empathizing with the caller's consternation, Dr. Anders gently guided him through the dilemma, suggesting a possible alternative between "doing nothing at all" and "working overtime to persuade" his daughter. He encouraged the father to "lengthen [his] time horizon indefinitely," trusting more fully in God and his providence. God is at work in his daughter's life, and he will strive to bring her home—in his own time. This will "take some of the onus off yourself and throw it back on God and the action of the Holy Spirit, where it belongs."

While we should seek to cooperate with God in the process, we don't have to do most of the heavy lifting, according to Anders. As parents, we naturally feel responsible for our children, but we need always to remember that God has an even more vested interest in their salvation than we do, and far greater power. So we need to turn away from trying to control the situation and let God do his work.

Dr. Anders suggested the father "generously" live out the Catholic Faith in his own life, both as an example to his daughter and to be equipped to share the fruits of his Catholic life with her. For example, if his daughter comes to him with a question or a problem, he will have the wisdom of his faith to help her—which could strengthen their relationship and potentially make her more open to the Faith. In the end, remaining in relationship with our children and loving them is what God is asking most from us.

WHY DID WE EVEN TRY?

Another caller shared that he and his wife had raised their two sons in the Catholic Faith, but both have since fallen away. The caller, sounding defeated, then suggested that it might have been better if they had not raised their children in the Catholic Faith in the first place, so that they would not have had anything to walk away from.

Dr. Anders gently assured the father that he had made the right decision. He reminded him that he and his wife's moral obligation was to raise their sons in the Faith to the best of their ability, not to ensure their sons would use their freedom wisely. In the end, it was their choice to leave the Faith, which is not something any parent can control.

A CULTURE HOSTILE TO RELIGION

As Dr. Anders told this forlorn father, "Keep in mind, you're in confrontation with a very anti-religious and hostile culture. It is perhaps more difficult to transmit the Faith through successive generations today than it probably has ever been in the history of the world."

Dr. Anders said that parents trying to raise their kids in the Catholic Faith today face "a great battle" and will not be judged on the fruits of our fidelity; they will be judged on their fidelity to God. As St. Teresa of Calcutta (Mother Teresa) once said, "God does not call us to be successful but faithful." We need to see where our responsibility ends and where God's begins, "considering the broader forces at work, including an overpowering culture at odds with our very mission as Catholic parents." In the end, "God is the judge of souls, not us."

HANGING ON GOD'S MERCY

Finally, Dr. Anders suggested this father's trial could be efficacious, reminding him that we "hang from cradle to grave on the mercy of God," and that our trials can be helpful for our own salvation—and ultimately, help lead our kids back to God and the Faith as well. As we continue along our journey, St. Monica will give us some helpful insights.

The faith journeys of our children can be mysterious. As parents, we ask, "What can I do about my child who has left the Faith?" often in resignation and in humility. We can be like spiritual beggars, searching for clues on how to square our emotions with the truths of the Church and the venomous culture that seems to have our loved ones in its grasp.

As Dr. Anders reminded the fathers—and all of us—the pain wrought through experiencing our children's apparent rejection of the Catholic Faith need not bring us to despair. We need to hold on to the hope that, in God's time, all can be brought to the good if we persevere to the end in faith.

14

Have We Been "Canceled"?

Some leaders of Catholic evangelization ministries have reported finding it difficult to successfully evangelize their own relatives. How can they help bring others to conversion but not their own family members? They seem to be living the truth of Jesus' words that "a prophet is not without honor except in his own country and in his own house" (Matthew 13:57).

As a leader of a major evangelization organization explains, "Your own family knows you so well that they don't think you have anything new to offer." We can see this in the life of Augustine. As a young boy, he was greatly influenced by his mother, and he was open to learning the Catholic Faith from her. But at age sixteen, while studying at the University at Carthage, Augustine became enamored with other ideas and came to discount the faith his mother had taught him that he had once embraced. At that point, in a sense, her faith had been canceled by him. Augustine was full of big ideas and put up a wall to anything his mother tried to tell him about the Catholic Faith.

His son, Adeodatus, was born in the year 372. It was around that time that Augustine read Cicero's *Hortensius*, which he credited with inspiring him to seek the truth. In Carthage, Augustine also came across the religion of Manichaeism, which dominated his life for the following decade. During this time, anything his mother tried to tell him about the Catholic Faith fell on deaf ears. He considered Christianity to be backward and lacking, so he "canceled" his mother's words to him.

Have your children "canceled" the things you have taught them about the Faith? Do they discount the religion you long to share with them? While we are experiencing it on a larger scale with society moving away from traditional Christian values, many families are finding their faith being canceled by their children, too.

As we have seen, Jesus is with us in this situation in a personal way. He too was "canceled" by his relatives and friends. In the sixth chapter of the Gospel of Mark, Jesus returns to his hometown of Nazareth, accompanied by his disciples, and begins teaching in the local synagogue. This presents a problem for those who knew him as he was growing up; they question his authority: "What is the wisdom given to him? What mighty works are wrought by his hands! Is not this the carpenter, the son of Mary?" they ask. Then, most telling, we read: "They took offense at him." Thus, "A prophet is not without honor, except in his own country and in his own house" (see Mark 6:2–4; Matthew 13:57).

Those words might really hit home with our own situation. When our children were young, they relied on us to provide and care for them, to give them their daily bread and guidance. Most of us took seriously the Church's admonition that we are the primary teachers of our children, especially in spiritual matters. To the best of our ability, we tried to instill the precepts of God in a living and active way.

When our children reject our spiritual guidance, we can feel like a prophet without honor in his own home. *This is hard.* But our Lord has given us perspective. In this story in Mark, we are reminded that within our own home, we may be misunderstood or discounted, perhaps more there than anywhere else.

CANCEL CULTURE

We can point to the early martyrs as examples of how long humans have been canceling one another. Their faith in Christ offended others to the point that they were tortured and put to death. For example, St. John the Baptist, who prepared the way for the coming of our Lord, angered Herodias by his condemnation of her immoral marriage to her brother-in-law, King Herod Antipas. After her daughter's dance pleased Herod, he promised her anything she wanted. Herodias seized the opportunity and prompted her daughter to ask Herod for John the Baptist's head. He was "canceled" due to his fidelity to the Lord.

The good news is that the antidote to this cultural toxicity is our Faith—one that is lived fully and with a dependence on God. We need to seek repentance through grace, with a heart that sees the dignity in all people—even those who disagree with us, or those who "cancel" us.

Being canceled hurts, but we can be comforted by the truth that God will never cancel us. The Catholic leaders mentioned at the beginning of this chapter seem to have a peace about their inability to evangelize their families. How? By praying for God to send someone who can get through to them, just as the preaching of Bishop Ambrose reached Augustine's ears and ultimately his heart.

15

Keep Your Chin Up!

The topic of this book touches one of the deepest parts of our soul. But God wants to offer refreshment along this vale of tears. So let us sit down together and drink a cool glass of lemonade—or whatever drink you prefer—and be reminded how much, and often, God thinks of us and our children, promising not to abandon us in our worry.

ROXANE: At the funeral of my Grandma Betty, who had just turned 101, her priest, Msgr. Thomas Richter, read from the notes she had scrawled in preparation for her death, which she had started many years before. It had grown into pages with different colored ink and writing. Grandma, an only child, had lost her parents fairly young and close together. She wanted to have things in order for her own funeral, so her children would not be left with too heavy a burden.

At the end of that list, she had encouraged people to keep their chin up, no matter what. Msgr. Richter did not believe this was just a note of optimism. "She was saying we need to keep our eyes on heaven. Chin up!" It is the kind of thing God would want us to hear right now, too.

GOD'S RESPONSE TO OUR REBELLION

In *The Bible in a Year* podcast with Fr. Mike Schmitz (day 177), we hear from Hosea, who reveals God's heart for his people despite their long history of rebellion. Chapter 11 begins, "When Israel was a child, I loved him, and out of Egypt I called my son. The more I called them, the more they went from me." We can hardly miss thinking about our own wandering children here. "Yes, it was I who taught Ephraim to walk, I took them up in my arms; but they did not know that I healed them," God continues. And then we come upon this greatly emotive utterance of God: "I led them with cords of compassion, with the bands of love, and I became to them as one who raises an infant to his cheeks, and I bent down to them and fed them."

When our children were young and our hearts filled with so much hope that they would stay near us, and God, we raised them to our cheeks, too, and bent down to feed them. What a tender, merciful picture this paints of God's unconditional love for us.

SARAH'S LAMENT

Sarah describes her estrangement from her adult children as "a deep ache," and one she shares with many others. She has fond memories of her early days of parenting, when she had faith that God would sustain her children through whatever challenges life might bring.

"I still remember when my middle child made his first confession," she says, noting that she especially loved helping her children prepare for the sacraments. "He was so nervous and had a stomachache because he was so genuinely morose about having to tell his sins to the priest. I prayed with him, out loud, to help him not be afraid, encouraging him to remember that moment as a happy occasion." When this son left the confessional, he had the biggest smile on his face. "He jumped up and down in the aisle of the church and shouted in front of his classmates, 'Yay! I have no sins!' I could hear our priest chuckling from the confessional. It's as clear now as when it happened nearly three decades ago."

Ultimately, though, the oldest two of her five children left the Catholic Faith for non-denominational Christian churches. At fifteen, this son who had been so excited about his confession stopped attending Mass. Her oldest daughter left the Church at eighteen, shortly after leaving a Catholic college she had begged to attend, according to Sarah. Both children were undoubtedly affected by their parents' divorce, she says, noting that her son, by this point, had moved in with his father, who did not enforce the Sunday obligation.

"Our middle child, after also leaving the Church and not speaking to me for ten years, has since returned and is now a vital part of our lives." Her oldest son, who also left at one point, has returned on a moderate basis, and her youngest son "thankfully never wavered in his fidelity to the Church." But for now, both daughters remain prodigals, she says, somberly adding, "They've left the Church, and they've left me."

GOD WON'T LEAVE US WITH EMPTY ARMS

As emotive as the verses in Hosea are—a true lamentation similar to what we have so often felt—God could never leave it there, and we should not, either.

Soon after his plea, the Lord expresses his undying commitment to his children—and our children—promising that he will not give up; he will fight to the end for them. "How can I give you up, O Ephraim! How can I hand you over, O Israel!" the Lord says in Hosea 11:8. "My heart recoils within me, my compassion grows warm and tender."

These are the heartstrings of God being yanked when his children leave him, and ours when we feel our children slipping away from God's grasp. But here, God promises that he will go after his dear ones, not in anger, but with love, and that they "shall come trembling from the west ... like birds from Egypt, and like doves from the land of Assyria ... *and I will return them to their homes.*"

In discussing these final chapters of Hosea, Fr. Mike says that the prophet is warning people to turn back to God, expressing that he is not finished yet; that he has not given up on his people, despite their rebellion. "Even though they keep turning away, he says, 'Return to the Lord ... *I will heal their faithfulness and love them freely.*'"

Can these words leave any doubt that God will fight with and for us for the souls of our children?

ALWAYS SUNNY ABOVE THE CLOUDS

Despite this assurance, in our vulnerability, we can still be tempted to lose hope along the way.

In one of Fr. Mike's prayers, tucked within *The Bible in a Year* podcast, he mentioned something critical following the reading of Psalm 88—

the only psalm, he said, that ends in darkness. Despite this, we need to remember that "the darkness is not dark for you," Lord.

Flying in an airplane above the clouds, it becomes apparent that the darkness upon the earth is only a shadow of a cloud, but above the cloud, it is always sunny. Though we, too, might feel darkness around us, it is just a cloud. And above that cloud, where God dwells, lightness abounds, forever.

Thank you, Lord, for reminding us that your light can never be extinguished. May we always rejoice in the pure gift of our children, as you always rejoice in us, remembering to keep our chins up!

PART II

PART II

16

A Tale of Two Churches

"Why doesn't the Church let gay people marry?" a daughter, now in college, asked her mother. "I don't like how it excludes them. Just because they are not 'traditional' doesn't mean they don't love each other and deserve to be happy, like anyone else."

The mother who shared this conversation said that, of all the issues her daughter has given for why she no longer feels warm toward the Catholic Church, marriage, as her daughter understands it, rises to the top. She just cannot shake her perception of the Church being hateful in its stance on marriage, along with its negative attitudes toward the LGBTQ+ community.

She is not alone. A Pew Research study from 2019 showed that two-thirds of white, mainline Protestants support same-sex marriage, and a similar portion of Catholics also do, at sixty-one percent—the same percentage as Americans overall.[37] These results illustrate a growing misunderstanding of certain fundamental realities, and division, in both the general population as well as within the Church itself.

The daughter cited what she calls the Church's "heavily patriarchal nature" as another reason for her growing aversion to the Faith that, in younger years, she had seemed receptive to and content with. Additionally, in her college courses, she said, she had come to see how women are demeaned, both through the Church and in Scripture. Finally, she commented that the Church seems full of hypocrites, and she feels judged at Mass.

Each of her complaints deserves a listening ear and a thoughtful conversation. For our purposes here, we can say that, from these examples, it is apparent that the Church we know and want to share, and the Church our children have experienced, observed, and believe to be true, may be two different churches in many ways.

When we think of the Catholic Church, an image comes to our minds that includes saints, sinners, and Christ at the center. Though our own unique histories and experiences will color our picture of the Church slightly, all of us can have an appreciation for its divine origin, having been established by Jesus himself and endowed with his protection, grace, and authority to teach in his name. Given its saving mission, Christ preserves the Church from error and offers the assurance that "the gates of Hades will not prevail against it" (Matthew 16:18). Throughout its two-thousand-year history, the Church has experienced its share of scandals due to the fallen, sinful nature of its members. Nevertheless, because it is ultimately a divine institution, the Church endures, preaching the truth of Christ, inspiring the rise of new saints through the ages, and proving, continually, to be a force of unfathomable good in the world.

Despite all we might have done to form our children in Jesus and in his Church, as they grew and began to experience life on their own, some may have developed a very different picture of what "the Church" means. In processing their departure and trying to understand what happened, it might help to consider that the Church from which they are fleeing does not necessarily match the one we have presented to them.

The Church has elements of brokenness because it is made up of sinful human beings. As a result, it has gone through periods of crisis in the past, as well as in recent times. But those of us who love the Church understand that it belongs to Christ and is holy *because of him*, even if some of her people do not always live up to their calling as its members.

MARRIAGE, ONE OF MANY REASONS

Kari Curtin, director of the Marriage Reality Movement, describes marriage as "the only institution that unites a man and woman with each other, and with any children born from their union."

Since Curtin understands all too well that many people today—particularly young adults—have a different idea of marriage, the Marriage Reality

Movement seeks to move them from an "adult-centric" view of marriage back to focus on family and children. The reality that children have a fundamental human right to grow up with their parents united in marriage needs to be re-presented to our culture, according to Curtin.

One Sunday after Mass, Curtin was in the vestibule of her parish at a table promoting the reality of marriage. A girl of about sixteen stopped by and glanced at the materials being offered. After perusing them for a moment, the girl said dismissively, "Oh, I'm not old enough for an organization on marriage!" Curtin saw this as an opportunity to share the truth about marriage with her.

She explained, "When a man and woman marry, they choose to become irreplaceable to each other, and to any children that come as gifts into their lives." The girl seemed genuinely surprised, saying, "That is so beautiful!" Curtin continued, "Would you want to marry someone who didn't believe in that description of marriage?" "No!" the girl replied. "Would you even want to *date* someone who didn't believe in that description of marriage?" The young woman said, "Oh, I see now what you mean," and she picked up one of the brochures from the table.

The girl had never heard marriage described that way, and she saw now how having a proper understanding of marriage applied even to her at sixteen.

Curtin also spoke of another young woman who, when she first heard about the Marriage Reality Movement, assumed it was "anti-gay." When Curtin described the actual work and aim of the organization—"to protect the fundamental human right of young people to grow up with their mom and dad united in marriage"—this young woman's perspective completely changed, and she expressed her support for its work.

Am I loving or using? is the key question we need to ask regarding marriage, according to Curtin: "We are using another when we are seeking intimacy that cannot actually be present in its deepest form, until we have made ourselves irreplaceably united in marriage. To truly love someone outside of marriage means to protect that future gift of self for both of you until after marriage. In doing so, we become more self-sacrificing." She added that this willingness to self-sacrifice for the sake of others is a vital attribute we should look for in a future spouse.

"The reality of marriage, and the way the Church describes and approaches it, is quite beautiful and compelling," Curtin said. "Many young people aren't hearing this truth. But I have seen many become more receptive after hearing what it is we really believe and try to convey."

In her exchanges with both the girl and the young woman, each of her listeners shifted their perspective upon hearing the real vision of marriage, rather than the way the culture spins it.

A CHURCH IN FLAMES OR SOULS ON FIRE

The cover of Ralph Martin's book *A Church in Crisis* displays a photo of Paris' Cathedral of Notre Dame in flames. On April 15, 2019, this ancient cathedral, dating from the thirteenth century, was severely damaged by an out-of-control blaze. Some Catholics saw this catastrophe as a metaphor for the Church's current engulfment in the flames of division, infidelity, and crisis.

If this is the picture our children hold of the Church—an institution in flames, at least figuratively—can we blame them for being tempted to flee? We need to help them understand that this is only a partial picture of the one, holy, catholic, and apostolic Church founded by Jesus Christ, "the way, and the truth, and the life" (John 14:6) and that the Church is more than the weaknesses and sins of its members. It is divine in origin. As Jesus promised St. Peter, "You are Peter, and on this rock I will build my Church, and the gates of Hades shall not prevail against it" (Matthew 16:18).

It is natural that we want the souls of our children to be on fire for God and his Church, rather than for any of them to be in danger of eternal fires of hell. We need to keep in mind, though, that our era is not the first in which flames have threatened to consume the Church.

ST. MONICA GETS IT

"I can find no words to express how intensely she loved me," St. Augustine would write after his conversion, "with far more anxious solicitude did she give birth to me in the spirit than ever she had in the flesh."[38]

But before attaining that perspective, St. Augustine had run from the Church his mother had tried to introduce him to. Though still in its relative infancy, the Church was, even then, controversial, for it has always been at odds with its surroundings.

Interestingly, our world today and the world of St. Monica and Augustine are, in a sense, mirror images of one another. The ancient world was post-pagan and pre-Christian, while our contemporary society is becoming post-Christian, with a subtle drift back into paganism in some quarters.

St. Monica had one vision of the Church in her heart—fashioned from her childhood, in which she was lovingly raised in the Faith—and St. Augustine held up another picture altogether. The one his mother tried to present to him was an impediment, in his mind, keeping him from the freedoms he wished to enjoy without guilt. Manichaeism offered a church in which people bear no responsibility for their sins. The wild, young Augustine, with his youthful hormones raging and his taste for alcohol, was attracted to this tantalizing "freedom."

"Such was my mind," he would later admit, "so weighed down, so blinded by the flesh, that I was myself unknown to myself."[39] It might be said he was fleeing not so much *from* the Church, but *toward* a church that promised a false, unconstrained liberty—just as the world promises our children today.

We cannot, on our own, change the vision in the hearts and heads of our children of what the Church is; the forces against us are simply too great. But we can hold firmly, resolutely, in place, trusting in God to quell the flames that lap at the door of our homes and hearts, and in his promises. "I keep the LORD always before me; because he is at my right hand, I shall not be moved" (Psalm 16:8).

We can also borrow assurances from just a few lines later in the same psalm, verse 11: "You show me the path of life; in your presence there is fullness of joy, in your right hand are pleasures for evermore."

Many words in our culture have been changed to mean something other than what they are, and the overwhelming saturation of the resulting ideas, spread through social media and other avenues, have lured our children into a world of mistruth that seeks to destroy the Christian faith and devalue marriage and the family. Our children, in part because they are still impressionable, malleable, and compassionate, are the prime targets.

The real truth is beautiful and can win them over—if they are receptive to hearing it. It will take more than our efforts to bring these two versions of the Church together, however. It will take God's grace.

17

Defending the Church amid Scandal

"Yeah, well, your priests like little boys," an ex-Catholic wrote under a social media post that was defending traditional marriage. This is a familiar, painful attack on the Church of late. While the ugliness of current scandals does not tarnish the beauty of Catholic truth, it has become a black mark on the Church and ammunition for detractors. By processing the scandals, whether regarding sexual abuse, financial impropriety, or anything else, we can cling to the Church founded by Jesus while neither excusing nor ignoring them.

We are addressing the sex abuse scandals because to some extent, we have all been affected by them. It may have also impacted our children's feelings toward the Church. The following interviews with an exorcist and three victims of abuse can help us separate scandal from Catholic teachings.

Any member of the clergy guilty of sexual abuse or covering it up commits an abomination against the victim, the family, and the Church. Although teachers, coaches, and other denominations have also had abusers in their midst, we tend to hear more about Catholic priests than the other groups. Does that mean the Church is picked on? Maybe, but priests *are* in the person of Christ, and the Catholic Church *is* the largest single Christian church. So, when a member of the clergy victimizes a child, this is an especially scandalous, horrendous sin.

Fr. Gary Thomas, an exorcist whose training in Rome is the subject of the 2010 book *The Rite: The Making of a Modern Exorcist* by Matt Baglio, addresses this situation in the article "How to Recognize Demonic Activity in the Church Scandals, According to an Exorcist" in the *National Catholic Register*.[40]

Fr. Thomas writes, "By sexually abusing children, Satan desires to destroy the icon of the kingdom of God. He wants to destroy the most innocent version of humanity, which is the child." He called on all Catholics to pray and fast and to act to triumph over the evil. He noted that he fasts and prays before his work as an exorcist. "Prayer, fasting, and the sacraments are efficacious," he said. "We want prayer to change us, and we are praying for a change in the whole Church, all the way up. And we are also praying for the victims who have gone through terrible trauma."

According to Fr. Thomas, Catholics need to be strong and be prepared to persevere. "However, our primary concern must be the victims who have been violated. There can be no tolerance for sexual misconduct perpetrated by clergy or lay people within the Church now or ever again."

PAUL'S STORY

Paul Peloquin, a Catholic clinical psychologist in Albuquerque, New Mexico, shares his story of abuse in the article "Victimized Family Finds Healing in the Church" in *Our Sunday Visitor*. He was abused as an 11-year-old by Fr. Earl Bierman. (It was later discovered that Bierman had abused many children in two different states. In 1993, he was sentenced to twenty years in prison and died there in 2005.) He explained that sexual abuse by a priest causes both physical and spiritual trauma. Peloquin left the Church for more than thirty years, but he now uses faith-based therapy to help victims to heal and return to the Church.

Peloquin explains that any family that suspects abuse should stay calm, listen to the child, and then go to the police. Reasons for the abused not telling anyone, he says, include repressing the experience, fear of hurting the parents, thinking no one will believe them, or shame because it's a seduction instead of a rape. "Because of the imbalance of power and immaturity of the child, there is no real consent, but the child will feel guilty and hide it. Then, where can they go? They are blocked from seeking reconciliation and blocked from the sacraments regardless of whether their parents are still making them go."

Peloquin began acting out, which he said is a typical response to abuse. He ended up being unruly and angry at his mother—who had been friends with the priest—and broke rules at home and in school. He ended up getting sent to a military-type boarding school to keep him under control.

Not until he began studying for his doctorate did Peloquin realize he had been blocking the abuse and entered into therapy. His return to the Catholic Faith came about slowly, over the course of several years, as his heart began to soften. Spending time at a Benedictine monastery in the mountains, surrounded by nature and soaking in the peace, helped him reestablish a relationship with God.

"We need good priests who want to live as servants. We cannot have the sacraments without them. The majority of priests are good; only a few are not," Peloquin says. "The Church has a lot of problems simply because it is made up of human beings," he said.

Peloquin's message to victims is: "Don't let the evil one imprison you. There is one who can set you free—Jesus—and heal you from our wounds. He is your hope and he never stopped loving you. He is there with open arms and thirsts for you to come back. If you leave the Church, you are leaving more than you realize; you are leaving your means for salvation."[41]

FAITH'S STORY

Faith Hakesley, author of *Glimmers of Grace: Moments of Peace and Healing Following Sexual Abuse*, was sexually abused at age fifteen in 2000 while working a part-time job as a parish secretary. Her rapist, the now-laicized Fr. Kelvin Iguabita, was sentenced in 2003 to 12 to 14 years in prison and then deported to his native Columbia.

Predators are good at gaining trust and manipulating and confusing the victim. As Faith shared in a *National Catholic Register* interview with one of the authors, "I was a shy and a socially awkward fifteen-year-old adjusting to high school and asked for his advice," Hakesley said. He had become my confidant; and by the time he struck, I was shocked and felt as if I must have led him on somehow. And the parish loved him, so why would they believe me? As so often happens to victims of abuse, I lived in a deep pit of fear, shame and confusion."[42]

The abuse came out when Hakesley saw a grief counselor following the death of her oldest brother from a heart condition in his early twenties when Hakesley was sixteen. "My counselor gave me the confidence to tell my parents," she said. "They believed me right away and never asked why I didn't come forward earlier. Eventually, I sat down with detectives, and the Archdiocese of Boston was alerted that something was up with Kelvin Iguabita." When the case went to court, seven women contacted Hakesley when they heard about it and said he did the same thing to them.

Having been raised in a devout Catholic family, along with three brothers, Hakesley says, "Faith was ingrained in me, but because of who my abuser was, the spiritual aspect of my life was betrayed. I kept my faith—though it was slight at times—through the sacraments. I could not let go of receiving Jesus in the Eucharist, even when I was mad at God. I tell anyone who is a person of faith that they can use that as a powerful tool to heal. ... In the midst of my suffering, there came a time when holding on to faith became a decision. I had to choose between abandoning faith or turning to the Lord, despite my doubt. I found more healing in my faith than anywhere."[43]

Hakesley is now happily married and the mother of three young children, and feels she has healed from much of the pain from her past abuse. She shares her own story to reach out to other victims and their families to give them hope and guidance but also to uplift the Church despite scandals that have unfortunately happened in recent years. Her message is that it is the sinner who has done wrong, but the Church still has the truth, and healing can be found there.

18

We Are All Broken

Because we are human, we are all broken. We all have to suffer the effects of original—and personal—sin in our lives. We come from broken families with broken histories, which ultimately reach back to the sin of our first parents, Adam and Eve. Thankfully, Jesus Christ, though perfect, allowed himself to be broken in his passion and crucifixion out of love for us for our salvation. Through him, our brokenness can be healed.

On day 151 of *The Bible in a Year* podcast, Fr. Mike Schmitz reflects on Ecclesiastes 7:1–4, noting that it is not the beginning of our lives that matters but the end. Sorrow can bring us wisdom. As we read, "Sorrow is better than laughter, for by sadness of countenance the heart is made glad. The heart of the wise is in the house of mourning" (Ecclesiastes 7:3–4).

We might have come into this world in brokenness, but Jesus and his Church offer us a way to be healed and become wise. Through sharing some of our own stories of brokenness, perhaps we can help one another do just that.

ROXANE'S STORY

Growing up on the Fort Peck Reservation in northeast Montana, I saw brokenness everywhere I looked. Poverty was rampant, and alcoholism was a major problem, along with crime. In the mid-1980s, during a rash of stabbings, it was widely believed that our small town had the highest murder rate of a community of its size in the nation.

We had moved there for my parents' teaching jobs when I was not quite two, and that was where I spent my entire childhood. My parents stayed many years beyond. Even before I left for college, I had begun to see that all the brokenness outside was inside our home as well.

My father left teaching because his drinking made it hard for him to keep up with the rigors of grading papers and being in a proper state of mind for his responsibilities as a junior high English teacher. For years, every day at five p.m., he would leave for the bar, and my sister, my mother, and I would eat dinner alone at home. A piece was missing from my life. Though I knew Dad loved me, this one-time seminarian with a once-fervent faith had lost some hope, and it colored his life's path in despair.

After my sister left for college, things got worse. Dad's disease progressed, and he began blacking out. We could no longer avoid this unpleasant truth. I often went to bed crying, believing he would die in the night.

Eventually, during my freshman year of college—through what seemed divine intervention—my dad went to treatment and became sober. Many things changed then, including his return to the Church after thirty-five years. But all those years growing up with a father who struggled to hold down a job and battled depression started to show its effects in my relationships. Though I did not realize it for a while, as the daughter of an alcoholic, I had been caught up in the mental aspects of the disease and needed some major healing.

Eventually, I dug deep and sought that healing. It was the hardest work I have ever done. But some of these wounds still sneaked into my marriage and early years as a mother. Additionally, my husband brought his own wounds. Though our parents had both stayed married, we suffered from some of their discord and struggles. Not knowing better, we transferred some of these learned, negative behaviors to our own relationship, and, sadly, onto our children.

Thankfully, God never left us, though we wandered away from him at times. I can only explain how we made it through our toughest years by pointing to the Cross—at Jesus' unfathomable love for us—along with the sacramental graces we received through participating in the life of the Church. But certainly, our own years of struggle and woundedness have had an effect on our children.

As I look back and see the broken shards of our lives glistening along the path behind us, my hope comes in remembering that God is the great healer. I have done the best I can to this point to repair what was broken, finding solace in drawing close to our Lord, his mother and the great saints who inspire and bring hope.

Now, I can even see how the trials we have experienced have humbled us and brought us closer to the Cross. Here, we find redemption and a path forward. And I know we are far from alone.

IF ONLY WE WERE LIKE THEM

Sometimes, we look at families around us who seem to have it all together and wish we could be like them. In comparison, we are tempted to feel like failures.

PATTI: I once heard a talk by a well-known Catholic speaker and ended up feeling sad. The speaker and his wife were a beautiful example of a faithful couple whose grown children were all Catholics and one became a priest. Although the speaker admitted that their family was far from perfect, while they shared some of their family traditions, I felt inadequate. They mentioned activities with extended family which we would never be able to arrange because of distance and willingness of relatives to participate in such activities. The longer I listened to their talk, the more out of their league I felt. I turned off the recording. I could not make us that kind of family, and hearing about it at length only rubbed it in. Yet, I told myself that God can make up for what is lacking, so I prayed for that then and continue to pray for whatever holes there were in our efforts.

St. Monica lived with brokenness, too. She must have lamented not being able to surround her family in faith and virtue. After all, she did not have a husband willing to work alongside her to create a wholesome, Catholic environment. Instead, Patricius was known to have a violent temper and to be unfaithful. Yet Monica remained faithful to her family and to God, offering alms, deeds, and prayers that vexed the proud Patricius. In time, she won him over with her charity, and he converted to Christianity a year before his death.

Monica's faith became her unshakable anchor through much disappointment. Other women began to notice. It was not uncommon for suffering wives to come to her for strength and comfort in their own difficulties.

ELIZABETH'S STORY

All five of Elizabeth's children have left the Church. "I feel like there needs to be a miracle to reach my children," she lamented. Although her husband, Dan, faithfully went to Sunday Mass and prayed the Rosary every day, he was not a strong, fatherly example. Despite taking great care to find a faithful Catholic husband to avoid being abandoned like her mother was, Elizabeth's marriage still ended in divorce. The problem: Dan believes he is a woman and has chosen to live like one.

Although Dan was never unkind during their thirty-year marriage, over time, Elizabeth's cross grew heavier. While running three businesses from home (two marketing companies and a Catholic bookstore), raising five children, and caring for her husband, she often felt as if she were drowning. Though Dan began having serious health problems, his growing desire to be a woman understandably burdened Elizabeth most of all.

Dan and Elizabeth's marriage began full of promise. They had met in college, and they became engaged in church before the Blessed Sacrament. *This is going to be the Catholic marriage that my mother never had*, Elizabeth thought. Soon after they were married, though, it became clear that Dan had an unusually low sex drive.

"My gut told me we had a real problem," Elizabeth says. "But I knew nothing about gender identity disorder. I thought my role was to be understanding. He was sensitive and artistic, and looked masculine, but he wasn't."

Over the years, they went to counseling several times. "The Catholic counselors we met with affirmed that sacramental marriage is between a man and a woman, and that God endows each of us with an identity of beloved son or beloved daughter," Elizabeth said. "Our gender is written by God into the DNA of every cell of our body."

Four years into their marriage, Elizabeth became pregnant. She had been promoted to the upper management of a telemarketing company, but she wanted to be a stay-at-home mother. She babysat and found other ways to make money at home while Dan worked as a social worker. He soon became ill, however, and his doctor diagnosed him with a serious adrenal disorder. He never returned to work. Their youngest child was only two at the time.

Elizabeth found a way to do marketing work from home, and even later opened a Catholic bookstore there. Amid all her busyness, she tried to block out her husband's troubling inclinations, but they kept resurfacing. By the time her youngest children were in high school, Dan began acting out more. But Elizabeth told him, "You've chosen marriage and children, so you don't have a right to act on those desires." Finally, she gave him a choice: stay married or live as a woman. He chose the latter.

When Dan began using a female name, grew his hair long, and started wearing women's clothing, Elizabeth consulted with several priests, one of whom was a canon lawyer. She was told that a marriage between a wife and "wanna-be wife" would be a lie. "I came to see that Dan and I had a beautiful friendship but never a true marriage," she says.

Though Elizabeth filed for divorce, she was determined to love Dan. She told him, "There will be landmines for sin in our path ahead—selfishness, bitterness, unkindness, and anger— but let's make an agreement to help each other to avoid sin."

Of their five children, two support their father living as a woman, two do not, and one is non-committal. But all treat him with kindness, something Elizabeth tried to instill in them. She challenges those who are upset with their father to forgive him or they will take their bitterness into every relationship. She says, "There will always be those who disappoint and hurt us. Most often people are sincerely trying to do the right thing. It's our choice whether we will be offended and bitter or realize that we also have hurt others and we all need forgiveness."

Elizabeth says she has come to a degree of healing she did not think possible earlier on. "Part of that healing is asking the Lord to help me continue to love him as a brother in Christ, even while not accepting the disorder," she shared. "We can't approve of disordered actions. Love can only be found in truth. Christ wants to bring all of us into order and abundant life. It helps me to picture Jesus' eyes looking at him, and all our frail humanity with profound love. It's easy to look on the surface and see the face of the offender, but love requires us to look deeper to see the suffering soul. I believe that's what God is asking each of us to do."

REACHING THE KIDS

Elizabeth says her children did not receive the Catholic Faith as readily as she had hoped. It did not help that Dan was militant about praying the Rosary every night but lacked a fatherly relationship with his children.

"They have been so immersed in the Church, maybe over-immersed," Elizabeth said. "I share my experience, but I no longer catechize them or try to convince them." Her daughter, having met some of Elizabeth's friends, recently commented that they are amazing, saying, "It's like they have something special." By this witness of peace and goodness among her relationships, Elizabeth hopes her daughter—and her other children—will become curious about its source: the Catholic Faith.

"The race is not over until it's over," Elizabeth continues. Her father's deathbed conversion encourages her to never give up hope. Years after her father left her mother and her two siblings, he returned home suffering from liver cancer. Elizabeth's holy mother took her ex-husband in and cared for him when he had nowhere else to go.

"I learned the lesson of forgiveness and mercy when I saw my mom being merciful to my dad over and over," Elizabeth explained. Her mother brought a hospital bed into their home, and Elizabeth and her siblings lived nearby and helped.

In conversations with her father, he admitted that he thought he would be going to hell.

"Dad, I've spent my entire life without you; I do not want to spend all of eternity without you, too," Elizabeth pleaded. "All you have to do is ask God to forgive you. Be humble and go to confession." He finally relented, "Well, honey, I'll do whatever you want me to do."

Soon thereafter, a priest was called in. "Jesus, have mercy!" Elizabeth prayed. "I claim his soul for Christ!" She kept praying until the priest opened the door and invited her and her mother in to pray. "A new person was there," Elizabeth said. "The look on his face was beautiful. I was convinced that my dad was right with God. We prayed with him, and he was able to receive Communion three or four times before he died a few days later."

Her father passed away right after Elizabeth's mother finished praying a Divine Mercy Chaplet at his bedside. "We knew the race was won and the struggle was over," Elizabeth said. "It was the most amazing experience of my life."

A CONDUIT OF GRACE

During his Sunday Angelus homily on December 27, 2020, Pope Francis said, "The holy family was holy because it was centered on Jesus." Despite the fact that Jesus' family began in an imperfect situation, with a young, pregnant mother whose husband, who had not taken part in Jesus' conception, almost left her, they became whole through focusing on God, he explains.

Pope Francis concludes his reflection by asking everyone "to pray for all the families of the world, especially those that, for various reasons, are lacking in peace and harmony" and to "entrust them to the protection of the Holy Family of Nazareth."[44]

God accompanies us in our brokenness. In our imperfections, we can find a conduit of grace for our salvation. We may be tempted to wish our family were less broken. But this is the family God has given us. In some mysterious way, it is through our families that we are saved, and it is through our brokenness that we come to experience our need for salvation—and seek healing and freedom in Jesus.

19

When We Are Tempted to Compromise Our Faith

Can there be no distinction between what the world accepts and what we are called to accept as followers of Christ? In recent decades, we have become increasingly aware that we must tread lightly and lovingly on certain issues—because we do not always model Christian charity as well as we should. The Church has been working to show greater understanding, charity, and support for various groups who struggle with its moral teachings. For instance, ministries such as Project Rachel (which helps women who have had abortions) and Courage and Encourage (which serve those with same-sex attraction and their families, respectively) were founded to accompany people through often painful life situations.

Nonetheless, Catholic moral teaching is sometimes portrayed in the harshest, most uncharitable light—as intolerant, cruel, unkind, opposed to love, etc. Our children can be affected by these strong cultural currents; they can even begin to view the Church as the "bad guy," as out of touch and just plain "wrong" on issues such as same-sex marriage or abortion. In order to foster a relationship, parents with children who have left the Church might be tempted to sympathize with their view and even follow them down that same path. It might seem easier to acquiesce than to sow further discord.

WHEN TEMPTATIONS ARISE

Gloria's son was a seminarian. She was proud of him, and she looked forward to the day when he would serve God as a priest. He ended up dropping out of the seminary, though, and announced that he was sexually attracted to men. Now, Gloria defends her son's choice to live in a same-sex relationship. She went from being a committed "cheerleader" of the Church to a fervent critic of its teachings against her son's lifestyle.

How can we stay devoted to the Catholic Faith given the pressure to bend to the whims of our culture? How do we navigate difficult moral situations without alienating others, particularly our own children? In some cases, these situations may actually involve our children. What do we do then?

A LESSON FROM TOBIT

In the book of Tobit, we have the story of a man who was taken into captivity by a tribe at odds with his ancestral people. During his captivity, Tobit's life became increasingly challenging, but he was committed to staying faithful to the Lord. As he says, "I, Tobit, walked in the ways of truth and righteousness all the days of my life" (Tobit 1:3).

Tobit's heart yearned to stay true to God, but those around him lived contrary to the ways of the Lord: "All the tribes that joined in apostasy used to sacrifice to the calf Baal, and so did the house of Naphtali my forefather. But I alone went often to Jerusalem for the feasts, as it is ordained for all Israel by an everlasting decree" (Tobit 1:5–6).

Upon his captivity, his relatives succumbed to the surrounding culture, and his brothers and relatives ate the food of the Gentiles. But Tobit did not, saying, "I kept myself from eating it, because I remembered God with all my heart" (Tobit 1:11).

Not only did Tobit give bread to the hungry and clothing to the naked, but if he saw someone from his tribe lying dead and discarded behind the wall of Nineveh, he would bury them—often secretly, knowing he could be put to death himself for doing so.

Tobit did not always have it easy. Soon, he would become blind from bird excrement that fell into his eyes. Poor guy! At times, we can feel like we are being dumped on, despite our fidelity to God. Yet the Lord calls us to remain faithful, even when things are difficult, with the help of his grace.

MONICA'S FIDELITY, DESPITE HER SURROUNDINGS

Monica's situation was not so easy, either. Despite the light of the Christian faith now shining through the darkness of the pagan world, her surroundings retained deep imprints of pagan culture. These influences had entrapped her son Augustine. Carthage, where Augustine studied, was considered second only to Rome in its culture and education—and in its corruption.[45]

As Forbes writes in *The Life of Saint Monica*, "All that was worst in the civilization of the East and of the West met and mingled. The blood combats between men and beasts, the gladiatorial shows that delighted the Romans, were free to all who chose to frequent the amphitheater of Carthage, with horrible rites of the Eastern religions practiced openly."[46]

In the schools themselves, lack of discipline reigned, with wealthier students often taking advantage of their positions. They actually worked at developing—and reveling in—their bad reputations, earning nicknames such as "smashers" and "upsetters" after destroying classrooms and raiding the schools of professors they disliked.

Augustine got caught up in it all, even if he did not always join in completely, frequenting the theater. As Forbes says, "His pleasure-loving nature snatched at everything that life could give." Only in later years would he lament this exorbitant, unmerciful existence, crying, "My God, with what bitter gall didst Thou in Thy great mercy sprinkle those pleasures of mine!"[47]

Meanwhile, back home in Tagaste, Monica, knowing that the world had enraptured her son, wept and prayed for him all the more. Unlike Patricius, she did not excuse her son's behavior, nor brag to others about his gifts—not when he was living in a state of sin.

When Monica learned that Augustine had fallen in with the Manichaeans, she clutched her heart. As Forbes reports, "This was a blow for which she had not been prepared; it crushed her to the earth. She would have grieved less over the news of her son's death." Nevertheless, she did not relent, but "bent her broken heart to God's will, and hoped on in Him, 'Whose Mercy cannot fail.'"[48]

A SHINING EXAMPLE OF GOODNESS

Commenting on day 192 of *The Bible in a Year* podcast, in which the aforementioned reading from Tobit emerges, Fr. Jim Chern notes that much of the Old Testament features "very broken people who fail in spectacular fashion." In Tobit, though, we have a family living in the midst of a pagan world yet remaining faithful to God, much like Job.

Even in exile, Tobit, unlike others in his tribe, holds to kosher regulations, following ordinances to care for the poor and bury the dead. As Fr. Chern notes, "In all of this, we see a shining example of striving to remain faithful to God's Word against all odds. Just because he couldn't do everything that God commanded his people to do, that didn't mean Tobit couldn't do some of the things that were in his power to do ... Tobit helps us to see that God's efforts of reaching out to us were not in vain. Not then. And not now."

STAYING STRONG

As parents, loving our children can be mixed at times with accompanying them down a wrong path. A particular wound from our past might keep us from doing what is right, leading us to support behaviors contrary to Catholic teaching, such as cohabitation before marriage, embracing a same-sex lifestyle, having an abortion, or using contraception, among others. Perhaps we ourselves are struggling with the Church's teaching on a particular issue.

Loving our children unconditionally does not mean unconditionally accepting their choices or lifestyle. If we really love them, we will be honest about where we stand and why. This means we must understand the teachings of the Church correctly and be able to explain them in a way that is relatable to our children. In the end, we need to stress that the Church's mission, given by Jesus himself, seeks to present the truth of the gospel—which is the path to freedom, happiness, and salvation. "You will know the truth, and the truth will make you free" (John 8:32).

ANOTHER WAY

"When I became Catholic in 1998, I was an especially naïve nineteen-year-old. I didn't know any other gay people who were willing to accept the Church's teaching on sexuality," Andrey Kuzmin shares in a recent article.[49] "Since then, I've been able to watch the startling development of gay Christian communities that accept the traditional teaching that sex is reserved for marriage between one man and one woman."

Kuzmin said that most are like her—they need to take the Church's teaching on trust. "God calls everyone to love," she writes. "He chooses which paths of love are open to us, but there is nobody who is left without any means of pouring out their life in giving and receiving love. Once I accepted that God wasn't calling me to a lesbian partnership, I started to look around and find other, neglected pathways."

She notes how far people have strayed from the varieties of love found in Scripture, such as the extended family of Ruth and Naomi; the familial, sacrificial love of the early Church; the covenant of friendship of David and Jonathan; and the love Jesus had for Lazarus and his disciples, especially for John, "the Beloved Apostle." She also shared that many with same-sex attraction struggle to love themselves because they have often been treated as if they do not love God or are not feminine or masculine enough. It is a reminder for Christians to "lead with love." As Kuzmin offers, "Our life with all its challenges is a gift that it is our duty to receive with gratitude, trusting that God has given it to you for your own good."

A MOTHER'S UNWAVERING LOVE

Carmen's youngest son has same-sex attraction. She says that she clings to the truth and advises other parents to care more about their child's soul than anything else:

> More than a decade ago, our son announced: "Mom, I think I'm gay." I was devastated! I told him he just needed time to get through his confusion. But he was resolute, saying that if we tried to change him, he would leave. As soon as I got off the phone with him, I crumbled to the floor, and wept long and hard to the point that I could scarcely breathe.
>
> When I finally gathered myself and stood, trembling from head to toe, I looked at the large-framed image of Madonna of the Street and cried out, "OK, Blessed Mother, apply the graces where needed." I offered up this horrific heartache to Jesus, uniting my suffering to his own.
>
> Over time, Ben returned to the practice of his faith. Soon, though, he said, "Mom, I realize I only came back to the Church to gain approval from the family. I don't really believe in God."
>
> "That's OK, son," I said. "He still believes in you. And I believe he has a great plan for you." I told him that I loved him too much to say, "OK,

son, what if you told me that you're attracted to snakes, especially the poisonous kind? I don't think you really expect me to say, 'Alright, if that's what makes you happy, son.'"

There have been other struggles in my dear son's life and there were numerous times that he could have died—from alcohol poisoning or driving under the influence. A few years after his announcement, his dad, my dear husband of thirty years, passed away. Ben took his father's death very hard, and he got behind the wheel drunk. He hit a parked truck while speeding—and ended up with just a badly bruised knee.

Days later, I told him, "God protected you because you have a divinely appointed mission awaiting you." After this, he made another attempt at the sacraments but when life did not unfold neatly for him, he bailed once again. I told him that as long as he was not doing what is necessary to grow in relationship with Christ and carry his cross—as we all must do—he would continue to feel a void in his heart. "God is not going to zap you and make everything seem great," I told him. "You have to do your part by prayer and spiritual reading."

One day, Ben told me, "Mom, I'm tired of being alone and lonely; I need someone in my life." These words came to me: "Son, the male love you actually crave is Jesus Christ and he wants your love even more."

Many more hardships came after this but by the grace of God, a lot of Rosaries, daily Mass, and sacrifices, Ben entered rehab and broke off a same-sex relationship. I am seeing a new maturity in him that formerly was woefully lacking. He is even praying before meals again and thanking me when I tell him that I'm praying for him.

I do not know what lies ahead for him, but I do know, by faith, that in the end, he will know that he has been unconditionally loved, especially, by God. I believe that as Ben grows in a relationship with Christ, he will find peace and healing to whatever extent God wills.

Though the culture surrounds, even having snared some we considered upstanding members of our Catholic community, we can, following St. Monica and Tobit, lean on God to help us stay resolute.

Lord, help me stay true to you, even in the midst of an unbelieving world. Bring your grace, so that I might not cave to the pressure, and still love my child truly, just as surely as you have loved me—in all my days.

20

Addressing Questions of Gender Identity Discordance

According to the American Society of Plastic Surgeons, approximately 11,000 "gender confirmation or sex reassignment surgeries" were performed in 2019 in the United States, a fifteen percent increase from the previous year. These figures are anticipated to continue growing. One report shows that $361 million were spent on sexual reassignment surgeries in 2019 worldwide, a total that is projected to increase to $1.5 billion by 2026.[50]

The questions of gender identity discordance we are currently experiencing do not seem to be going away anytime soon. It is now a topic discussed on a daily basis in high school and college classrooms, in homes, and throughout the media.

It is now even discussed on Catholic radio, as Dr. David Anders, host of *Called to Communion* on EWTN, knows too well. On his July 22, 2021, show, for example, a caller had a pressing question, one that was causing him a fair amount of anxiety. His question was: "How should I handle conversations with a fellow parishioner and coworker who recently began the process to transition from male to female?" As the caller explained, "I want to lead with love, but I also don't want to shy away from what I know to be the truth." He asked Dr. Anders how he should navigate this delicate situation.

This questioning caller could represent any of us, as we talk to our children about the issues of the day that divide us most—including those they might know who consider themselves to be transgender.

Dr. Anders acknowledged the profound suffering individuals grappling with gender issues endure. During his conversation with the caller, he suggested some resources, including the Vatican document *Male and Female He Created Them*.

Ultimately, Dr. Anders recommended responding with deep love and a profound acceptance of the person—which does not mean accepting the solution they have proposed—along with patience and a sincere desire to accompany them, rather than being judgmental.

This conversation might be helpful as we continue to process the ever-changing and shifting cultural tide that threatens to pull our children away from the Catholic Faith. Sometimes, all we need is a fresh approach as well as a lot of charity.

THE CHURCH WEIGHS IN

Our faith is clear that transgenderism contradicts God's moral law. In September 2015, Pope Francis decreed that transgendered individuals cannot carry out the responsibility of godparents in the sacrament of Baptism.[51] In addition, the Congregation for the Doctrine of the Faith has stated that "transsexual behavior publicly reveals an attitude contrary to the moral imperative of resolving the problem of one's sexual identity according to the truth of one's sexuality."

In his post-synod letter on marriage and the family, *Amoris laetitia* ("The Joy of Love"), Francis states that children should be taught "respect and appreciation" for sexual differences:

> Beyond the understandable difficulties which individuals may experience, the young need to be helped to accept their own body as it was created, for "thinking that we enjoy absolute power over our own bodies turns, often subtly, into thinking that we enjoy absolute power over creation ... An appreciation of our body as male or female is also necessary for our own self-awareness in an encounter with others different from ourselves.

> Only by losing the fear of being different can we be freed of self-centeredness and self-absorption. Sex education should help young people to accept their own bodies and to avoid the pretension "to cancel out sexual difference because one no longer knows how to deal with it.[52]

In October 2017, Pope Francis addressed the topic before the Pontifical Academy for Life's general assembly in Rome: "The biological and physical manipulation of sexual differences, which biomedical technology allows us to perceive as completely available to free choice—which it is not!—thus risks dismantling the source of energy that nurtures the alliance between man and woman and which renders it creative and fruitful."[53] He denounced how new technologies are making it easier for people to change their genders, saying this "utopia of the neutral" jeopardizes the creation of new life.

Such advances in biomedical technology, he said, "risk dismantling the source of energy that fuels the alliance between men and women and renders them fertile."

A CATHOLIC ANSWER

When asked the Catholic view of being transgender, Catholic Answers apologist Tom Nash replied that those who espouse transgenderism take the position that humans are all assigned a gender at birth through observed anatomy. When a biological male identifies as female and has related surgery, they speak of it as "gender confirmation" rather than "gender reassignment," believing their anatomy now reflects their true human identity.

According to Nash, "The Church has a different take on it, one that is grounded in genuinely confirmed reality." Here, there are two possibilities: we are either born male or female. "This also applies to hermaphrodites who, though they manifest both male and female anatomical aspects at birth, are either biological boys or girls."[54]

In this light, he said, the Church recognizes that every human person is created in the image and likeness of God, male or female, citing Genesis 1:26–27. Rather than supporting people in a disordered attempt to reject their undeniable biological identity, he said, we should help them discover their true identities as children of God.

STICK TO THE PREFERRED NAME

Nash advised against using "preferred pronouns" and to simply call a person by their preferred name. As he explained, "I once received a call from a man who had had sex-change surgery and now identified as a woman. He referred to himself as 'Mary.' At that point, I decided to refrain from asking him the name his parents gave him at birth or insist on using his birth name in our conversation. After all, he had called a faithful Catholic apostolate to receive genuinely Catholic counsel, so if I wanted to have hope of giving a fruitful witness, I couldn't let minor details derail things. In other words, I couldn't let style get in the way of substance."

Instead, while using this person's preferred name, Nash gently explained how everyone is called to live a chaste life. In this case, that meant not just "ending a sexually intimate relationship with a Christian man who wanted to continue the relationship despite having learned about Mary's surgery, but refraining from dating altogether and living a life of complete continence."

As a result of Nash's witness—which included the reminder that Jesus loves them, despite their struggles—the person recommitted to living a chaste life. As Nash explained, "If we give faithful witness to the teachings of Christ and his Church, then using a person's preferred name will become a moot point. In contrast, if we insist at the outset on setting them straight on which name we will use to refer to them, we will likely lose the opportunity to give them a faithful witness through which Christ can soften their heart to receive and embrace the gospel."

Armed with knowledge and a heart attuned to Christ, we can bravely enter into these challenging conversations and situations, not only with strangers, but with our children, who need to somehow survive this culture they are newly entering as adults. We might not know the answer to their question or challenge right away, but if stumped, we can offer to research it, perhaps talk to a spiritual director or someone else who might help us sort through the facts, and come back with something that, through prayer and enlightenment, can become not a dividing point, but a drawbridge that, as we let it down, will allow our children to walk across, and back into God's gentle arms.

21

Spiritual Warfare for Parents

We are in a spiritual tug-of-war. Our children may have stopped "pulling for" the Catholic Faith, so we are taking up the slack. In the end, it is they who will choose sides. By uniting ourselves with Jesus Christ, who loves them even more than we do, and calling on all the forces of heaven to employ our arsenal of spiritual weapons, we can take up the fight in earnest.

PRAYERS FOR PROTECTION

Those who have walked away from the Faith are not seeing things clearly, so they might be easily led astray into dangerous areas, such as occultic practices. Unfortunately, the occult and demonic influences are strong in our modern culture.

Msgr. Stephen Rossetti, chief exorcist of the Archdiocese of Washington for more than a decade, notes in his book *Diary of an American Exorcist: Demons, Possession, and the Modern-Day Battle Against Ancient Evil* that our society is showing signs of demonic oppression, with all its anger, division, confusion, occultic practices, and celebration of sin. He believes that the significant decline in the practice of the Catholic Faith has resulted in a loss of graced protection.

But all is not lost! It has always been that the small barque of Peter with a little band of the faithful on deck can turn back divine judgment and "coax" the Almighty to shed extraordinary graces on the people. The redemptive graces of Jesus' death and resurrection are infinite, and our merciful God wishes to shed those graces upon us.

"What must we do? Love God and love the people—completely. Judge no one, left or right, liberal, or conservative, Republican or Democrat, black or white. Pray constantly. Invoke the Blessed Virgin. Pray that our little prayers and sacrifices will be filled with the Spirit and share in the redemptive action of Jesus. Thus, they will become immensely fecund.

God will not abandon the United States. I believe it has a special role to play in the divine plan of salvation. But the influence of the demonic these days is palpable. The country needs us and our prayers right now."[55]

SPIRITUAL WARFARE FOR FAMILIES

In her book *A Family Guide to Spiritual Warfare: Strategies for Deliverance and Healing*, Kathleen Beckman shares her knowledge gained from serving for twelve years as part of a diocesan exorcism team, which offers prayer support for an exorcist's work, often being present during an exorcism.

She notes that the devil often aims for the family member who feels unloved, so we must not lose our focus of love to will the good of one another. Beckman says that demons attack families because of their enormous significance in God's plan of salvation, but that parents can call on their God-given authority and trust in the power of Jesus Christ to conquer evil. She also advises us to turn to Scripture for guidance, put on the armor of Christ, and remain in the state of grace to be protected and be productive in our efforts.

Beckman points to St. John Paul II's 1981 document *Familiaris consortio*: "At a moment of history in which the family is the object of numerous forces that seek to destroy it or in some way to deform it, and aware that the well-being of society and her own good are intimately tied to the good of the family, the Church perceives in a more urgent and compelling way her mission of proclaiming to all people the plan of God for marriage and the family."[56] Similarly, Pope Francis writes, "The devil does not need to possess us. He poisons us with the venom of hatred, desolation, envy and vice. When we let our guard down, he takes advantage of it to destroy our lives, our families, and our communities."[57]

As Beckman notes, "If you are seeking for a way to protect yourself and your family, look no further than the Person of Jesus Christ. He is the way! Think, act, and pray like Jesus Christ. In spiritual warfare, it is your incorporation into Christ that ensures victory over sin and evil." She quotes Acts 19:11–15, when an itinerant Jewish exorcist failed to exorcise a demon, who replied to him: "Jesus, I know, and Paul I know, but who are you?"

Beckman and Msgr. Esseff both advise the following:

- Seek always to remain in the state of grace by avoiding deliberate mortal sin.

- Receive the Eucharist frequently and offer up your Communion for the conversion of our loved ones.

- Pray the prayer the angel taught the children of Fatima: *My God, I believe, I adore, I hope, and I love you. I ask pardon for those who do not believe, do not adore, do not hope, and do not love you.*

- Pray the Chaplet of Divine Mercy frequently.

- Read Sacred Scripture every day.

- Offer personal sacrifices in reparation for your sins and those of others.

- Have a blessed crucifix in your home as a reminder of Jesus' love for us.

- Forgive. Don't let anger and resentment open you to evil influences. *"Forgive us our trespasses, as we forgive those who trespass against us."* Therapy and good spiritual direction may be necessary to help accomplish this.

- Use holy water to bless yourself and the rooms of your home. (Fill a bottle at church.) The blessings that a priest puts on the water extend through the places you sprinkle the water. It represents our baptism. Exorcists report that people who are possessed show a revulsion to holy water and blessed objects.

- Spend time praising and thanking God, especially for our children.

- Pray for spiritual protection with the Prayer to St. Michael the Archangel and St. Patrick's Breastplate Prayer.

- Review your own life and repent of any occultic practices you may have been involved with. Such practices include horoscopes, tarot cards, palm reading, and séances. Occult practices are forbidden by the first commandment and prohibited by the *Catechism of the Catholic Church* (see CCC 2117).

- Say the name of Jesus aloud several times. In the New Testament, we see that the demons were powerless and were cast out in Jesus' name (see Luke 10:17; Mark 16:17–18). Healings occurred in his name (see Acts 3:6, 3:16, 4:10), and salvation comes in his name (see Acts 4:12; Romans 10:13).

- Pray to St. Joseph, who has been given the title "terror of demons."

- Take authority in your home by claiming your children for God. Say a prayer to consecrate them to God and consecrate them to the Blessed Mother for her protection.

22

When the Debate Is Over

The caller to the Catholic Answers radio show shared his troubled heart with that day's guest, Catholic psychologist Dr. Ray Guarendi, about the state of his two adult sons' souls. Since they are both engineers with master's degrees, the caller and his wife believed they had succeeded in helping their sons get an education, but they did not do as well in helping them realize their purpose in life—which is eternal salvation. He asked, "Can we still help them to reach their purpose?"[58]

Dr. Ray, author of *Raising Upright Kids in an Upside-Down World*, called this issue a "longstanding byproduct of the culture's misshaping," noting that many adult children these days are making the decision that "the whole God thing just doesn't belong in their lives."

It is a decision he understands all too well. Dr. Ray explains, "I have kids who have drifted from the Faith also. For the most part, I keep my mouth shut. I'm not going to preach and I'm not going to nag. If any type of moral topic comes up, I'll engage them. But I have to decide whether I'm causing more harm than good by engaging in these kinds of interchanges that create friction."

When our children reach adulthood, our parenting role changes, he said. Now, their own God-given free will dictates their course. "They can do anything they want regarding the Faith." Sometimes, an opening presents itself where he might offer his kids a book to help address questions and concerns, especially those who are still at least marginally in the Faith. But those who are hostile toward it? "I really have to tread lightly regarding when to bring the subject up."

Dr. Ray suggested the father create "a smooth, decent relationship" with his sons. "And be careful about pushing the Faith too hard," he cautioned. "Usually that pushes them further away—especially if they think they're so smart, as engineers, that they don't need to deal with this God stuff," considering it a "throwback to simpler thinking."

THE TIME FOR ARGUMENT HAS PASSED

St. Monica, intent on making up for her husband's lack of faith, took the initiative for her children's spiritual lives. Like any conscientious Christian mother, along with her everyday modeling of the Faith, as they grew through the years, she gladly offered guidance to help her children stay oriented toward God.

But at some point, when it came to Augustine, the good advice began to fall on deaf ears. As Fr. Falbo notes, "This, then, is what had become of Monica's advice: illegitimate sexual relationship, concubinage, and a child outside of marriage."[59] The lectures were no longer having an effect. But his departure from the Christian faith hurt even more than all this.

Once Monica realized she had lost control of the ability to guide her son well, she fell to the one thing she could control: prayer, and much of it. And, as Falbo notes, "The Lord did not despise her many tears and would ultimately grant her prayers."[60]

Though she felt compelled to turn him away from her home for a time in his adulthood due to his transgressions, a prophetic dream made her reconsider, and Monica accepted Augustine back. During that phase, at the end of each day working in the school Augustine helped start in Tagaste, he would be warmly greeted by his mother. But she would avoid any doctrinal discussion, Falbo notes. She had done enough discerning to know that, despite her own sharp mind and ability to convey clear thoughts, the time of debating had passed.

BITING OUR TONGUES

Rose, whose story of her daughter's departure from the Faith we saw earlier, expressed the need to bite her tongue at times for the sake of peace. Several priests have affirmed the need to be cautious in divulging her feelings with her daughter. "They have advised me not to discuss my heartache with her, saying it is not my job, and that a lasting conversion has to come from her own experience, not through pressure from her mother," she says. "They reminded me that she is a married woman, and that this is her journey with God. While I recognize their wisdom, at times I still struggle to fully separate her choices with my desire for her to have a love for the Catholic Faith. I love her intently, but I sometimes experience her rejection of the Church as her rejecting me."

Though Rose knows that her daughter still loves her, "she just cannot face me. It is kind of like Adam and Eve in the Garden. They turned away when they realized they were naked and knew they had done wrong. A few years ago, when [my children] came over at Easter, I saw no joy on their faces, and I realized that they had not gone to Mass. I saw that they were running and hiding from the Faith, and my heart ached."

Even so, Rose knew her best recourse was prayer, not pleading. "I find comfort that their story is not done, and that my daughter's journey was never meant to be a replica of my own. I have a strong personality, whereas she is gentle and sensitive. I have to remember to stop and listen, not react, and ask questions."

NOT THE ARCHITECTS OF OUR CHILDREN'S SOULS

On day 212 of *The Bible in a Year* podcast, Fr. Mike Schmitz shares that "God writes straight with crooked lines." We simply have to trust his way of doing things. As we journey with our adult children, we cannot take the approach we did when they were young and needed a sharp and bold warning about the dangers ahead. They must discover and internalize God's path on their own.

As an assurance, Fr. Mike notes, "Everything in the world belongs to God, even if people don't know it." Contemplating this, it can be easier to let go, knowing God will pick up where we left off. In moments, that can still be scary. Free will, a beautiful thing, can be used to lead us—and our children—astray.

DIDN'T WE GIVE THEM TO GOD?

On day 51 of *The Bible in a Year* podcast, Fr. Mike also says that "nothing given to the Lord is ever wasted." The materials God consecrated in Old

Testament days were ordinary, he reminds, until they were anointed. At that point, they became holy; God became present in them.

"We, too, are ordinary, yet when we are consecrated, we are made extraordinary," he says. "God says to us, 'You dedicated it to me, so just let it be mine.'" But often, when we dedicate something to the Lord, he says, we are inclined to try to take it back. We must resist this, he said. If we have given something to the Lord, it is now his. This dedication, this consecration, cannot be undone.

If true with things like holy vessels and tabernacles, how much more when it comes to our children—God's precious creations? At Baptism, we offered them to God. They were washed by sanctifying water, and anointed by God through the words of the priest, "I baptize you in the name of the Father, and of the Son, and of the Holy Spirit." At that moment, their souls were placed in God's care, forever. No matter what it might seem to us, this is an indelible truth that cannot be reversed. They are his, as we are his.

A PARTNERSHIP WITH GOD

Sarah, whose story we saw earlier, said that throughout her years of raising children, she viewed her role as a partnership with God. "In our kids' younger, most tender years, I homeschooled all five, brought them to daily Mass, and delighted in their milestones," she says. "My children kept me humble and encouraged me on my quest for holiness. I wanted to be a good role model in our domestic church."

The family became close friends with many of the priests who served their parish, along with the nuns and Franciscan brothers who assisted on Sundays. "I wanted our children to be holy, moral, and honorable members of society," she says. "I wanted to give them some of the things I had missed as a child." Despite her best efforts, two of her children have not spoken to her in years. Sarah has no choice but to let go, and to bring her deep hurt—and hope—to God.

It is not always easy, she says. "Each time one of our children began walking away from the Faith, I felt like a failure, both as a mother and a Catholic. As a longtime Catholic journalist, I sometimes feel like a farce. I write articles to affirm and uphold the Faith yet have been unable to keep my own children connected." Over time, however, turning to God in her consternation has helped her cope and keep hope alive. "Not a day goes by that I don't think about and pray for my daughters. I have had a novena going for fifteen years, asking God to bring my youngest daughter home. More recently, I added my oldest one to that long, persistent prayer."

Sarah reminds herself to count her blessings, focusing on the strong relationships she maintains with her sons and their children. "I see the three granddaughters who live closest to me every week, and they greatly enrich my life. We cook and bake together, and I've been teaching them how to sew. I have a sewing machine just for them to use, and they know how to lay out the fabric, cut, pin, and sew simple garments and other items," she says. "They also enjoy hearing stories from when I was a little girl, especially the times I got into trouble! Our moments together are so precious."

NO DEADLINES HERE

Despite the ruptures in her family's relationships, Sarah says she has never felt abandoned by God. She finds reassurance in various passage of Scripture, especially Proverbs 22:6: "Train the young in the way they should go; even when old, they will not swerve from it."

"From this, I feel hope, for I believe that someday my daughters will return to the Faith, and to me," Sarah says. "Though it might not be until after I have passed, I believe they will come back."

As we have seen, Dr. Anders advises that we might need to employ a different mindset, to "lengthen the time horizon indefinitely," and relent to another plan. He reminded the father that his daughter's conversion, should it happen, "might not be in a way that would make sense to you, or be on your timetable."

EATING WITH SINNERS

Learning to let go of debate does not mean that we have given in or now agree with everything our children say or do. Rather, this places our relationship with them before everything else. Tweaking our perspective can lead us to a deeper trust and more fulfilling relationship with our Lord, and help us maintain a relationship with our children.

During a segment of *The Doctor Is In*, Dr. Ray responded to a mother whose daughter—who had only recently begun speaking to her parents again—was about to enter into a marriage with a man sixteen years older than her. The mother asked Dr. Ray what she should do.

"If you want some kind of healed relationship with your daughter, you're going to have to fake it," Dr. Ray responded. "Be pleasant and civil and take whatever joy you can in their relationship ... or you won't see your daughter anymore. And then you can't know which direction she's headed. You'll be on the outskirts."

Not everyone would agree with this advice, he said. In some situations, parents might need to "call wrong, wrong." But in this case, the relationship is already strained, and the parents are limited. "If you are civil and even friendly, does that mean you are wholeheartedly agreeing?" he asked. "No, not at all."

Jesus was criticized by the religious authorities of his day because he ate with tax collectors and sinners. In that culture, he said, it indicated a closeness with those people. "That's why the religious leaders were scandalized," he said. "But did that he mean he approved of what they did? No, not at all," he said, concluding, "Our Lord's model is that I can still love you and not approve of what you're doing. We conflate the two sometimes."

NO WAY AROUND LETTING GO

Another lesson from day 212 of *The Bible in a Year* podcast is from Isaiah 46:9, where we hear the story of a man using a tree trunk to cook his meals, warm himself by the fire, and carve an idol to worship, which the author of the book declares as utterly foolish.

"How often do we tell God, 'Here's how things should be!'?" Fr. Mike asks. "We are treating the true God like he is our toy, like a magic wand or a crystal ball, basically thinking we can give God counsel, or criticize God." He noted, "This man is in all of our hearts."

So, too, when it comes to our wayward children. We must let God be God, and allow him to be the architect of their souls. As a friend puts it, "God is not a snowplow," ready to move all the mounds of snow that have built up after the latest blizzard. Obstacles will come on our children's unique searches for God, but we cannot order God to clear the path for them.

OFFERING OUR HURTS TO HIM

Sarah says that all the hurts she has experienced have pointed her more and more to God, who alone can resolve these situations: "While pouring out my heart to God, I have pictured myself holding each of my daughters, and my four grandchildren I don't know. I have given them to Jesus for safekeeping, and one by one, I have named them and lifted them up to Jesus' arms, with the request that he care for them, love them, and, when the time is right, reunite us all."

She also draws inspiration from the saints—especially St. Monica. "She suffered greatly for years due to her son's behavior, but through time on her knees, Augustine transformed, becoming a saint," she says. "With God, anything is possible, including my daughters' return. I wait in hope, trusting in God's love for us all."

23

I Surrender!

Monica was quite young when she began learning that she needed to surrender to circumstances beyond her control—a spiritual state of mind that would serve her well throughout her life. One of the first such lessons came at age twenty-two, when her parents gave her in marriage to Patricius. Without recourse, Monica "took her new trouble" to the only place that seemed to offer solace—the Lord.

In *The Life of Saint Monica*, Forbes writes, "Kneeling in her favorite corner in the church, she asked help and counsel of the Friend who never fails … And now, it seemed that it was she who would have to be strong for both; to strive and to suffer to bring her husband's soul out of darkness into the light of truth."[61] Later, the same would be true of her son.

Praying in the church, Monica raised her voice to heaven. She prayed again and again through her tears, "You in me, Lord." As she made her way home later that night, she knelt at her bedside and "laid the ideals of her girlhood at the feet of Him who lets no sacrifice, however small, go unrewarded. She would be true to this new trust, she resolved, cost what it might."[62]

Like Monica, we have fallen to our knees at points in this journey with our children, either literally or figuratively, as we find ourselves at the end of what we can do to bring them closer to God. We realize the little control we have had all along, and that God alone can carry the weight that bears down on our hearts. We are not without recourse in this. Jesus modeled this ultimate act of surrender to God on the Cross.

As it turns out, surrender, far from being a weight, becomes a freedom as we place everything in the hands and heart of the One who brought this world into being, and knows it, and each of us, best. Will we, like Monica and so many saints, learn the lesson of surrender? God willing.

FROM HEARTBREAK TO SURRENDER

ROXANE: From the passenger seat of my car, I fumbled in the dark through my overnight bag, grasping for something I thought I had packed. "I am sure I put it in here," I said to my husband, who was driving us to the hospital. In just a few hours, a medical team would be cutting open his chest.

Though Troy was the one facing open-heart surgery, experiencing this trial with him had been frightening to me, too, though in a different way. He had said it best. "If I die, I'll be in a better place. But you? You'll be left here to parent our kids alone."

Now where was that Surrender Novena card? The dread we had both been feeling in the last weeks rose steadily in my body as I searched. Finally, I felt the sought-for trifold at my fingertips. Pulling it out, I asked, "Are you ready to do day 9?" We knew the final day of the novena would be on the day of surgery. But my husband decided to change plans. "Let's wait until tonight. I want something to look forward to."

Patti had introduced this novena to me during one of my trips to Bismarck to visit my mom. "I have only a few of these prayer cards left, but I just feel like I should give one to you," Patti had said that day. "Thanks," I said, tossing it onto my car's dashboard before the three-hour drive home. At the time, I had no clue how I would come to depend on it, not only in facing Troy's health trials but those we would experience with our children.

A few weeks later, Troy went to the walk-in clinic to deal with a persistent cough. "You've got a heart murmur—quite a whopper in fact," the physician had said. "I'd like to schedule an echocardiogram." That test would reveal a significant leak in my husband's mitral valve, making him vulnerable for a stroke. The only viable remedy seemed to be open-heart surgery to repair the prolapsed cords. At 49, my husband, who was more fit than most his age, would be undergoing one of the most delicate, critical surgeries possible. A medical team would traverse a place in his body where only God usually has access—the center of his heart.

The night of the news, still in shock, my husband noticed a little card of the Sacred Heart of Jesus I had taped to our bedroom mirror months ago. "Look at that," Troy said. "Jesus' heart was broken, just like mine is." How could I help him through this, I wondered? Immediately, I remembered the novena card with the heart on the cover, and ran out to the garage, relieved to find it clipped to my car visor.

Though I had long been a proponent of the Divine Mercy Chaplet and its famous phrase from St. Faustina, "Jesus, I trust in you," the Surrender Novena seemed to go a step further in offering solace by asking Jesus to "take care of everything."

It was these words to which we clung in the days leading up to a procedure that would last six hours—three more than expected. Troy's heart had stopped the moment the surgeon cut him open and needed to be physically massaged back to life. Pacing the waiting room floor as the hours stretched on, I began begging God to save my husband, even as the words of surrender flowed from my lips.

In intensive care that night, I cried tears of joy and gratitude. Sitting next to him, I tenderly touched his nearest hand and tried conversing with him through the fog of anesthesia and intubation, which made the simplest phrases strenuous. After a while of this, and seeing his frustration, I remembered the novena.

"Ready to do day 9 now?" I asked, holding up the card. He nodded, and I read: "A thousand prayers cannot equal one single act of surrender," a prayer that would carry us through the recovery ahead.

Just after celebrating Troy's one-year anniversary of his surgery, he scheduled a follow-up appointment. "I just feel like something isn't right yet," he had said. "Like I could fall asleep and just not wake up." I had not wanted to admit it, but his skin coloring had begun to look grayish. We soon would learn the murmur was back, along with signs of serious anemia. Another open-heart surgery would be needed.

This time around, we wasted no time in getting the Surrender Novena going. As before, we prayed the words together each night, holding hands in bed in the dark, the light from my cell phone illuminating the prayer that brought such calm. This time, Troy decided he did not want to wait until after surgery for day 9. He said, "Let's finish it all before, but as I'm going under, I'm going to say the words: 'O Jesus, I surrender myself to you. Take care of everything!'" If it would be God's will for him to not come through, he wanted these to be his final words on earth, and what Jesus would hear first.

Eventually, Troy made it through his second surgery, and our lives returned to some normalcy. But our shared heartache of seeing some of our children lapse in their practice of the Faith became more prominent. When a friend gave me the idea of inserting our children's names into the prayers to place them in God's care, we readily added this to our novena routine. "O Jesus, I surrender *[child's name]* to you. Take care of everything."

I have realized over time that, though God gave us this prayer as a way to bring us through the trials we would face with Troy's health, ultimately, it was just as much for our children. Troy's broken heart had drawn us to this prayer, but it has helped calm our hearts in journeying with our children through their faith wanderings, too.

Recently, Troy drove our oldest son hundreds of miles from our house to his new residence. My husband struggled to let go, sharing with me how much he dreaded the goodbye with our first-born "baby." "Say the Surrender Novena," I reminded him. "Yes," he replied, "I've already started."

Just as when Troy faced the cold surface of an operating room table, now, we could grasp the same, powerful words while facing the often-cold world our children were entering—a secular world that wants to claim their souls for its own.

As Servant of God Fr. Dolindo Ruotolo, who wrote the Surrender Novena, heard Jesus say many years ago, "Leave the care of your affairs to Me, and everything will be peaceful." My husband and I now see these words as consolation from Jesus as we walk always in hope. "I say to you in truth that every act of true, blind, complete surrender to Me produces the effect that you deserve and resolves all difficult situations."

How powerful to think that in turning our children's lives and futures over to God, even the gates of hell themselves cannot prevail against them or us. What a solace to say anew, and with great expectation, each day, "O Jesus, we surrender ourselves and our children to you. Take care of everything."

LOOKING DEATH IN THE FACE AND SURRENDERING

PATTI: Accepting the inevitability of death demands surrender. I know that; I accept it in my mind. But not knowing if our son was dead or alive was a horrifying moment. My body shook uncontrollably as I prayed, "Your will be done, Lord, but if it's possible, please save him." I knew God could do anything. What I did not know was if our ten-year-old son Tyler was already with God. It seemed possible. The thought flashed through my mind. "But I didn't even get to say goodbye," I cried.

We had gathered with our then-six children, my husband's parents, and two brothers and their families on a lake in Minnesota for a family reunion. It was the end of the first day, night by now, actually. And it had been a very long day. We left for the six-and-a half-hour drive before sunup. The day was filled with getting reacquainted with relatives, swimming, fishing, and barbecue.

Mark awakened me yelling, "Something's wrong with Tyler. He's not breathing! I'm going to get Scott!" His brother in the cabin next to us was a doctor. Our oldest, Mike, was sharing a bed with Tyler when he noticed his brother struggling to breathe. "Tyler!" he yelled, wanting the suffocating sounds to stop. They did but only because Tyler had stopped breathing. Mike yelled for help. Mark ran in and carried Tyler to the floor. He was turning blue. Still no breathing. That is when Mark yelled for me.

"I can't remember how to do CPR," I cried, desperately. "I remember from Boy Scouts," Luke, two years older than Tyler, said and stepped in. But his airways were blocked. Mike and I shook and prayed. I yelled for Scott to hurry, despite knowing Mark was over there. It seemed an eternity.

When Scott ran into our cabin, Tyler had begun gasping for breath. As he struggled to suck in air, his color returned until finally the breaths came easily. We took him to the emergency room at a hospital thirty minutes away, but they found nothing. And so, we returned to our cabin trying to shake off the horror of what had happened and to get some sleep. "Thank you, God, for giving us Tyler back," we prayed. "Help him to be OK."

There was fear in not knowing what had stopped his breathing. Could he pass out on the boat and fall into the lake or have a recurrence while swimming? But he felt fine and spent the week binge-fishing with Luke and their cousin Joey.

Later, back home, an electroencephalogram showed that Tyler likely had a type of seizure disorder that could hit randomly, most likely at night when asleep, and is usually outgrown by the age of fourteen. It never happened again. He is a father of four in his thirties now.

But our family had experienced death that horrifying night. We experienced how quickly life can be gone, without warning. We had a glimpse of that now.

The next day, I learned that while Mark pounded on his brother's cabin door, he and I were united in prayer. He too thought that maybe Tyler was already with God. He too understood it was God's will, not ours, that mattered. *But if it's possible, please save him!* he had prayed.

We have nurtured a faith that precedes us. It guides us through fears, emergencies, good news and bad, conflicts and blessings. Life has taught us that we are not in control. Even at times when we said that we knew we were not in control, we have had to learn it better. Perhaps our biggest lesson in life has been the need to surrender. It is hard to do but makes life easier. Yet, it's a lesson that needs continual learning.

Mark and I continue praying with one mind and heart for eternal life for our children who are now all grown. They have all grown to be kind and successful adults, and those who have children are loving parents. The lesson of surrender, however, is the recognition that our children have free will, but we surrender whatever ties and influence we might have over to God. We often pray novenas, surrendering our lives and our children to God. One that has become a favorite is the Surrender Novena. It helps us to abandon everything to the care of God. At the end of each day's prayer, you pray ten times: "O Jesus, I surrender myself to you, take care of everything." Even when we aren't praying the novena, those words have become our guide.

24

They Surrendered

We can always use a miracle worker in our lives. The list of saints we can turn to for their powerful intercession is long, but some had a special heart for families and were strong examples of surrender. The following saints offer messages especially pertinent to parents of children who have left the Faith.

FR. JEAN PIERRE DE CAUSSADE: ALL FROM THE FATHER'S HAND

Fr. Jean Pierre de Caussade, SJ, a French Jesuit who lived in the late 1600s to mid-1700s, has been described by some as "the Eckhart Tolle (author of *The Power of Now*) of the eighteenth century." Fr. Caussade believed in what he termed "the sacrament of the present moment," and for decades, his compilation of letters on this theme, compiled into the book *Self-Abandonment to Divine Providence*, was widely used and recommended by spiritual directors.

Though not an earthly father, Caussade "parented" many young people of his time into a richer, more abandoned and peaceful relationship with our Lord, especially through offering spiritual direction to a community of religious sisters, the Nuns of the Visitation in Nancy, France. Through this ministry, he gained keen insight into the consternation of the soul of human beings. He also learned how to console them, by constantly encouraging them to place their worries in the capable hands of the

Father, reminding them that our peace and power lies in the present moment—and only there.

The evil one thrives on catching us either ruminating on the past, stuck in regret, or obsessing anxiously about the future over things that may never come to be. How many hours we waste wringing our hands over a worry that simply will never manifest; time that could have been spent praising God.

Parents of children who are away from the Church might need this reminder when our thoughts carry us in either of these directions, bringing anxiety and fear and a lack of trust in the Lord, who knows all and has promised to be with us every moment of our waking and sleeping.

In a letter he wrote to Sister Marie-Thérèse de Vioménil from Perpignan, France, in 1740, he said, "I am convinced by faith and by many personal experiences that everything comes from God, and that he is powerful enough and a good enough Father to bring all issues to the best advantage of his dear children. Did he not prove that he loved us better than his life when he laid it down for love of us? And can we not be assured that, having done so much for us, he will not forget us?"[63]

Caussade goes on to say that he "expects success with confidence, but also with calm ... not in accordance with my own impatient desires, but at the time of divine Providence, which regulates and arranges everything for our greater good, although we usually understand nothing of what it is doing."[64]

If we accept all, both the good and bad, from the hand of our good Father, Fr. Caussade teaches that "he will keep us in peace in the midst of the greatest disasters of this world, the fashion of which passes away in a flash. Our life will be holy and tranquil in proportion as we trust in God and abandon ourselves to him."[65]

In summarizing St. Thomas Aquinas' *Summa Theologica*, Peter Kreeft speaks of the reality of *nunc fluens*, or "now flowing." As he writes, "The past is no longer actual, the future is not yet actual. The 'now flowing' (the present moment in the life of a temporal creature) is more akin to eternity (the 'now standing still') than it is akin to past or future. Eternity touches time only in the present."[66]

Here, we can deduce that the richest, most hopeful, most real moment we have is the one we're in right now—the present. Nothing else compares, and nothing else can bring us back to our senses when we become distraught over what was, and what could be.

Caussade offered further perspective in a letter to Sister Marie-Antoinette de Mahuet in 1742:

> What is a little longer or a little shorter stretch of life, a few more or a few less tribulations, in comparison with the eternal life awaiting us to which we walk—we run—without a pause and which already is within hand's reach? ... It is time, then ... to make ready my little provisions for eternity. Now, crosses lovingly borne and great sacrifices made to God's will are the best such provisions. Nothing will comfort us so much in death as our humble submission to the various plans of divine Providence ... The vicissitudes that he allots you of good fortune and of bad, of health and of sickness, are well calculated to keep you wholly dependent upon him and to constrain you to perform the most meritorious acts of trust.[67]

By staying in the present and surrendering everything to our Lord, we can allow God to make good on his promise from Romans 8:28, that "all things work for the good for those who love God, who are called according to his purpose," trusting that he will lead our children—and us—lovingly into the future, which he has prepared for us all.

God provides perspective such as this to bring us, and our children, back to his heart, where abundance awaits. As the prophet Isaiah says, "The LORD will guide you continually, and satisfy your desire with good things, and make your bones strong; and you shall be like a watered garden, like a spring of water, whose waters do not fail" (Isaiah 58:11).

FR. WALTER CISZEK: THE REFLECTIONS OF A PRISONER FOR THE LORD

As a young seminarian, Walter Ciszek could not have foreseen that one day he would be falsely accused by the KGB of being a Vatican spy, sent to a Soviet prison, confined for five years in a gulag, and stripped of all freedoms except silent prayer. Neither could he have predicted how God would bring him from the brink of despair, helping him see every moment of that excruciating journey as from the Lord's hand.

After nearly twenty-three years of imprisonment, Fr. Ciszek returned to American soil, forever changed. The cause for his beatification and canonization has been opened. The harrowing story of his confounding, trying—and at times exhilarating—years in Russia have been detailed in his book *He Leadeth Me*. Fr. Ciszek's insights might help us as parents grieving our children's lapsed faith as we learn to surrender each day—and even each minute—to God.

God is constant, even in turmoil. Even the trials of the Jewish people in salvation history were a manifestation of God's special providence, Fr. Ciszek says. "He was leading them through every trial and in every age, to the realization that God alone is faithful in all tribulations, that he alone is constant in his love and must be clung to, even when it seems all else has been turned upside down." God alone is constant in love, our only sure solace, even for those of us watching our children slip further away from the Faith we know will save them.[68]

Belief in divine providence. Fr. Ciszek was pulled from total despair by his untiring belief in divine providence, and that no man, and no situation, is without worth and purpose in God's eyes. "Under the worst imaginable circumstances, a man remains a man with free will, and God stands ready to assist him with his grace," he wrote, offering assurance for us that even when our children seem to be letting go of their only sure anchor, God remains near them, and us, especially when we act in accord with his will.[69]

Looking beyond hopelessness. In the hostile environment of a Russian prison, Fr. Ciszek learned that our sense of hopelessness in situations over which we have little control arises from our tendency to inject too much of self into the picture. In prison, he realized he was being asked to accept the circumstances, forget about his powerlessness, and set about the task of looking to the immediate needs of those near him: "It was all I had to do, but it was plenty—and it could not be done while I sat feeling sorry for myself ... I had to learn to believe that no matter what the circumstances, and to act accordingly—with complete trust and confidence in his will, his wisdom and his grace."[70]

Every moment is ordained by God. Fr. Ciszek came to see that God works out his purpose in our lives minute by minute, day by day. Our task is to prepare ourselves continually to be open to his grace through our choices—to seek his will and act accordingly. As Fr. Ciszek's choices seemed to shrink further in solitary confinement, he often had nothing to do but ruminate over his past life and future fears. "But above all, I prayed." Often, he found that a simple "Our Father" was the most perfect prayer. "The human mind could not elaborate a better pattern in prayer than the one the Lord himself gave us," he concluded. It contained everything needed to live a whole life, ordering everything rightly.[71]

Bearing burdens patiently. Despite feeling many of his prayers were going unanswered—even asking for basic needs, like food—Fr. Ciszek realized that prayer might not remove bodily pain or mental anguish. "Nevertheless, it does provide a certain moral strength to bear the burden patiently. Certainly, it was prayer that helped me through every crisis." He defined the purest prayer as "the spontaneous outpouring of a soul that has come to realize—however fleetingly—that it is standing at the knee of a loving and providing Father."[72]

Only God can save. Fr. Ciszek also learned that no matter how much we desire it, we cannot bring others to salvation. "For just as surely as man begins to trust in his own abilities, so surely has he taken the first step on the road to ultimate failure," he said. "The greatest grace God can give such a man is to send him a trial he cannot bear with his own powers—and then sustain him with his grace so he may endure to the end and be saved.[73]

Full surrender. "Only when I had reached a point of total bankruptcy of my own powers had I at last surrendered," Fr. Ciszek said. "God is in all things." He came to the point of discerning this in every situation and circumstance in order to accept each circumstance and situation, letting himself "be borne along in perfect confidence and trust."[74]

Actions, not words. Despite the difficulty of daily toil, Fr. Ciszek came to see that every moment, and in every encounter with every prisoner, the will of God was manifest, and that prisoners responded less to preaching God and religion and were drawn more by simple respect and kind acts. Only slowly do we come to know the workings of the spirit in ourselves, he observed. "How much more slowly, then, do we begin to detect the workings of that same spirit in others?"[75]

Our grief can help others. Fr. Ciszek discovered that our moments of grief can become the sacrifice needed in the passion for saving souls, and as we recognize our suffering as being part of God's redemptive plan for the universe and each individual soul, we can adjust our attitudes more easily, not shunning trials when they come, but bearing them in the measure grace is given. "The dedicated soul instinctively realized ... that what was most important in the Father's eyes was total surrender to his will," he added, noting, "Whatever he inspired or commanded became paramount, not the human effort or the wisdom or the work resulting from personal initiative."[76]

No suffering is lost. Through profound trials, Fr. Ciszek came to understand that "no man's life, no man's suffering, is lost from the eyes of God."[77] All, without exception, have been created to praise and serve God, and by this means to save our souls and help in the salvation of others.

BLESSED SOLANUS CASEY: HUMBLE MIRACLE WORKER

PATTI: *This is so like God,* I thought, looking up at the jumbotron display in Detroit's Ford Field on November 18, 2017. "Whoever humbles himself will be exalted" (Matthew 23:12). On the giant screen was a portrait of the thin, scraggly-bearded Capuchin priest, Fr. Solanus Casey, being honored by the sixty thousand who had gathered for his beatification. The apostolic nuncio to the United States, Cardinal Amato, four other cardinals, twenty-eight archbishops and bishops, and three hundred priests were present to concelebrate Mass.

I am originally from the Detroit area, so I traveled from North Dakota to cover the beatification for the *National Catholic Register*. Most Catholics from Detroit, where Fr. Solanus served the poor for twenty-one years, knew him from the many reported miracles attributed to him. When he died there July 31, 1957, more than twenty thousand mourners came to view his body at St. Bonaventure Monastery, and eight thousand attended his funeral Mass, overflowing onto the streets.

The Solanus Center was later built adjoining the church, where his tomb lies. Because Fr. Solanus has been connected with so many answered prayers for conversions, we want to introduce him to anyone not familiar with him.

WHO WAS FR. CASEY?

Born Bernard Francis Casey on a Wisconsin farm to Irish immigrant parents on November 25, 1870, the sixth of sixteen children, Casey struggled in his studies at a seminary in Milwaukee due to a lack of formal education. After praying a novena to the Immaculate Conception, he said he heard the voice of the Blessed Mother tell him to "go to Detroit."

He arrived at the city's Capuchin monastery on Christmas Eve 1887 and, in 1904, was ordained a "simplex" priest, without faculties to hear confessions or preach homilies due to his poor academic performance. He took the religious name "Solanus" after St. Francis Solanus, a sixteenth-century Spanish saint with the gift of miracles.

Fr. Casey became renowned for his gifts of miracles and prophecy. People lined up for blocks to see this humble priest, who was always ready to listen and known to encourage others to "thank God ahead of time." Even in his semi-retirement at St. Felix Friary in Huntington, Indiana, busloads of people came from Detroit on Sundays to meet with the beloved Capuchin priest. He returned to Detroit for medical treatments in 1956 and died from erysipelas, a skin disease, at eighty-seven.

At St. Bonaventure, Solanus Casey served as a doorkeeper, just as he had done at three previous assignments in New York. He also worked in the soup kitchen and visited the sick in hospitals. He counseled people to accept God's will since not everyone received the favors they asked for, but many did. Of the six thousand entries of prayer requests Fr. Casey entered in his log—only a fraction of total requests—he recorded seven hundred cures and reported on many conversions and resolutions to problems.

Before the beatification, I had interviewed Gerarda Tobin, chairwoman for the Fr. Solanus Casey Beatification Committee, who told me her ninety-four-year-old mother was planning to attend. "My mother grew up across the street from a man whose eyesight was healed," she said. "As a young man, Clarence Umlauf was losing his eyesight, and the doctor said that nothing could be done about it. His parents took him to see Fr. Solanus, who said: 'Do not worry about your eyes; your prayers have been answered.' His vision returned, and the following week his doctor said: 'These are not the eyes I saw last week.'"

Fr. Larry Webber, one of the two Capuchin vice postulators of his cause, told me he has twelve drawers full of thousands of reported favors attributed to Fr. Casey's intervention. In the spring of 2013, several of the strongest cases were sent to Rome for review by the Congregation for the Causes of Saints.

The approved case involved the healing of an incurable skin condition that occurred at the Solanus Casey Center in September 2012. Fr. Webber happened to be present. He explained that Paula Medina Zarate, visiting from Panama, had worked at the Capuchin mission there for many years and had come to Chicago and Detroit to visit some of her Capuchin friends. While touring the center, Zarate asked why there were papers on top of a table. She learned they were prayer intentions and that it was not a table, but the tomb of Father Solanus. In 1987, his body was exhumed and found incorrupt, although water had seeped in and rotted the insides of the coffin. His body was moved into a crypt in the chapel of the Capuchin monastery adjoining the Solanus Casey Center, where it is now.

"She [Zarate] filled out fourteen or fifteen papers for other people's intentions," Fr. Webber said. "The friar showing her around told her it was time to go to lunch. But then she heard a voice say: 'What about you? What do you need?'"

Zarate was overwhelmed and knelt back down, telling God she was sorry for not thinking of herself. Then she prayed for the intercession of Fr. Solanus to heal the very painful genetic skin condition from which she had suffered since birth. When Zarate continued to the cafeteria for lunch, she soon felt strange and excused herself to her guest room.

"In her room, all these scales of skin were falling off her, and there was baby skin under it," Fr. Webber said. "She was stunned and went back to the cafeteria and explained what happened." A report was filled out that day. Ultimately, five doctors determined no natural explanation for the healing could be found.

During the beatification Mass, Cardinal Amato said in his homily that the holy priest favored the poor, sick, indigent, and homeless. He shared a story of when the soup kitchen that Fr. Solanus helped open during the Depression ran out of food. "More than 200 people were still waiting to eat. He began reciting the 'Our Father,' and then a baker appeared at the door with bread and other things. When the people saw this, they began to cry with emotion. Fr. Solanus simply stated: 'See? God provides. No one will suffer if we put our trust in divine Providence.'"

God, we thank you ahead of time for the blessings you will bestow on our families. We trust you with your great love for them, and desire to bring them home to your heart.

Blessed Solanus, pray for us!

25

Lord, If This Is How You Treat Your Friends …

An often-told story about St. Teresa of Avila shows our human tendency to complain about suffering. As she was traveling by horse to visit one of her convents, Teresa fell off her mount while crossing a cold stream. She lost her footing in the strong current and was almost carried away.

Complaining about this situation and the constant trials in her life, like most of us do when we vent out loud, she heard the Lord reply, "Do not complain, daughter, for it is ever thus that I treat my friends." Teresa, ever witty, responded with her typical humor, "If this is how you treat your friends, Lord, no wonder you have so few."

As we travel the journey of parenting children, we may feel similarly slighted when things do not turn out as we hoped. This can be a source of particularly painful suffering. But life in general offers other struggles as well. Regardless of its source, our suffering can be offered up for the conversion of our children.

PATTI: At ninety-six, my father is joyful and faithful … and he suffers. One might not be aware of this as he pushes his walker down the hall of his assisted living facility to play cards or join in a sing-along with fellow residents. He smiles at everyone, embraces life, and frequently finds ways to bring God to others in conversations, often when staff admire the many religious images on his wall.

Recently, our family wondered if his time was at an end after a medical event had him admitted to the hospital. He had no interest in eating or drinking for three days. "It might be time for hospice," my sister who heads his care told me.

When he was released from the hospital, he was very weak, and it was painful for him to get out of bed into his wheelchair. I had flown in for a ten-day visit. On my last day, Dad was using his walker and exercising with light weights to increase his strength. As long as he is on this earth, he works to be his best both physically and spiritually. Another sister has been there for a month, and as of this writing, he is well enough to be taken to Mass with his walker—his great joy—and participate in many activities. But ninety-six is ninety-six!

He shared, "When I was in the hospital, I could not pray, so I just kept saying the name of Jesus." His two biggest intentions are for the unborn and the conversion of those—especially friends and family—who have turned away from God. He does not want to waste a moment of his suffering.

Blessings come to us in both joy and suffering. Even the Blessed Mother suffered alongside Jesus, but her suffering was never one of desperation or despair. If we are able to transcend our suffering, we can have something powerful to offer to God for the conversion of our children. Suffering is a treasure that we can spend on them.

"Your sufferings, accepted and borne with unshakable faith, when joined to those of Christ take on extraordinary value for the life of the Church and the good of humanity," St. John Paul said on the occasion of the World Day of the Sick, a day for "prayer and sharing, of offering one's suffering for the good of the Church and of reminding everyone to see in his sick brother or sister the face of Christ." This day was instituted on May 13, 1992, and is celebrated on February 11, also the memorial of Our Lady of Lourdes.

In 2001, John Paul II was diagnosed with Parkinson's disease. He had already written a great deal about suffering, particularly his 1984 apostolic letter *Salvifici Doloris*, in which he discusses Christ's salvific suffering on the Cross and the redemptive suffering we can take part in.

"LOW-GRADE" SUFFERING

In *When You Suffer: Biblical Keys for Hope and Understanding*, Jeff Cavins speaks to the power and even joy that can come with suffering. According to him, real life is often irritating and full of unmet needs. "When real life collides with your ideal life, things can get ugly," he writes. "You might react in a less than Christ-like way. ... But what if instead you could live 100% of your life? What if real life could be transformed into an opportunity to love, an opportunity to grow, an opportunity to become more like Christ?"[78]

Where can we sign up, right? Cavins reveals that the first step is recognizing that real life involves suffering, especially low-level suffering in the form of all those daily inconveniences. "The mystery of suffering is that out of this weakness and emptiness, out of this less-than-ideal life, can come incredible graces," he says. "Christ is the key to transforming suffering into much more of an ideal life than you could ever imagine." Cavins explains that transforming your life in this way is one of the greatest opportunities that Christ wants to give us, and it is an opportunity to help others.

We cannot escape suffering, but there is a redemptive aspect to it, Cavins points out. In joining our sufferings to those of Christ and loving as he does, suffering can begin to truly make sense, he explains. And in suffering, God will give us the graces that we need.

EVERY DAY CAN BE IDEAL

Jesus' life was full of discomfort and suffering, but every day was "ideal" because he was accomplishing the will of the Father. Even the day of his passion and crucifixion was an "ideal day" because he was fulfilling his Father's will for our salvation.

With this understanding, we can begin to view our suffering as a way to grow in closer union with Jesus—to die more to ourselves and live more fully in Christ. As Cavins writes, "And [suffering] truly becomes a gift. You give Jesus your suffering. The consolation we receive is the knowledge that something marvelous is happening in our lives, even if we don't feel anything or see the results we had hoped for. This is Christian maturity; this is walking as Christ walked. Suffering gives you the opportunity to grow."[79]

To put suffering in perspective and see it as uniting ourselves to Jesus, Cavins asks us to consider what the worst thing that could possibly happen might be. He answers, "The crucifixion of Jesus"—but the day of Jesus' crucifixion turned out to be the greatest day in the world. It brought about our salvation. So too, when we unite our suffering with that of Jesus on the Cross, we can bring about holiness and salvation in our lives—and the lives of our children.

SORROW AND PAIN ARE GOD'S MESSENGERS

In *Good News About Prodigals*, author Tom Bisset notes that personal brokenness has been one of the principal means by which God has revealed himself to his people. "The idea is utterly contradictory if you think in human terms, yet it has proved itself again and again to the followers of Christ yesterday and today: Sorrow and pain are God's messengers," he writes. "What's more, they bring with them the seeds of our healing and restoration so that we can bring not only praise to God, but blessings to others."[80]

The pain and mess that we experience with children who have fallen away from the Faith has meaning, Bisset offers. "In this picture, God is at work in our children and in us, trying to accomplish his purposes," he says. "If we deny the pain and tragedy, or seek its removal at any cost, we miss what God is trying to do in our lives."[81]

In Isaiah, we see that the Lord waits for us to come to him so he can show us his love. Could it be that God is waiting for us parents as well as our prodigal children? Might God be "working both sides of the street?" Bisset asks. "I think so. When it comes to prodigal children, I believe that God is waiting both with us and for us. The story is not one-sided. ... In the mystery of God's purposes, our prodigal sorrows become our blessing that in turn bring praise to God."[82]

26

No One Is Beyond God's Reach

St. Augustine was a handful—bright, strong-willed, and on the wrong path. Like St. Monica, we are concerned about the path our children are on. Some parents have a child who has simply grown lukewarm in his or her faith, while others have children who seem hopelessly far from the Church. Regardless, we know that no one is beyond God's mercy. For that reason, we want to share several especially dramatic conversions to bolster your spirits.

FROM SATANIST TO SAINT

Although Bartolo Longo was raised by devout Catholic parents who prayed the Rosary daily, he strayed so far from the Faith that he became a satanic priest. When he turned back to God, his conversion was so dramatic that he has been beatified, and his writings became St. John Paul II's inspiration for the luminous mysteries of the Rosary.

Bartolo was born in the small town of Latiano, Italy, on February 10, 1841. A bright and active child, he became unruly at age ten, following the death of his mother. When he entered the law school of the University of Naples, many of his professors were ex-priests preaching against the Church. Influenced by them, Bartolo soon jumped on the anti-Catholic bandwagon and convinced others to leave the Church. His spiritual void was filled by attending seances and visiting mediums—something people still do today.

This opened the door to the occult. Though many are unaware, mediums deal in the occult, and anything occult leads to the devil. Exorcists often see the results of this; once invited in, the devil does not want to leave.

It was a short path from the occult practices to outright satanism for Bartolo. He went so far as to give his soul to the devil and became a consecrated satanic priest and an ardent enemy of the Church. He presided over satanic services and participated in diabolical activities of every sort, including performing blasphemous black masses and participating in orgies.

It is hard to believe how far Bartolo had gone. But no one goes from praying and going to Mass one day to orgies and satanism the next. The dark path unfolds step by step, leading further and further away from God.

During those dark years, the Longo family stormed heaven for Bartolo. He started to become overwhelmed with extreme depression, paranoia, confusion, and nervousness. One day, when Bartolo felt he was having a breakdown, he heard his dead father beg him to return to God.

Bartolo was a mental and physical wreck. His family called on the help of a friend, Professor Vincenzo Pepe, who taught at a university near Naples. "Do you want to die in an insane asylum and be damned forever?" Pepe asked. Bartolo was ready to listen. Pepe connected him to a strong support group of educated Catholics. One of them, Dominican priest Alberto Radente, tutored Bartolo in the Catholic Faith, including the writings of St. Thomas Aquinas.

Bartolo publicly renounced his past and returned to the sacraments. On the feast of the Annunciation, March 25, 1871, he became a member of the Third Order of St. Dominic and took the name of Brother Rosary in honor of his new devotion. As penance, he chose to work for two years in the Neapolitan Hospital for Incurables. Still, he could not shake the guilt or feel worthy of salvation.

One evening in Pompeii, as he walked near the chapel, Bartolo had a mystical experience, which he wrote about later: "As I pondered over my condition, I experienced a deep sense of despair and almost committed suicide. Then I heard an echo in my ear of the voice of Friar Alberto repeating the words of the Blessed Virgin Mary: 'If you seek salvation, promulgate the Rosary. This is Mary's own promise.'"

Bartolo fell to his knees and promised to spend the rest of his life promoting the Rosary and living out its gospel messages, beginning in Pompeii. He built Pompeii's famous Basilica of Our Lady of the Most Holy Rosary with the financial support of the Countess. He also founded orphanages, technical and elementary schools, and wrote novenas, prayer manuals, and books on the Rosary.

He promoted the Rosary until his death on October 5, 1926, at the age of eighty-five. St. John Paul II beatified this "Apostle of the Rosary" on October 26, 1980, with more than thirty thousand people in attendance. As the Holy Father remarked, "Rosary in hand, Blessed Bartolo Longo says to each of us: 'Awaken your confidence in the Most Blessed Virgin of the Rosary. Venerable Holy Mother, in you I rest all my troubles, all my trust and all my hope!'"

THE UNWAVERING PRAYERS OF LACHITA CALLOWAY

As a high school dropout with an affinity for drugs and crime, Fr. Donald Calloway seemed more likely to end up on a "Most Wanted" poster than wearing a Roman collar. (In fact, he actually was "wanted" by the authorities in Japan at one point.)

But with God, all things are possible. Calloway was ordained a priest on May 31, 2003, at the National Shrine of the Divine Mercy in Stockbridge, Massachusetts. He currently serves as the vocations director of the Marians of the Immaculate Conception and is the author of a dozen books, including five on the Rosary. His most recent work is *Consecration to St. Joseph: The Wonders of Our Spiritual Father*. This former high school dropout now holds a doctorate in Mariology.

Fr. Calloway's autobiography, *No Turning Back: A Witness to Mercy*, reveals that he was a parent's worst nightmare. So we will now turn to the reflections of his mother, LaChita, who shared her story in the Ascension book *Amazing Grace for Mothers*. Her thoughts will be interspersed with those of her son, as expressed in the Ascension book *Amazing Grace for the Catholic Heart*.[83]

> *LACHITA:* I was only eighteen when I had Donnie, so I went from a teenager to a mother. When Donnie was ten years old, I married Don Calloway, an officer in the Navy. The two Dons in my life took to each other with great affection. Don soon adopted my son as his own. A year after our marriage, our son Matthew was born. Donnie was ecstatic. As Matthew grew, the boys spent hours together playing.

Because Donnie seemed to be his same old self when we lived in California, I never saw the dangerous changes taking place. But shortly after our family transferred to Japan, the problem became obvious. Donnie lost no time getting acquainted with the local criminal element. We were at a loss for what to do.

During this time of conflict, some friends in the Navy invited us to attend the Catholic Church on base with them. Religion had been largely absent during my childhood. But I did have fond childhood memories of my beloved Catholic grandmother taking me to Mass. The moment I walked into that church, peace filled me. I knew that I had found a home. Don felt it, too. The Catholic Church became our comfort and grace to get us through what awaited us.

After we had been in Japan for two-and-a-half years, Donnie ran away. We did not search alone for our son, however. The Japanese government also wanted him. It did not take long for them to figure out that the white boy frequently witnessed at crime scenes was responsible for them. The military transferred our family to Pennsylvania to get us out of there. Although I felt incomplete leaving Japan with just one son, my newfound faith gave me confidence that my prayers would be heard.

As I boarded the plane in tears, Don looked at me and promised: "I will not leave Japan without Donnie." He was true to his word, but it took a pair of handcuffs and a police escort to get him on the plane.

FR. CALLOWAY: During my early years, I experienced many changes in family life. My mother was always a loving and caring woman, but my father drank a lot, eventually causing them to separate when I was about four years old.

When I was ten, my mother remarried, and that same year, she and my stepdad had me baptized into the Episcopal church. It was my first memory of anything related to God. Though I was newly baptized, religion did not become a part of my family life. I was so illiterate when it came to religion, I had no clue who St. Joseph, the angels and saints, or the Blessed Mother were. I thought Jesus was a mythical character who showed up at Christmas along with Santa Claus.

My stepdad was in the Navy, so we relocated often. My parents had my little brother during the first year of their marriage. By the time I was thirteen, living in California, I was already involved with girls and drugs. When my dad became stationed in Japan—it was a chance to get me away from bad influences. Instead, I became such a bad influence on my own that the country of Japan kicked me out. It took a month for the military police to find me after I had run away from home. My dad's tour of duty ended nine months early. I was creating an international scene.

LACHITA: Donnie agreed to be admitted to a drug and rehabilitation center in exchange for the Japanese government not pressing charges. He did not like us any better than before he had run away, but my heart rested in the faith that God would take care of Donnie. And Don and I were determined to do everything possible to help him.

In Pennsylvania, we officially became Catholic. "Dear God," I often prayed. "Please help my son. And hear the prayers of the Blessed Mother of Our Lord and Savior, Jesus Christ. She gave us the gift of your Son. Now I plead to you that my own son be saved."

Upon completion of Donnie's rehabilitation program, he seemed better, and our new membership in the Catholic Church brought us much comfort. But before long, Donnie was back to his old ways. During his junior year, his school performance was so poor that he finally just gave up altogether and dropped out. Waist-length hair, an earring, and a Grateful Dead tattoo gave an impression of my seventeen-year-old son that I refused to accept. I knew that underneath the rough exterior was still my kind and loving son.

We had often tried to encourage Donnie to turn to God, but he would have none of it. "I will never set foot in your church," he once announced. Another time, he had been embarrassingly rude over the phone when our pastor called.

After he dropped out of school, his life continued on a downward spiral. On his own, he chose to enter drug treatment for a second time. It did not take. Shortly after completing the treatment program, Donnie left for Louisiana to bum around with a friend. He had another brush with the law and continued down the wrong path. Donnie called only sporadically. My heart broke that he was so far from us both physically and spiritually. My prayers were unceasing now. Not half an hour went by that I did not talk to God about my son and ask his Blessed Mother to keep praying for Donnie. He returned home at nineteen. If nothing else, at least he was home with us, I thought. Shortly thereafter, my husband was transferred to Virginia. Donnie came with us.

Matthew settled into fourth grade at a Catholic school, Don was sent out to sea on a six-month tour, I kept up my never-ending conversations with God and the Blessed Mother, and Donnie returned to his destructive lifestyle. Then, suddenly everything changed overnight.

FR. CALLOWAY: One evening, while planning for a night out with friends, a terrible feeling came over me. Something was coming for me, and I could only imagine that it was death. I canceled my plans. The feeling lingered. I realized it did not matter what I did that evening. I was going to confront something. Whatever it was, I wanted to be home when it happened.

Sitting in my room, I became restless. I wanted to go out but did not dare. Fighting boredom, I walked into the hall and scanned my parent's bookshelf. One book caught my eye. I pulled it out and scanned it. It was a book on apparitions of the Blessed Mother. "My parents are into some kind of cult!" I thought with horror.

I took it to my room and began reading. At three a.m., I closed the book, having read it from cover to cover. I had no idea who the Blessed Mother was, but when I started to read about things like prayer, fasting, Jesus Christ, and his death on the Cross for me, I was overcome with a sense of love and joy. Much of it I did not even understand. When I put the book down, I said to myself, "This woman is the woman I have been looking for. This Virgin Mary is perfect. Her God is my God. I will listen to what she tells me."

My euphoric excitement made sleep impossible. My whole life had been flipped upside down. I could not wait until my mother woke up.

LACHITA: "Mom," Donnie said as I passed by his bedroom early one morning. "I want to talk to a priest." I stopped in my tracks. This was the moment I had waited for so long, but when it finally happened, I was shocked.

"What did you say?" I asked, afraid to believe my own ears. Donnie repeated his request. There was a light in his eyes, and his face was radiant.

Dumbfounded, I just stared at him. "Mom, I read this book last night," he said, holding up a book of mine on apparitions of the Blessed Mother.

"You read *that* book?" I asked, amazed.

"Mom, I consumed this book," Donnie said. Somehow, through the beauty and love of the Blessed Mother, Donnie was overcome with the reality that her God was his God.

I made arrangements for him to talk to a priest on base. Donnie flew out the door and ran the half-mile to the chapel. Something miraculous had happened to him that night. My spirits soared in wonderment as I thanked God. Words cannot describe my joy—it was so complete. Now I prayed that what had begun was for real and would continue without distractions.

FR. CALLOWAY: I tried to tell the priest everything in a few sentences. Not knowing what to do with me and having another appointment, he gave me a crucifix, a picture of the Sacred Heart of Jesus, and one of Pope John Paul II and told me to return the next day.

At home, I got five big garbage bags and filled them with music, drug paraphernalia—anything I was attached to. I hung a crucifix and pictures around my room. Then I did not know what to do. A desire welled up in me to talk to God and Our Lady, so I knelt in front of the Sacred Heart picture and watched. I had no idea what prayer was all about and expected God to appear to me.

As I looked upon the image of Jesus, however, I became flooded with real contrition and joy. Tears poured down from my eyes for at least an hour, leaving my clothes soaked. I was completely convicted of my sinfulness and of God's love. I knew there was hope for me. I knew I would never be the same. The old me had died the night before.

LACHITA: Tears of joy dripped onto the letter I wrote to my husband. "You will be coming home to a very different Donnie," I wrote. After that, everything happened very quickly. Donnie immersed himself in Catholic books and began practicing the Faith. It would be another six months before he could be fully received into the Church, but during that time, his all-consuming zeal never let up. Donnie told us early on that he had a great desire to serve God for the rest of his life.

FR. CALLOWAY: In 1993, after only ten months as a Catholic, I said good-bye to the happiest mom in the world, on my way to be a priest with the Congregation of the Marians of the Immaculate Conception. This radical life of poverty, chastity, and obedience—the very things I once ran from—I now embrace.

My calling to the priesthood is like a marriage covenant with God. The honeymoon—the high of my conversion—lasted four years. It was as if God gave me a lollipop experience so I could taste the sweetness of his love. Then he took the lollipop away, so I had to struggle and still choose him. That is where the real love is; to remain faithful when it is not always easy. Our Lady is the one who brought me to Jesus, and I continue to go to him through her. I've been saved by Jesus with the cooperation of his Blessed Mother.

LACHITA: On May 31, 2003, ten years after he became Catholic, I cried tears of joy again as I hugged my son, the priest. "I love you, Fr. Donnie," I told him after the bishop had congratulated him and introduced him as Fr. Donald Calloway. My son had become a priest for life with the Congregation of Marians of the Immaculate Conception.

So many people prayed for Donnie on his journey to the priesthood, especially from our church, Immaculate Conception Parish in Clarksburg, West Virginia. And, of course, our Blessed Mother Mary has interceded every step of the way on this journey of faith for our entire family. She understood a mother's pain and now she celebrates with us the conversion won by her Son.

PART III

27

Worry Is Not Prayer

Monica was in trouble. She was on the verge of becoming what we today call a "helicopter parent": one who hovers over her child so closely that he is not able to "breathe his own air."

Thankfully, God intervened, and what happened next changed everything.

Monica had been growing ever more weary about the state of her son Augustine's soul, even following him from city to city to make sure she could keep tabs on him and influence his steps. She met with a bishop named Antigonus, who was passing through Tagaste, where they were staying. At the time, the city had no bishop in residence. Here was Monica's chance, she figured, to pour out her heart to someone who might have influence over her son.

As Monica approached Antigonus, she began explaining the situation to him. Apparently, Augustine's fame as an expert public debater and orator had preceded him; the good bishop had heard of him already. Monica begged him to meet with her wayward child to convince him of his wrong path. But the bishop responded with great prudence, as Augustine would later state.

As Fr. Falbo writes, "Antigonus remarked to Monica that it was not only a case of a doctrinal dispute with someone arrogant and unwilling to listen to others; Augustine was a brilliant speaker who had already confounded capable and educated men."[84] He advised Monica to be patient and wait, assuring her that "using no other weapon than prayer, she would one day see her son finally realize his error and return to sound principles."

But Monica could not let go of her worrying, and began now to weep, persisting in her plea that the bishop do something for her son. Rather than give in, he encouraged her, confiding that as a child, he, too, had fallen into the errors of the Manichaeans, but eventually returned to his Christian faith. This would be Augustine's fate as well, he said.

Monica still would not relent. Falbo writes, "Finally, the venerable bishop lost his patience and, weary of her nagging, brusquely told her, 'Go away now; but hold on to this: it is inconceivable that he should perish, a son of tears like yours.'" It was as if Monica had been slapped gently upon the face, for these words not only woke her up but gave her real hope, perhaps for the first time in this journey with her son. "Monica received these words as if from heaven," Falbo notes.

God wanted to console Monica and relieve her of her worrying. It was time for the mother to rest and for the Lord to take over. Without this intervention, Monica may have stayed on Augustine's heels, causing him to push away even further. But, as he later contended, her retreating was the right decision.

WORRY IS NOT LOVE

Julie, a mother of an adult child who has left the Church, says that in sorting through her grief with trusted friends, she was given insight into how the evil one can whisper lies into our ears, such as "worry feels like love."

"I realized that when I worry about my children, it feels like I'm loving them," she says. "But that's not true. As Padre Pio says, we are supposed to pray, trust and not worry. I've now gotten to the point where I don't worry about her salvation. I simply pray and trust."

One day, before she had reached this understanding, her daughter did something drastic, packing up everything she owned, including her mattress that she tied to the top of her car. Without a job, she then moved hundreds of miles from home. Watching her drive away, Julie was beside herself with worry.

"I said to God, 'I need a sign, and I need it this week,'" she shares, noting that she felt called to be specific in her request. "I said, 'The sign I want is that someone will send me a card or a letter in their own handwriting, addressed to me, in the mail—something that isn't an advertisement.'" Within a short amount of time, three notes from three different people came in the mail, two mentioning her daughter specifically. She had told no one of her prayer pleas, only God. "I had told him, 'I need a sign that her moving is part of your plan for her eternal salvation,'" Julie says, "and that is what he gave me."

Does that mean every day has been easy since? "No, it's been hard and scary," she admitted. "But I have great hope and confidence. God has blessed me with very clear signs of peace about it," she said, "and I realize that he loves her even more than I do."

LOVE AND WORRY ARE OPPOSITES

Deacon Jim Keating, in a presentation to a women's group at St. Louis' Kenrick–Glennon Seminary in January 2021, says that we sometimes get confused and think that worry is a sign of love. But love and worry are actually opposites. Jesus himself says that love and worry can never exist together because "perfect love casts out fear" (John 4:18).[85]

In faith, we need to learn to place our worries for our loved ones in Jesus' Sacred Heart, because "fear is useless" (see Mark 5:36), the deacon adds. "Sometimes our worries are like the bees mentioned in the psalms," referring to Psalm 118:11–14: "They surrounded me, surrounded me on every side. ... They surrounded me like bees. ... In the name of the LORD I cut them off!"

We can let our worries consume us in this way, but we must ask the Lord for the grace to truly believe that fear is useless—and that worry is not a sign of love. Rather, worry is a sign of feeling alone, powerless, and emotionally isolated—which is the opposite of love. "We must go to the Source, the Font of Love, and place all of these fears into it."

TOBIAS' MOTHER WORRIED, TOO

On day 196 of *The Bible in a Year* podcast, Fr. Jim Chern mentions a saying he saw on a sign in an online marketplace: *Mothers don't sleep. They just worry with their eyes closed.* "With apologies to my mom, personal experience validates that there is an element of truth here," he says.

This saying came to mind while reading chapters ten to twelve of Tobit, which describe the wedding of Tobias and Sarah. The couple marry after Tobias travels to Sarah's home, but they are delayed in returning, and Tobias' parents start worrying. His mother, Anna, "immediately imagines another possible reason—that he's been killed," Fr. Chern says. "It seems even saying the words unleashes grief and mourning for the poor mother." But soon, Anna anxiously looks down the road for her son's return. Even in her distress, she still has hope.

Soon thereafter, as Fr. Chern notes, "The days of mourning and grief turn into the happiest of homecomings. Not only has Tobias returned, but he brings home his wife, and is able to share the miraculous remedy to his father's blindness."

According to Fr. Chern, faith should help us recognize God's presence, no matter what the situation or outcome: "Whether God brings about healing or is able to use that suffering to transform us and those around us, or ultimately, brings us to himself, he is with us." Worry, he adds, only causes us to doubt and forget what Scripture continues to remind us over and over again: that God loves us.

A RECEPTACLE FOR WORRY

Deacon Keating says that when worry fills our minds, we often bring it to Jesus in prayer as a recording in our head, making prayer a time of anxiety, rather than a time for healing and peace. This, in turn, can become an emotional affliction. But Jesus wants to carry our worry for us, and for that to happen, we must deepen our faith.

"Come to me all you who labor and are burdened, and I will give you rest," he said, quoting Matthew 11:28. "One of Jesus' deepest desires is to give us rest and not have our worries continually circulating, processing them over and over in the echo chamber of our minds."

THE MAILBOX ANALOGY

The deacon offered an analogy to help us think through worry, using the visual of putting mail into a mailbox. It would be odd, he says, if we waited around until the mail person came to empty the contents, or followed the truck to its destination to make sure it was properly delivered. "And then further, to wait on the recipient's front porch until he or she opens the door to retrieve the mail and take our letter." Why mail the letter in the first place if we do not trust the one we gave it to to do what is proper and purposeful with that letter?

Spiritually, the proper receptacle for our worries is Christ's heart. "We should treat Christ's heart at least as trustingly as we treat the post office. Once it's placed in his heart, the proper receptacle, he will take care of it."

Does this erase Jesus' request that we be persistent in prayer? No, according to Deacon Keating. Persistence is not the same as obsession and control. At the wedding of Cana, Mary was persistent, but "in the form of deep trust born of a relationship that she had with her Son ... and because she was depositing what she noticed in the greatest receptacle of love that has ever existed—the Sacred Heart of Jesus—she could trust that her son would do what she was noticing was proper, what was for the good of all."[86]

THE SOURCE AND SUMMIT OF RELIEF FROM WORRY

Through the Resurrection, Jesus took all of our worries and fears upon himself, having conquered the very origin of fear and worry itself—death. As Deacon Keating says, "Because [Jesus], being life and love itself, tamed death, emptied it of its power, and redirected our fears into hope."

Even the smallest worries flow from death, he said. But Jesus penetrates this, going where death can no longer define us, and we become defined by communion with him.

In the Crucifixion and Resurrection, we "move away from dead and dying things." We can experience this every single day at daily Mass, tapping into the greatest power available to us on earth by "staying in communion with [God] in a disposition of gratitude."

RELEASING OUR WORRY AT MASS

Deacon Keating suggests four things to help decrease our worry and increase our reliance on God at Mass:

1. Before Mass, in silence, let your burdens rise up, and lay them at Jesus' feet.

2. During Mass, when inspiration comes, place your worries into the Sacred Heart of Jesus.

3. If your burden or worry returns to your mind, remember that you already gave it to Jesus during Mass. Then move forward with your day.

4. If you find relief from worry in this way, tell others about it.

God wants to help relieve our worrying, especially over the lapses in our children's practice of the Catholic Faith. "Let's pray that a new trust arises in our hearts," Deacon Keating concluded, "and that we will believe him that he has come to relieve our burdens."

28

God's Timing:
An Eternal Perspective

At the end of her life, Monica was only in her mid-fifties. Today, this is considered a young age to die. Not so much in ancient times, but God could have kept her on the earth longer, granting her more time to enjoy the fruits of her laboring for the soul of her son Augustine. What some might consider a slight of years, though, Monica did not, for she had accomplished the main thrust of her life by then: to see to it that all her children were firmly in God's grasp.

Just before her death, with her son having been fully converted to the Faith, Monica's heart was full. "Son, there is nothing in this world now that gives me any delight," she said to Augustine. "What have I to do here any longer? I know not, for all I desire is granted. There was only one thing for which I wished to live, and that was to see you a Christian and a Catholic before I died. And God has given me more than I asked, for He has made you one of His servants, and you now desire no earthly happiness. What am I doing here?"

Days later, she was overcome with fever. "You will bury your mother here," she said to Augustine. At that point, even the place of her death did not matter to her, despite previously having had her sights set on being buried at Tagaste beside Patricius. "Oh, why are we not at home where you wish to be," cried their friend and traveling companion,

Navigius. "Do you hear what he says?" she asked Augustine. "Lay my body anywhere; it does not matter," adding, "This only I ask—that you remember me at God's Altar wherever you may be."

Monica could die peacefully wherever she took her last breath, knowing her son was now bound for heaven, where she, too, hoped soon to be. She had fixed both mind and heart firmly on eternity.

DISCOVERING GOD'S PERFECT TIMING

ROXANE: Betrayal. The word hit me hard that December night. Even at only seventeen, I grasped what it meant, and this night—at the intervention we had planned in advance to lure my father to an alcohol treatment center—it sank deep into my bones.

We had a secret, and Dad was not *in* on it; he was the *center* of it. But soon, all in the name of something my uncle had called "tough love," he would know. He would come to understand that we had not been blindsided after all.

I could feel my heart beating through my hoodie as we sat in a circle in my grandma's living room—my mother, grandmother, sister, and me—along with our visitor, my father's older brother. He, too, had been deeply broken by alcoholism, but had come out of the pit. And now he was here with us to help save his brother.

Though I desperately wanted my father to go to treatment, I felt the least sure that he would. No one was more stubborn than Dad. Instead, I thought he would choose a more drastic route, possibly ending his life on this cold, dark night.

"Well, Bob, I'm not here just to visit tonight." These words of my uncle shattered the façade. It was about to become real. As we shared our testimonies, my father's face revealed his pain, embarrassment, and anger. We had surprised him, and he seemed like a wounded animal caught in a trap with no way out. Would he see the love on the other side of our actions that now had him feeling pinned down, realizing we were not doing this to hurt him, but free him?

Through blurred memories, I recall my sister and me leaving the room to give Dad time to process everything. As I walked away, I caught sight of my father's look of abandonment, which seared into my heart. Soon, we heard our mother's voice. "Girls, Dad is going and wants to say goodbye." For a moment I assumed the worst, but then I realized what was happening. Against all the odds, Dad had agreed to the plan; he was going to treatment!

My father's story is one of redemption. It is the story of a man who, as a little boy, the youngest son in a family of nine, had yearnings of becoming a priest, even entering the seminary. He left, though, not long after receiving a telegram with the stark words: "Your mother has died." Like Monica at her death, Grandma Mary was only in her fifties, dying from a preventable infection. My father was devastated. He would go on to serve in the US Air Force, work as a chaplain's assistant in Japan, and finally, meet my mother one summer while working at the North Dakota State Capitol in the insurance department. Mom, working as a receptionist in an office across the hall, said their occasional sightings of one another from across the way led one day to a meeting and, later, to their first date.

A few years later, my own story would begin. But Dad was still in the middle of his, with all the pain he carried deep inside. By then, he had turned to alcohol to numb life's sorrows. Though he expressed his love to his two daughters, my dad carried these wounds with him into our lives. Eventually, alcohol would completely pull him off track—from his work as a teacher and from his faith. For thirty-five years, Dad abandoned his commitment to God and the Church.

I have reflected on my father's story many times—of how his sobriety helped awaken and revive his memory of God's love for him and led to his eventual return to the Church after more than three decades. Until recently, though, it had not occurred to me how Dad's story could shine a light in my heart of what is possible within my own family. One day, while working on this book, it struck me that my father's story of redemption and return to the Church after so many years could be how God wants to offer hope by reminding me of his patience, fidelity, and goodness.

During my teen years, as my dad's disease got progressively worse, I would go to bed believing by morning, he would be dead. When he stopped attending Mass with us, this brought an additional ache to my heart. "Pray for me," he would say as we walked out the door. How could he encourage us to remain close to God while refusing to approach the altar himself? Ultimately, though, this made his eventual return all the more blissful.

In 2013, my father passed away at the age of seventy-seven from the effects of pneumonia and diabetes. Before he passed, he met—and played with—his eight grandchildren. He engaged them with life, getting down on the floor with them when they were little and making funny sounds and expressions that prompted delighted giggles. Following his hard-won reversion, God gave him the gift of time.

The story of my father's return to God after years of wandering has been one of my life's greatest gifts. It took my father decades to return to the Church, and that gives me a deeper understanding of God's economy of time.

As I held my father's hand as he lay dying, only a few things mattered. I knew he loved me, and I knew he loved God and had accepted his love. The journey had been painful for us all, but here was the prize: a holy death, wrapped in the love of God, blessed by having received all the sacraments, and with a tear in his eye—which I took to be a sign, when he could no longer communicate in words, that he had a vision of heaven. I sensed his last words to us were "I love you."

The mercy of God is great. While painful to watch those on a prodigal journey struggle, having watched my father's ascent back to his Father, I firmly believe that if we allow God to do his invisible work and trust in his compassion, in the end we will sing with the choirs of heavenly angels. "I tell you, there is joy before the angels of God over one sinner who repents" (Luke 15:10).

29

It's Not All Bad

After Patricius' death, and before she set out after Augustine in an attempt to influence his conversion, Monica discovered something that can help us as we wait for our children to come home: God will not let the desires of a willing heart be wasted.

In early widowhood, despite her grief, Monica found joy in serving the sick. As Forbes writes, "She would kiss their sores for very pity as she washed and dressed them, and their faces grew bright at her coming."[87] Some even called her "mother," appropriately, for she interacted with them with a motherly affection.

Additionally, she would gather the orphan children at her knee and teach them the truths of the Catholic Faith, bringing some of the poorest ones into her own home for a time, feeding and clothing them. She said, "If I am a mother to these motherless ones, [God] will have mercy and give me back my boy; if I teach them to know and love Him as a Father, He will watch over my son."[88]

Indeed, it seems that God notices our desires to give, and even if we cannot receive the precise gift we so yearn for right now—the conversion of our children—our Lord will allow our outpouring of love to be used for the good, if we remain open to it.

A CHANCE TO CLING TO GOD

As Monica learned, though grief brings suffering, it can also bring opportunity. If we look deeply enough, we might find that this arduous journey we are on is not all bad.

While praying for her daughter's conversion, Rose discovered something she might not have realized otherwise; that this cross has kept her husband and her more fervently focused on Christ. "We're constantly praying for our children," she says, and for the children of others. "Adding prayer upon prayer doesn't thin out the prayer or make it less powerful."

One of Rose's friends, whose children are "living the gay lifestyle" and not practicing the Faith, she says, seems to have relented to the culture, despite being "a good, Catholic woman." Rose has implored her at times to not give up hope. "A parents' prayers are powerful!" she has reminded her.

Holding onto God, her anchor, has given Rose the solidity she has needed in her own waiting, she says. "Does it make me sad that our children are taking this crooked, crazy road? Yes, but I pray for the right people in their lives to bring them home."

Over time, Rose has begun looking at the glass half full. Her husband, a convert, modeled a robust faith for his daughters as they were growing up. "We have been going to Adoration together for twenty-five years, along with daily Mass. He had a deep conversion, which the girls have witnessed."

Rose holds all these hopes near, while recognizing that even in this suffering, a great good arises from the rubble: the absolute need for an ongoing appeal to God. She also credits her husband for added perspective. In reacting less emotionally about their daughter's departure, he has helped her see that, rather than getting stuck in sadness, bringing their disappointments to God can be much more efficacious.

"We started praying together several years ago for this need, starting with a fifty-four-day Rosary Novena," she says. "The intention was for our children to return. I think that's part of the answer. We never stop praying."

They also have prayed numerous novenas to St. Joseph at her husband's suggestion. "He is much better about leaving it in God's hands," Rose admits. "Though I do not know everything he internalizes, I am grateful for our prayer time together. It is quite beautiful to hear your spouse praying for your children. Praying with him in this way has brought a peace, a letting-go. Otherwise, I think, it would just eat at my soul."

While she does not lose sleep over her daughter's salvation, Rose says, she still laments the losses. "I just want her to have everything that the Church offers—the Eucharist, Confession, the Mass," she says. "People sometimes ask me if I have a personal relationship with God. How much closer can you get to that than our sacraments? That is what I want for everyone, but especially my own children."

OUR WILLING HEARTS

As with St. Monica, God notices how much we would like to see our children back in the Faith and will not let this desire go to waste.

As Michelle began praying for and desiring her children's conversions more and more, even as they moved further and further from the Church, other young adults began drawing near her, asking about the joy she seemed to carry with her so often. "I have had many conversations with young adults and teens who want to hear about the Catholic Faith. Some have even met me for coffee to talk more deeply about it," she says. "It is beautiful to see them wanting to grow in their faith walk."

Though she sometimes wishes it could be her own children who have her rapt attention, Michelle says, she has come to believe that while waiting for this prayer to be answered, God has nudged others whose hearts are ready her way. "It has made it so much more tolerable knowing that my love for him and the Church are having an effect on others. It has been like a salve on the wound of my heart," she says. "I pray that someday, it will be my own adult children I am talking to in this open way about our Lord and his Church."

SEEKING THE OTHER LOST

As Tom Bisset echoes, "our love is not wasted." We continue to play an important role in the return of our fallen-away children to the Faith, no matter where they are and what they have experienced in their wayward journey.

"The fact that mediating persons play an essential role in the return of prodigals means that we should actively seek prodigals," Bisset suggests.

"We need to be like the devoted shepherd in Luke 15. This amazing man, full of a sense of duty and care for his flock, refused to rest until all of his sheep were safely in the fold. So, we, too, should give time and energy to finding (other) lost prodigals."[89]

Bisset says Christian parents who feel the loss of their wayward children cannot help but think of and pray for them daily. This love, he says, is beautiful to contemplate. "I believe it is a love that compares to and even surpasses all the loves known to humankind."[90]

In our suffering over our children's wandering from the fold, our love, in a sense, grows even stronger, and our longing for God more powerful. He, in turn, does not overlook a moment of our hearts' unmet desires.

APPRECIATING THE BREADCRUMBS

Sharon likes to think of them as "bread crumbs," little slices of goodness that God offers in the waiting. Like the times she has offered to pray for her son, who says he no longer believes in God. "Even though he isn't sure if God exists, he has not argued when I've offered to pray for him in times of distress. I'll take that as a victory."

Another bread crumb might be an insight she feels came from God— like the day she realized that even though some of her children are not practicing the Faith, they have been claimed by God for all eternity through their baptism and confirmation, indelible marks on their souls that bind them to the Faith.

"Just having this insight that God, the hound of heaven, is pursuing them relentlessly helps me let go," she says. "I might not be able to control my children's choices, but I can choose to be hopeful and think of things differently. I can choose to see each day as another chance to pray for them and their conversion."

Sharon suggests other parents in waiting mode stay awake to all that God is doing in them in this desert time. "This isn't wasted time. He will bring you closer to him, too, if you let him."

WE HAVE BEEN BLESSED

A case in point, as we began sharing the burdens of our hearts with one another, and in praying about writing a book to console other parents, we realized that God has allowed us to use our suffering to connect with and, hopefully, help bless others. Journeying together with each other in mind has focused our souls on what is most important—not on our disappointments but on the love God has for us, as we unite our prayers with others on a similar journey.

We do not cry out to a deaf God but one who "leans down to hear our whispered pleas," as Bisset says, referencing Psalm 31:2. "The Spirit helps us in our weakness; for we do not know how to pray as we ought, but the Spirit himself intercedes for us with sighs too deep for words ... the Spirit intercedes for the saints according to the will of God" (Romans 8:26–27).

Considering all this, we can say, "It's not all bad," as we await, with great hope and a growing love of God and others, the day of our children's return.

30

The Hidden Workings of God

As the discussion about abortion and the work of sidewalk advocates who pray at abortion facilities across the country continued, the radio host felt a tug on her heart. She had her own story to tell, and this seemed the perfect time.

She opened up and shared the following with her listeners: "You know, I'm the mother of two children, but both are dead from abortion." After a pause, she collected her courage and continued. "And I remember the people on the sidewalk. They said they were praying for me."

At the time, she admitted, she felt nothing but negativity toward these people, even giving them a dismissive, offensive gesture. "I so believed the world, and the Planned Parenthood message that *they* could solve the problem," she recalls. "I was certain they had the answer—*not* those people praying."

However, that day was not the final word. "The thing is," she said, "I could not un-see them in my life. Maybe it took ten or more years for their prayers to come to fruition in me, but they did." In time, she said, she was healed—not by Planned Parenthood but by God and the Church. "I always tell people on the sidewalk outside the clinic, 'Thank you for just saying you were praying for me—and for being there. ... even though we weren't able to save the child that day, I couldn't un-see you, and you always stayed with me in those prayers.'"

She added that the prayers of those who had shown up on the sidewalk "were like a candle they lit interiorly," the last light she had to hang on to as she moved into the darkness ahead.[91]

ROXANE: I have often shared this story in describing the prolife sidewalk ministry in which I am involved. I relay it also to new sidewalk advocates, who might wonder if our prayers are going unheard. After all, many more women come out with empty wombs than with a conviction to have their babies.

I share with them, "We can't always see what God is doing, but he is always doing something. The more I pray here, the more I have begun to trust that. We just have to show up; God will work on the hearts that are open."

While this lesson has become firm in my mind and helped me through many moments of frustration over learning another little life has been banished from the earth through abortion—knowing, too, that the mothers, fathers, and anyone connected also suffer the effects in some way—I have not always applied it to other situations, such as the wanderings of our children from the Faith. But if God can work silently in the soul of women like the radio host in the story, using our prayers, even if it takes months and even years for them to take effect, can we trust God enough to do the same in the souls of our children?

EVEN WHILE THEY SLEEP

As Tom Bisset notes, "Even while we are anxiously waiting and wondering, God is at work in [our children's] lives. His plan is filled with events and appointments that are leading to the consummation, the return of the prodigal to the Father's house."[92]

He continues, saying, "[God] alone knows how long it will take to get through to an angry, strong-willed son or what is required to bring healing and hope to a daughter who is spiritually disillusioned."[93]

But God does know, and he will act in our children, through our prayers and his love.

The point, Bisset said, is to remind praying parents that their dearly loved children, who seem so far from God at times, are not far at all. "He or she is as close as the Scripture verses, gospel songs, and Sunday school lessons that lie deep within their minds and hearts," he writes. "The God who is there is really there. He is seeking your children in ways you cannot imagine whether they are awake or asleep."[94]

RETURN TO THE ROSARY

Tiffany shares a story about her daughter, who seemed far away from God. Shortly after college, her daughter began to experience medical symptoms that could be signs of cancer. "One night, she called me in a panic about this. I did what I could to comfort her, but nothing seemed to suffice," Tiffany says. "Finally, hesitantly, I asked her if she had prayed about it. I knew she might be upset about this suggestion, given other conversations we had had in the past. I knew I had to move tenderly."

To her surprise, however, her daughter said, "Yes, I have. I even prayed the Rosary last night." Tiffany was shocked. Despite her daughter having been born on the Feast of Our Lady of the Rosary, she had not seemed at all drawn to the Church's sacramentals and prayers for so long. But in her moment of consternation, she had turned to her Rosary beads—and to Mary, who, as a little girl, she had seemed to be so trustingly drawn toward.

"I know it wasn't much, but to me, it was everything," Tiffany says. "I just held tightly to that little moment, realizing that even though she is not currently attending Mass or availing herself of grace through the sacraments, in her worry, she went to the best place she could—straight into Mother Mary's beautiful lap."

In the end, her physical issues turned out to be no cause for concern. Tiffany said that whenever she begins to lose hope over whether her daughter will ever return to her practice of the Catholic Faith, she remembers this moment and trusts that, no matter what it might seem, God is firmly entrenched in her daughter's soul.

TRUSTING IN GOD'S WHISPERED WORK

James reports that when his son stopped going to Mass as a young adult, he felt like a failure. Since he is the eldest, James worried about the example he was setting for his younger brothers and sisters. Mostly, though, he is just grieved over his son's loss of faith.

The summer this was unraveling, James was given a book about end-of-life conversions. He was amazed, though, by how many of these apparent "conversions at the last minute" turned out to be not so "last minute" after all.

As James says, "In story after story, each person had been advancing toward God all along. They just, for whatever reason—societal pressure, family unrest—could not quite get there, until the very end, when they were on or near their deathbed. Reading these stories, I realized that I really knew very little about what was going on in my son's soul. This gave me a reason to hope that, just [like] the individuals in these stories, God is working in my son's life in ways I cannot imagine. It gave me perspective that has helped me let go of my fears and trust the Lord."

TRAVERSING THE HEART

ROXANE: After my husband's second open-heart surgery, something clicked in my mind that had not been as apparent the first time. I had become more aware of how the surgeon had traversed a place in my husband that ordinarily only God can access. This realization left me in awe.

A friend whose son had been born with a faulty heart valve, requiring numerous surgeries throughout his life, had read the post-surgery report I had sent her through text, and she responded, "Isn't it breathtaking?" Normally, I would not have grasped how something that had caused such consternation just weeks earlier could be described in this way. But now, I understood.

Earlier that week, in anticipation of my husband's surgery, I read Ecclesiastes 11:3: "Just as you know not how the breath of life fashions the human frame in the mother's womb, so you know not the work of God which he is accomplishing in the universe."

This passage gripped me, and while contemplating the word "universe," I applied its vastness not to the physical universe but to the "universe" within my husband's body, understanding God was already there, within his very heart, just as he had been from the beginning. I felt assured God would work silently for the good.

From there, I imagined the Divine Physician guiding the surgical team, trained in a science ultimately rooted in God's wisdom, through the inner chambers of my husband's heart. I realized that, as amazing as this medical team was, they would only be glimpsing what God already knew intimately. The hidden work of God, who fashioned the universe, was now guiding the hands of my husband's surgeon.

This same God is guiding our children each day through the journey they have been asked to take. May his adept and skillful hands lead them back to his heart.

31

Spiritual Fathers Offer Healing and Peace

Here, several priests offer some encouraging words to deepen our faith and trust in God as we patiently wait and pray for our children.

FAITH AND BOLDNESS IN HEALING

On June 27, 2021, Fr. Joshua Elhi, pastor of the Cathedral of the Holy Spirit in Bismarck, North Dakota, gave an inspirational homily on Mark 5:21–43. In this passage, Jesus raises the daughter of Jairus from the dead, and he heals a woman afflicted with a hemorrhage for twelve years after she had reached out and touched his cloak. Both had faith and acted in boldness. Fr. Elhi encourages us all to do the same.

> We know that Jesus healed. We just read about two extraordinary accounts. The woman with the hemorrhage for twelve years and the daughter of Jairus who was ill, died, and then was raised.
>
> It is an historical fact that Jesus healed. But I have a question for you. So what? Is he done healing? You know the answer. He is not done healing because he is not dead. We know that the same Jesus who healed two thousand years ago, is as alive and present now as he was then. When he healed Jairus's daughter and when he healed the woman with the hemorrhage, it's the same Jesus, and the same desire ...

His desire is to heal. Right now. Today. Tomorrow. But there is a prerequisite, Brothers and Sisters. We must be like Jairus and believe that he can and will. That's faith. It's the same Jesus. Believe that he wants to heal ... We must have faith and the boldness of the woman with the hemorrhage. Having a hemorrhage back then meant you were unclean. For twelve years and she had gone to all sorts of doctors, spent all her savings and what does it say in Scripture? She got worse! It made her unclean so that meant she could not approach Jesus or anyone else for that matter for that would make them unclean. That meant no more temple worship. She had no business touching him. She was not worthy, but she was bold. "I've got nowhere else to go." She was bold, and she was going to touch Jesus and did not care about the consequences. That's boldness, and Jesus likes it.

We think we are unworthy: *He wouldn't heal me; he wouldn't do something extraordinary for me because I'm just lowly.* Baloney! None of us is worthy. Neither was the woman with the hemorrhage, but she went forth and touched the hem of Jesus' cloak and was healed. Faith and boldness. He will do today what he did two thousand years ago. If we don't have it, ask him. Say, Jesus, increase my faith. He can and will.

Now we know that Jesus does not always heal the body. That's his business. But I promise you if we ask for any sort of healing—physical or otherwise—something will happen. That's a guarantee. Do you think Jesus is going to say, "No, sorry, I can't help you today?" No, he's going to find some other way, but we have to ask with faith and boldness, and he will do it ...

I leave you with this story. It's not a story of physical healing but it is a story of healing. I got a call on Wednesday from the daughters of a sixty-eight-year-old man who on Monday was not feeling well and was admitted to the hospital. By Wednesday, he learned that it was serious. Really serious.

This man of sixty-eight had supported his two daughters in their Catholic faith. He had supported his now deceased wife in her beautiful Catholic faith. But himself, for whatever reason, had never been baptized. His daughters asked him, "Dad, do you want to be baptized?" And he said, "Yeah." He opened his heart just a little bit to the Lord.

They called me and I rushed over and took a little water, put a couple drops over his sweaty head and said a few words—"I baptize you in the name of the Father and of the Son and of the Holy Spirit" and his soul was healed. And I took some chrism oil and put it on his head, said a few words and confirmed him. It gave him all the strength he needed for that journey.

I said, "That's all he needs right now. If anything happens, let me know."

On Friday, I got a call. "Father, Dad's not well. It will be any moment."

I rushed over with the oil of anointing and gave him a third sacrament, the Anointing of the Sick. And then I took a small piece of Jesus from the host and placed it in his mouth and gave him the fourth sacrament, the Holy Eucharist. Then I whispered a few words and gave him the Apostolic Pardon calling upon all the treasures of mercy from all the saints and from Jesus himself. I left and an hour or so later he died.

This is a story of healing, and that is a guarantee. Do I have any doubt of where his soul is? Not a one. Jesus healed that soul and did extraordinary things for him. And he's not done, but we must ask in faith and in boldness. Jesus, thank you for bringing your healing to the world. Thank you, Jesus, for all you do for us.

JESUS IS ALWAYS PERSONAL

The same weekend, in a homily given at the Maryvale Convent in Valley City, North Dakota, Fr. Don Leiphon commented on the same readings, noting how Jesus was always personal when he healed people. "Jesus didn't want these healings to be anonymous, to seem like magic," he said. "He wanted to look into the eyes of the people he was healing and touch them."

Fr. Don said that as the crowd drew around Jesus after he healed the hemorrhaging woman, "a mob of animosity was all that the apostles could see." But Jesus saw more, allowing an intimate encounter to take place. Further, he used the term "daughter" to talk to her, "one of the most tender references in all of Scripture."

We are more than anonymous figures in a crowd. We are God's beloved children. We are not strangers without an identity, but the objects of his pursuit, the focus of his concern, and love.

Jesus desires to heal whatever is broken in us and in our loved ones. The good things we want for our children, Jesus wants even more. But we must, and our children must, take the first step to seek his healing touch. "We can approach Jesus, confident of his care and desire for good for each one of us," Fr. Don affirmed. "He works this way—for our sake and that of others."

When we reach out to God for healing, he reaches back to us, calling us by name. From there, we pray it is only a matter of time before that touch will find its way to our children's weary souls, too.

INTERIOR FREEDOM

In his book *Interior Freedom*, Fr. Jacques Philippe explains that, even in the most unfavorable circumstances, we possess within ourselves a space for freedom that nobody can take away, since God is its source and guarantee. If we learn "to let this inner space of freedom unfold," he says, even though many things may well cause us to suffer, nothing will really be able to oppress or crush us.[95]

So, even as we watch our children seeming to leap headlong into the world, far away from the sanctuary of our Savior and our soul's deepest longings for them, we need not despair.

Philippe offers the added perspective that even in seemingly disastrous situations, invisible things are also happening: the glory of God from on high is present, along with his angels' protective wings. Gently, he helps us from our place of frozenness and fear onto a path of peace.

ACCEPTING OUR SUFFERINGS

First, Philippe suggests, we must accept whatever suffering we experience, examining the situation not from external appearances but from inward truth. True freedom of the soul does not depend on external circumstances at all, but "something primarily internal."[96]

In our search from interior freedom, he says, we often believe we must eliminate anything that seems restrictive or limiting. But while some obstacles do need to be remedied, this does not provide a lasting solution. Even when we successfully remove some of the impediments, "we shall always come up against painful restrictions."[97] True and lasting freedom must come from within, he says again, in the form of a close relationship with God. Here lies our antidote and hope.

To demonstrate, he points to St. Therese of Lisieux, who spoke so often of the suffering she experienced in her life at a Carmelite convent in France in the late 1800s. Despite her hardships, all of these were "overtaken and transfigured by the intensity of her inner life."[98] How? By Therese's love of God. As she says, "Love is a mystery that transforms everything it touches into beautiful things that are pleasing to God. The love of God sets the soul free."[99]

Without such an approach, we can become imprisoned in our fear. As Philippe says, "It is we who need to change, to learn how to love, letting ourselves be transformed by the Holy Spirit ... that is the only way of escaping our sense of confinement."[100]

CONSENT IN MEETING DIFFICULTY

Philippe points to three approaches we can take in the face of a difficulty or challenge—rebellion, resignation, or consent. Only the final option, consent, actually helps us. By consent, he means an interior change of attitude, not acquiescence: "We say yes to a reality we initially saw as negative, because we realize that something positive may arise from it. This hints at hope."[101]

Our consent does not mean "agreeing with" negative circumstances, but rather relegating them to the future, where God already dwells. As Philippe says, "We can, for example, say yes to what we are in spite of our failings, because we know God loves us; we trust that, out of our deficiencies, the Lord is capable of making splendid things."[102]

AN "ATTITUDE OF THE HEART"

It all boils down to the attitude of the heart, Philippe concludes. For consenting means trusting in God, who created us as we are. "Where grace is accepted, it is never in vain, but always extraordinarily fruitful."[103]

May our consent to reality, when placed capably in the Lord's hands with utmost trust, bring freedom to our souls regarding our own children. We need to remember that Jesus came and gave himself up for them, so that they might "not perish but have eternal life" (John 3:16).

32

Visions of Hope

For a moment, it felt to Monica as if all hope was lost. Through word of mouth, she had become newly aware that her oldest son had fallen into the trap of the Manichaean heresy. At this, her heart cried out in sorrow.

When Augustine returned home on break shortly thereafter, Monica felt she had no choice but to announce her limits, turning him away from a place to rest in their family abode: "The Christian in Monica rose above the mother; her horror of heresy was for the moment stronger than her love for her son."[104]

That night, she cried to God for help, falling, exhausted, into a deep sleep. Her dream was as vivid as one had ever been. As Forbes recounts,

> It seemed to [Monica] that she was standing on a narrow rule or plank of wood, her heart weighed down with sorrow as it had been all through the day. Suddenly, there came toward her a young man radiant and fair of face. Smiling at her, he asked the cause of her tears. "I am weeping" she answered, "for the loss of my son." "Grieve no more then," he replied, "for, look, your son is standing there beside you." Monica turned her head. It was true; Augustine stood at her side of the plank of wood. "Be of good cheer," continued the stranger, "for where you are there shall he be also." Then Monica awoke; the words were ringing in her ears; it seemed to her that God had spoken. In the morning she went straight to Augustine and told him of her dream.

"Perhaps," suggested her son, anxious to turn it to his own advantage, "it means that you will come to see things as I do." "No," said Monica firmly, "for he did not say, 'Where he is you shall be,' but 'Where you are there he shall be.' "[105]

Forbes describes Monica's dream as being "like rays of light in the darkness," through which she drew fresh hope and redoubled her prayers. Indeed, it buoyed Monica's spirits, allowing her to better bide her time, renewed in hope in the Lord and his perfect timing.

Occasionally, God allows our dreams to be a consolation to our hurting hearts, offering us a vivid way to wait more patiently as we journey through this life. Like marathon runners provided "pit stops" for refreshment—a cool drink of water and snack to replenish needed physical energy—God can provide ways to keep our souls replenished through dreams. Let us be watchful for these gifts, which often come in unexpected ways.

PATTI'S STORY

The pink line that emerged on the test strip, indicating a positive result, took my breath away. I would be forty-seven when the baby was due. We had recently added an orphan boy from Kenya, so now we were a family of eleven.

"Hey Mark, we're going to have another baby," I announced to my husband, showing him the pink line. We looked at each other, wide-eyed. We shared a strong understanding that each little soul is a gift from God that will last an eternity. Still, I would be forty-seven and Mark forty-eight. As we adjusted to the news, I discovered that our willingness to accept new life led us closer to God. Instead of thinking of things like money, the opinions of others, and our ages, we would trust God to provide for us in this transitory world.

The younger kids were ecstatic. I thought the older kids would be taken aback. (One was in college, three in high school, one in junior high, and four in grade school). But they all said that given my history, they pretty much expected it.

Then, at three months, I miscarried for the first time. The enormity of the loss did not fully hit me until I was alone at morning Mass a couple days later. I had requested that our kids ask God to let us know the sex of the baby. The oldest suggested I give it a unisex name and leave it at that.

"I would really like to know who it was," I explained, "so please ask God to somehow let us know."

Just before Mass, two days after the miscarriage, I suddenly felt a deep sense of knowing that the baby had been a boy—Matthew. Realizing I had a son suddenly filled me with a deep awareness that my very own child was very likely with God now. I knew there was no greater place to be, but still, a maternal sadness washed over me. Our little Matthew was our only baby we did not get to hold in our arms in this world.

I shed a few tears but was filled with peace that I knew who our baby was. Then, after Mass, before leaving for home, the thought occurred to me that although I was convinced that I had a son in heaven, other family members (especially the teens) might say: "Mom, you really don't know for sure."

I sent up a prayer. "Dear God, it would mean a lot to me if you would somehow let the others know the baby was a boy." I wanted my husband to know his son, and the children to have a relationship with a little brother in heaven. I did not know how God could answer my prayer, but I trusted he could find a way.

Shortly after I returned from Mass, our oldest called me from where he attended college and was living for the summer. "Mom, I'm in a big hurry, but I just wanted to call to tell you I know the baby was a boy." He had dreamed two nights in a row of a baby. In the first dream, a baby had died, and that confused him. The next night, he had the same dream, but this time, when he looked at the baby, he knew it was his little brother. I was in the dream, too. He looked at me, and we nodded at one another in understanding. "I've never had a dream that continued the next night," he told me. It had been so powerful; he was certain he had a little brother, Matthew. It confirmed our earlier experience and had given our family a sureness that Matthew is in heaven waiting for us.

Another significant thing happened that morning while sitting in the car before I drove home. I felt God letting me know that Matthew was in heaven to pray for the rest of us, his family. It was a deep knowing that filled me. At the time, we were all one in faith. That is no longer the case. But thinking of Matthew interceding for us in heaven is a comfort. We are his family, and he would want us together with God one day. God knew we would need Matthew to help prepare the way and pray for the rest of his family.

ROXANE'S STORY

The last place I wanted to be on Mother's Day 1999 was church. We had just lost a child through miscarriage the week before, and I still felt extremely tender. I didn't want to have to see people and hear the well-meaning responses that could reopen my hurt. It took all the courage I could muster to walk into the sanctuary that day.

I never envied those who were pregnant at the same time as I was who carried their babies to term. I was happy for them. But the cries of a baby at the rear of the church awaiting baptism pierced my heart, reminding me of what would not be.

Several things brought solace, but one of the most healing thoughts was the realization that our baby was in heaven. Imagining our little one shining a light for our family, attaining what we are called to and strive for as believers in Christ, left me in hopeful awe.

In each loss of family or friend since, I have been able to rejoice in thinking of our loved ones reuniting with our little Gabriel, whom I believe was there to welcome them at the pearly gates. While I feel at peace now about him, there are no guarantees for his five siblings here on earth still in the thick of their journey toward God. Despite all our efforts to lead them to heaven, at times I wonder, will we all end up together in the end?

A friend once said that heaven cannot possibly be a place worth going to if every member of our family is not there with us. The possibility that all might not make it is a difficult possibility to reckon with. While I remain positive, the uncertainty often keeps me on my knees in prayer.

This same friend and I were lamenting this over coffee one day, sharing different ways it appeared we might be failing, at least on the outside. I shared, "But we have to remember that only God knows everything that's going on in the soul." A book I had read recently about deathbed conversions had convinced me that even those who appear to be far away from God may be closer to him than we think.

My friend then said something that consoled my heart: "My mom always says our kids are going to get to heaven on our coattails." I sat for a moment with that image and, smiling, pulled it in close. I said, "I'm going to remember that." Now, whenever I begin wondering about whether our whole family will make it to heaven, I just turn straight to that visual, and it brings me comfort.

Even if it appears the world has our children in its grasp, can anything be more powerful than God's love for them—and our own? If we have shown love to our children and done our best to lead them toward God, I believe that when they are faced with that final decision of choosing to live with him, and us, eternally, or dwell in a place of darkness without us, they will make the right choice.

Oh, I imagine there might be some holdouts hemming and hawing, but at the critical moment, I trust they are going to grab ahold of our coattails and hang on tight, to come along with us to the place where Love resides, forever.

CECILIA'S STORY

It had been a long journey for Cecilia and her husband with their oldest child, who was adopted and had come into their family with a multitude of wounds. As Cecilia's daughter grew into adulthood, these wounds began to surface in striking ways. Moving far away, without a job, she had strayed from the Church. Nevertheless, she seemed to have retained a deep awareness of God. In time, though, she became involved in a relationship with an abusive man. Understandably, Cecilia's heart was deeply grieved.

During that time, Cecilia and her husband went on pilgrimage to the Holy Land and had the chance to attend Mass at the Church of the Holy Sepulchre in Jerusalem, traditionally held to be on the site of Calvary, where Jesus was crucified, as well as the tomb where Jesus' body was laid before the Resurrection.

"The night before the Mass, I had a profound dream," Cecilia shares. "In the dream, my daughter was standing in front of me, naked, her body covered with gashes. I looked at her and said, 'Please stop your behavior.' She gave me a look that said, 'Stay out of my life.'"

Cecilia woke up, got dressed, and walked to the Church of the Holy Sepulchre along with the other pilgrims. The priest who celebrated Mass asked her to proclaim the Scripture reading. "As I was reading, God brought to my mind an image of himself rising from each wound in the body of my daughter that I had seen in my dream the night before," she says. "And there was a glorious light coming from every one of her wounds."

Cecilia says that moment changed the way she thinks about her daughter and her journey with God. "I no longer worry about her. I love her where she is at," she says. "Do I stop praying? No. I can't even count the number of times a day I pray that she will have a conversion back to the Faith. But is God outside of her life? By no means, I am now convinced."

Reflecting further on that day, Cecilia adds another gift that came as a result. "In my mind, my daughter had become a problem. Her identity to me had become a problem," she says. "And in that moment, God, as he was rising out of her wounds, he was at the same time showing me his love for that daughter of his, the one he'd entrusted to me. And her identity in my heart changed." Now, she was seeing her daughter as "beloved," just as God did. "It was as if God were saying, 'She's not your *problem*, she's your *beloved daughter*, and mine.'"

Because of this and other consolations God has given her, Cecilia says, she has great hope and confidence, based on these very clear signs, that God loves her daughter abundantly and has her in his hands at every moment.

She adds, "A counselor once told me, 'Cecilia, there is one savior, and you are not him.' And it's true. We try to save our children, but that work isn't to be done by us, and we have to receive that gift of God in trust."

33

Praise and Thanksgiving Change Everything

We have children who are away from the Church. *Praise you, Lord Jesus!* Wait, *what!?* God commands us to praise him in *all* circumstances. All means *all*, not just some. Scripture attests to the power of praising and thanking God, even in desperate moments. As a matter of fact, it is a way to turn those desperate moments into success.

In his book *Praise God and Thank Him: Biblical Keys for a Joyful Life*, Jeff Cavins says he has witnessed the power of praise and thanksgiving over and over again. In the Bible, even after people complained over their circumstances, he notes, they often praise God for his greatness and thank him for his mighty deeds. "What are you facing today that seems impossible?" Cavins asks. "Can God turn situations around that make you feel penned in on every side? The answer is a resounding yes!"[106]

He says, "The pattern [of praising God] in Scripture is consistent. When faced with difficulty, people responded in a specific way for success. To be victorious, they responded with praise. Hebrews 13:8 tells us that Jesus Christ is the same yesterday, today, and forever."[107]

According to Cavins, when we actively praise God and give him thanks, "our hearts will find the resting place that we so desire. There will always be problems, but how we respond determines our success in our walk with God or whether we will become even more frustrated with the difficulties that we face."[108] We need to intentionally hand our lives and circumstances over to God, especially in the most difficult times, when we feel there is no hope.

According to Cavins, the Lord says, "I can do things in your life that you think are impossible. I know this situation better than you do, and I know you. Just cooperate with me, and we will do this together. You are my child, and I am your God. Let me show you who I am—let me demonstrate my strength in your life. Allow me to guide you with my wisdom. Let me show you how when others have failed, my Son was successful."[109]

In all times and situations—whether good or bad—our response should be to turn to God with praise. As Cavins notes, "[This] may not change the situation right away, but it will change you!" Praising God with sincerity needs to begin with the sacrament of Reconciliation, for confessing our sins makes us humble and acknowledges our proper relationship with him. It helps us feel his presence in our lives.[110]

We can praise God from our heart, and we can reach out to him praying the many Scriptures passages of praise—especially the Psalms. "Praise the LORD! O give thanks to the LORD, for he is good; for his mercy endures for ever! Who can utter the mighty doings of the LORD, or show forth all his praise?" (Psalm 106:1–2).

Praise doesn't change God; it changes us. As Cavins notes, "It changes our perspective on situations. We move from our limited view to God's unlimited view, and this provides an open door for God to move."[111]

DON'T FORGET TO SAY THANKS

Praising God goes hand-in-hand with thanking him. We praise him because he is good, and we thank him for the good that he does. As Blessed Solanus Casey said, "Thank God ahead of time for answered prayers." Although he was a miracle worker, he taught that regardless of whether a person's specific request is granted, God hears and answers all prayers.

Jesus teaches us to be thankful. When ten lepers were cleansed but only one returned, he asks, "Where are the other nine?" It is a safe bet that most of us ask more than we thank God. If we do not get what we want, at least not immediately, do we still thank God for what he is doing? As St. Paul tells us, "Rejoice always, pray constantly, give thanks in all circumstances; for this is the will of God in Christ Jesus for you" (1 Thessalonians 5:16–18).

PATTI: Years ago, my husband Mark prayed fervently to get a job for which he had applied. It was a position that offered greater security and benefits for our growing family than his current radio job did. He promised God that he would pray the Rosary before the Blessed Sacrament for nine days if he got the job. He did not get it, though. It would seem, therefore, that he was not obligated to follow through with his pledge.

Nonetheless, it occurred to Mark that if he trusted that God always hears our prayers and does what is best for us, thinking that God had let him down by not getting him the job would show a lack of faith on his part. Mark decided to proceed praying nine Rosaries before the Blessed Sacrament. When he finished, he received a surprise phone call. The person who had been offered the job had turned it down, so they offered it to Mark after all. What a blessing! And what an opportunity God had provided by making Mark wait so that he had the chance to step out in faith despite disappointment.

Faith in God means trusting him in all circumstances, proclaiming, "Jesus, I trust in you!" As St. Paul says, we are to address "one another in psalms and hymns and spiritual songs, singing and making melody to the Lord with all your heart, always and for everything giving thanks in the name of our Lord Jesus Christ to God the Father" (Ephesians 5:19–20).

He also says to thank God with our whole hearts—always and for everything. "Whatever you do, in word or deed, do everything in the name of the Lord Jesus, giving thanks to God the Father through him" (Colossians 3:17).

GRATITUDE BLESSES US

For Fr. Russell Kovash, pastor of St. Joseph Parish in Williston, North Dakota, developing an attitude of gratitude has been life-changing. "I am more aware of all the blessings of my life," he said during a retreat he gave one Lent. "And now, I find I am thanking God for things that in the past I would not have done." He explained that over a decade ago, he integrated the habit of praying a nightly "Rosary of gratitude"—where one gives thanks for one thing on each bead— into his prayer every evening.

"It has dramatically changed my life with many fruits as I see how ridiculously good God has been in my life," Kovash says. "I thank God today for blessings that once, I would not have even thanked him for, or maybe I would have complained about them," he added, noting, "Now, I begin noticing God's blessings from the moment I get up in the morning."

Fr. Kovash offers an example of some of the things he thanks God for on his rosary beads: "Lord, thanks for my wonderful, comfortable bed, for hot showers, for modern plumbing ... Lord, thank you for my shoes, my clothes, my ability to talk and to walk, for the Mass, for the great sacrament of confession, for the Eucharist—your Body and Blood. Thank you for your patience with me, thank you for the Cross, thank you for the gifts of faith and hope and love. Thank you for my parents, thank you for the priesthood—for my priesthood."

Through the lens of gratitude, Fr. Kovash has even come to appreciate problems in his life. "Now, I'm thanking God when I'm throwing up with the flu. I thank him for my great health. I thank him for the slow driver in front of me, because maybe I need to slow down," he said. "I thank him for my crosses, it prevents me from becoming a spoiled brat which happens when we get everything we want."

He credits gratitude with increasing his love of God and the joy and zeal for life and seeing things through an eternal lens. "We will truly come to see what is really important in life—those things that have a bearing on eternity," he said. "When we have a passion for the mission of God, no longer will we be lukewarm. Gratitude will light us on fire."

As the *Catechism* reminds us, Jesus gives us an example of thanksgiving in Luke 22:19 when he took bread and wine and gave "thanks" (*eucharistia*). The Eucharist is a sacrifice of thanksgiving to the Father, a blessing by which the Church expresses its gratitude for God for his benefits, for all he has accomplished through creation, redemption, and sanctification. Eucharist means "thanksgiving" (see CCC 1360).

The Mass is filled with glory and praise. As Jeff Cavins writes, "The victory of Christ in the Mass is our victory as we are joined with him through his body. Every time we enter into the Mass with a sense of plight, we should exit with praise and thanksgiving in our hearts and on our lips."[112]

GRATITUDE IN STRESSFUL TIMES

How can we give thanks for stressful times? St. Paul encountered adversity, but he taught: "Give thanks in all circumstances; for this is the will of God in Christ Jesus for you" (1 Thessalonians 5:18). So even when he and Silas were in prison, they spent time praising and thanking God.

Our faith gives us eyes to see. The world sees suffering and pain; the Christian sees an opportunity to love like Christ. Likewise, our children leaving the Faith can become an incentive for us to go deeper into our own faith.

We can thank God for the blessings that we do have in our children, such as having a good heart, being employed, being fun to be around, etc. If the relationship is severed or difficult, we can thank God for our faith and for increasing our love and patience and for the opportunity to offer up our suffering for that child.

No matter how challenging life becomes, we can always find reasons to give thanks.

34

A Little Help from Our Friends

Monica got by with a little help from her friends. As we have seen, St. Ambrose proved especially helpful for her and ultimately played a significant role in her son's conversion.

Msgr. Jeffrey Steenson, a patristics scholar, says that Monica was "entranced with the teaching of Ambrose … [and he] basically took her under his wing … They prayed together and were very close. Ambrose even did some pretty powerful counseling with her. And Augustine, though he wasn't a Christian at the time, was fascinated by Ambrose—with how good he was, and what a wonderful speaker he was."[113] The Basilica of St. Ambrose in Milan, the very church they attended together, exists to this day. "It has a wonderful mosaic of Ambrose's brother," Steenson notes. "Ambrose's sister became a nun, and Ambrose ultimately was buried there; his grave is there in Milan."

Without the influence of St. Ambrose, and his willingness to take time out to listen to and bring hope to Monica, as well as guide her son—so much in need of a worthy father figure—we would not be writing this book.

KATHLEEN'S STORY

Kathleen, a widow, mother of eleven, grandmother of thirty, and great-grandmother of fourteen, began married life barely knowing any Catholics. Her parents divorced when she was three. Her father was

Greek Orthodox, and her mother believed in God but did not practice any religion. Kathleen attended a Catholic boarding school and through the inspiration of the sisters, became Catholic. "I knew from the bottom of my heart that I loved Jesus and wanted to become a Catholic."

Dan had a Catholic mother and Baptist father, and his parents often fought about religion and ended up raising their children without any. When he married, he fully intended to join his new wife's religion. As Kathleen explains, "The week Dan and I got married, he received four sacraments—Baptism, Holy Eucharist, Penance, and Matrimony." She says that they never argued about religion, mostly because Dan went about his everyday life without giving it much thought. He attended Mass only on Christmas and Easter, or when his children received their sacraments.

In 2004, they made a trip to Rome and had the opportunity to shake hands with St. John Paul II. "For the second time in our married life, Dan went to confession," Kathleen recounts. "When he came out, he announced that he just found out that it was a serious sin to miss Mass on Sunday. After this confession, Dan never missed Mass again unless he was sick. He also joined the weekly Rosary group that had been meeting at our house every Wednesday night."

Not long afterward, Dan discovered he had stage four cancer. Near the end of 2005, he received Last Rites, and surrounded by family, died peacefully. By then, Kathleen had a strong community of Catholic friends.

She had often leaned on their prayers and support while raising their family, especially during the heartbreak of a daughter who was addicted to crack and had moved across the country. Kathleen made the bold move of flying out to find her and convinced her to come home and receive treatment. "She's been sober for over twenty-five years and says I saved her life," Kathleen says. "She lives nearby now and takes such good care of me."

Among her other children, some left the Church for a number of years and have come back. Kathleen and her prayer group await the return of another child. Ironically, it was a Church event that led Angela into the cult of the Magnificat Meal Movement, a New-Age group with a mix of other traditions under the leadership of founder Debra Burslem, who claims to be a visionary. They operate in Vanuatu, an island country in the South Pacific Ocean where she can avoid facing charges of embezzlement and tax fraud from the Australian Federal Police.

Before the group was excommunicated, Debra traveled to unsuspecting parishes as a speaker. Kathleen was intrigued. When she returned to hear Debra at another church, she brought her daughter Angela along. "Angela was hooked right away," Kathleen explains, noting that the group seemed authentically Catholic at first. "But Debra started doing things, like changing the words of the Hail Mary and changing the sabbath from Sunday to Saturday."

Kathleen broke away from the group, but Angela remained committed. In 2016, she gave up her thriving real estate business, divorced her husband, and left her children. One of Angela's adult daughters now also lives in the cult in Vanuatu, while the other one lives near Kathleen.

"I did everything I could to talk her [Angela] out of it," Kathleen says. "One day I told her: 'Why don't we hold hands and pray and ask God to lead us to the truth?' She did it once with me." Kathleen continues to pray that prayer daily for her daughter, granddaughter, and Debra.

"Through God's grace, I believe this story will be a true St. Monica story," Kathleen says. Just as St. Monica had a dream that foretold that Augustine would be with her in faith one day, Kathleen dreamed of Jesus sitting with Angela at a table. "His eyes left Angela for a moment, and he looked over at me sitting at another table and smiled. I believe that was confirmation that one day, she will come back."

In the meantime, Kathleen's Catholic Faith brings her much comfort, as does her prayer group. "Monday mornings I go to Mass at ten and then we come back to my house and pray together," she says. "Where two or more are gathered in my name, I am in their midst. Our group has been together now twenty-nine years. We have seen answers from our smallest intentions to life-saving miracles."

SEEKING SUPPORT

Prayer can take many different forms. Online groups exist that offer to pray for anyone's intentions. For instance, a directory of cloistered nuns provides websites with contact information for prayer petitions. Most churches have Bible studies and prayer groups. If yours does not, call other nearby churches to see what they offer. In various areas, St. Monica's Prayer Groups have sprung up to specifically pray for this intention we all share—our children's return to the Faith. An Internet search might bring you to one of these groups near you, or help start a group on your own.

PATTI: An email group I began with a friend called "Mary's Moms and Dads," now numbering 120 people, involves sharing the saint of the day and a prayer every morning, and either doing a novena, or, in between novenas, praying a daily Memorare for all families in our group. Our single intention is for our families to grow closer to God. "But seek first his kingdom and his righteousness, and all these things shall be yours as well" (Matthew 6:33). I also occasionally participate in a mothers' prayer group after Tuesday morning Mass at our parish.

ROXANE: I discovered early on in my own parenting journey, some twenty-five years ago, the immense value of praying mothers joining hands. I first became involved with a faith-sharing group connected to our children's Catholic school and church, through which we read the readings for the upcoming Sunday, sharing how our lives relate to them, and pray for each other. Some of the women have become godmothers to our children, along with other vital sources of support. Another of my prayer groups studies and discusses Church documents but, even more importantly, exchanges prayer requests as we uplift one another through our trials and triumphs.

We both also have a couple of text groups we reach out to when we need immediate prayer support.

JULIE ALEXANDER'S CLUB 11

After bouncing back from the brink of divorce and coming to understand God's plan for marriage, Julie Alexander and her husband, Greg, started the Alexander House, where they serve as marriage coaches. They talk with couples together, and also Greg is there to support and coach husbands and likewise with Julie and wives. Julie also created an online community for women, Club 11, to grow spiritually and find support and purpose in their lives.

During the years her marriage floundered, she had no good Catholic friends to encourage her in the Faith. Now she understands how important such support is. "Club 11 came from a prompting of Mother Mary whispering to my heart about the need to pray for our husbands," Julie shared. "There are four specific areas: strength, courage, leadership, and protection for our husbands." They also offer prayers for one another's families and ask Mary to distribute their prayers for men who have no one to pray for them by name.

"It has been such a gift and a blessing to be able to place a quick prayer request to these special ladies and have them offer their prayers and intentions for such causes," Julie explains. "We have prayed together for almost ten years now and are blown away by the fruit, friendship, and comfort received from having prayer warriors standing in when we are too weak to carry the burden ourselves. When two or three (or eleven) gather in my name, I am there in their midst, Jesus tells us in Scripture— even if it is through texts."

We were never meant to do this alone, and thanks be to God, we do not have to. We are the body of Christ so that we can be a gift to one another. By seeking out support that reflects Christ, we are supported by him and through him. Praying for one another also multiplies our efforts and lessens our burdens as we head in the direction of salvation together.

35

Praying Our Loved Ones into the Kingdom

PATTI: Deacon Mike McKeown, who serves at St. Mary's Church in Sleepy Eye, Minnesota, is the father-in-law of one of my daughters. He is the father of six grown children, five of whom live nearby, and the sixth is a cloistered nun in Pennsylvania.

When he heard about this book, Deacon Mike shared that he gave a talk entitled "Praying Your Loved Ones into the Kingdom" during a Day of Reflection at the Abbey of the Hills in Marvin, South Dakota, in January of 2020. Although his own children continue to live their Catholic faith, some members of his extended family have left the Church. He acknowledged that parents have a role to play in our children's openness to the Faith, but we cannot control everything. He also shared that unhealthy anxiety for our loved ones or beating ourselves up over our mistakes is not helpful.

Here is a summary of his two talks on how we can intercede for our family.

———◦◦◇◦◦———

Most of us feel a special burden for our loved ones who don't practice their faith. *Why don't they take faith seriously?* Realizing the beauty of Christ in our lives, it's only natural to want to share that blessing with them. We may even wonder what will happen to them if they don't accept Christ into their lives.

Family members and friends can be the most difficult people to reach. When we are trying to share the beauty of a relationship with Christ with a family member, they can feel judged. Our adult children may even interpret our concern to mean that they don't measure up in our eyes. While it is important to share our faith, we need to be careful not to press too hard. Our main task in the salvation of our loved ones is to intercede and communicate God's love. Only Jesus can touch their hearts.

Many parents look at their children who have abandoned their faith and say: *My kids are basically good people, and God loves everyone, so I'm not really worried.* Yet, you are here today because you have a burden in your heart. That burden was put there by God; it is an invitation to a life of deeper trust and prayer in order to draw graces into your family.

I would like to share my own journey into this life of intercession. At nineteen, I had an experience of the Holy Spirit that changed my life. I wanted to follow God's will for my life, but I had a lot to learn about my Catholic faith. A few years later, it seemed like God pulled back the veil to show me the beauty of the Catholic Church. I was so awed by what he showed me. It is the main reason I became a deacon. When God touches you in a special way, it's only natural to want to share it with those closest to you; but often, they are the ones who resist you the most.

Having experienced this resistance from family members, I remember one day in prayer I felt God tell me that I am to be like Joseph from the Old Testament. If you remember the patriarch Joseph, he was sold into slavery and ended up in a high position of authority in Pharaoh's court in Egypt. Eventually, during a time of famine, his brothers came to him for food from Pharaoh's storehouse, and he was able to provide for them because of the position that God placed him in. In the same way, we are all called to be Joseph to those that we love. We are called to open up the storehouse of the riches of the grace that Jesus Christ won on the Cross. We are appropriators of that grace. If you feel a burden in your heart for the salvation of your family members, know that God has placed it there, and he is calling you to a deeper life of prayer. You can be that channel of grace and blessing for them by your intercession!

SURRENDERING OUR ANXIETY

One day, a woman asked me to pray for her. As we talked, she broke down sobbing: *My children no longer go to Church, I have grandkids who are not even baptized! I don't know what to do!* What heart doesn't break to hear that? There is something about the grief of a maternal heart that is deep. It is the same with our Blessed Mother; she is always ready to intercede for us.

It is good to be concerned about the salvation of our children, but we need to be on guard against anxiety. We can too easily confuse prayer with worry. Remember, worrying is not a form of prayer; it is actually a sign of a lack of trust in God.

St. Faustina Kowalska was a Polish nun who received messages from Jesus about his Divine Mercy. Her diary was published under the title *Divine Mercy in My Soul.* Here is what Jesus told her about anxiety: "My Child, know that the greatest obstacles to holiness are discouragement and an exaggerated anxiety. These will deprive you of the ability to practice virtue. All temptations gathered together ought not to disturb your interior peace; not even momentarily.[114]

God understands that we can become fearful or anxious, but there is a difference between a natural, human response to a situation and a persistent disposition where we live in constant anxiety. One person even told me, "I will never be at peace until my family is back in the Church."

We do not have the right to insist that God act according to our expectations or in our time frame. When and how he saves them is not up to us. Anxiety is not going to change anything. Constant anxiety is a sign that we are not trusting God. Jesus told St. Faustina, "Oh how much I am hurt by a soul's mistrust. Such a soul professes that I am holy and just but does not believe that I am mercy and does not trust in my goodness."[115]

At times, our anxiety stems from the knowledge that we are partially to blame for our children leaving the Church. We may even have failed our kids in a big way. For instance, one woman told me she was an alcoholic and that her children would often see her drunk or passed out. She felt terrible about how her children were affected by her poor example. Maybe you've experienced similar guilt over your failings. You may have had a conversion later in life where the light bulb went on and you thought, *Why didn't I see this before? Why did I do those things? I want to share God's love with them, but now they don't want to hear it.*

If you deal with similar feelings, there is hope. God is not limited by our mistakes. When we sincerely repent and offer our mistakes to God with the sacrifice of Jesus, he loves to turn them upside down and make something good from them. Let Jesus be the savior. It's why he came into this world! "We know that in everything God works for good with those who love him, who are called according to his purpose" (Romans 8:28).

These words of Scripture should encourage us to never give up hope for our loved ones, knowing that God is the one calling and inspiring us to unite our prayers with him. If we have faith in Jesus Christ and the power of what he suffered for us, we do not have to see the results in order to believe. We can continue to pray with faith and the assurance that God is at work and will continue to be at work. "And this is the confidence which we have in him, that if we ask anything according to his will he hears us" (1 John 5:14).

When we pray with confidence in God's desire for the salvation of souls, we are praying in direct union with his will and can have the assurance that what we ask him for is ours. Confidence, boldness, and expectation lead to grace being released in a powerful way. Jesus loves it when we pray with confidence.

THREE ENCOURAGING STORIES

To encourage you not to lose hope for your loved ones, here are a few stories of people who weren't reconciled with the Church until the very end.

My brother died around seventeen years ago. He had left the Church for another denomination and had a lot of animosity against the Catholic Church. When he got cancer and looked to be near the end, my mom asked him if he wanted to see a priest. To her surprise, he said yes. The priest came and heard his confession and gave him communion and Anointing of the Sick. He died within a few days later, reconciled with the Church.

My aunt also left the Catholic Church many years ago for another denomination. She had experiences that left her feeling hurt and misunderstood by those in the Church. She died this past year at age ninety-five. I was pleasantly surprised to receive a letter from her daughter describing her death: "Before Mom died, I asked her if she wanted to see a priest, although she hadn't been to a Catholic church in years, she said 'yes.' The priest came, gave her Anointing of the Sick, and heard her confession, and gave her communion." She also died soon after receiving the sacraments. God's mercy pursues us right up to the very end!

The Divine Mercy chaplet is an especially powerful prayer to pray at a dying person's bedside. Jesus told St. Faustina, "At the hour of their death, I defend as My own glory every soul that will say this chaplet; or when others say it for a dying person, the indulgence is the same."[116]

Even non-Catholics will normally give their consent if you offer to pray it with them. In the chaplet, we are offering up the sacrifice of Jesus to God the Father for our sins and those of others.

I used to be a furniture rep and traveled five states. One of my customers was a business owner. He was an alcoholic and pretty rough around the edges. I would see him every month, and we got along well. He seemed to respect the fact that I was a person of faith. He told me he was baptized Methodist but never went to church. When he got cancer, I would visit him at the hospital and later in hospice. One day, I asked if I could pray with him. Here is how our conversation went:

"Michael, they tell me I don't have long to live."

"Are you ready for that?"

"What do you mean?"

"Well, Dave, when we die, we all have to stand before Jesus and account for our life," I explained. "Are you prepared for that?"

"I don't think Jesus wants anything to do with me," he responded.

"Dave, you are wrong," I said. "Jesus wants everything to do with you."

Dave looked remorseful and said, "But I've done a lot of bad things in my life."

Seeing his turmoil, I said, "What would you say if I told you Jesus was willing to wipe the slate clean right now so that you would be forgiven when you stand before him?"

"How does that work?"

"You need to sincerely repent of your sins. Is this something that you want?"

Dave agreed that he wanted to repent, so I asked if I could pray with him.

As we began to pray, I asked him to think of everything he had done that offended God, and then I led him through a prayer of repentance. He repented of the ways he had offended God and expressed sorrow for his sins. He said he believed in Jesus and the sacrifice he made for his life. I led him through a prayer of surrender of putting his life in Jesus' hands. After we got done, he seemed to be at peace. "God is with you," I told him. "Do you mind if I pray the Divine Mercy chaplet?"

He wasn't familiar with the chaplet but wanted me to pray it. I prayed the chaplet and stayed with him a little longer. As I left, he thanked me, and I could sense the peace in his heart. He died within the week. I believe Dave received the gift of salvation that day. He repented, he wanted salvation, and he asked for it. He was reconciled with God because Jesus pursued him to the very end.

SURRENDER YOUR BURDENS TO THE LORD

If you are carrying a burden in your heart, not just for the salvation of your loved ones but a burden of guilt over your failings, I invite you to bring these burdens to Mass today and offer them up with the sacrifice of Jesus. Know that he wants to turn your failings into something good. But you have to surrender them to him. Today, during Mass, when Father offers the sacrifice up to God the Father, your prayers will be joined with the sacrifice of Jesus. This is the intercession that God is calling you to.

OTHER WAYS TO GIVE TO GOD

- Witness your faith to others when appropriate, but don't nag.

- Pray the Litany to the Precious Blood of Jesus, which is a powerful prayer for those who have left the Church.

- Make sacrifices and offer up your sufferings for others to return to the Faith. As Our Lady told the children at Fatima, "Pray much and make sacrifices for sinners."

- Seek the intercession of the saints for your loved ones. God allows them to share their graces with us when we ask them in prayer.

Remember, the burden you feel in your heart for your loved ones is an invitation from Jesus to intercede. He has already paid the price for their salvation, and he invites you to surrender your concerns to him and join in his intercession.

Jesus is not limited by our failures. I believe in God's goodness, that he is merciful, and he cares about my loved ones more than I do. Instead of giving God a deadline or insisting he meet our expectations, we need to let God be God.

Repeat after me: Jesus, you are the Savior ... I am not.

Lord Jesus, we come before you in a spirit of confidence in your great mercy. We thank you for the ways you are at work in our hearts and in the lives of our family even when we don't see it. Through the intercession of our Blessed Mother, we confidently surrender all of our loved ones and our concerns for their salvation into your merciful heart. We offer them in union with the perfect and eternal sacrifice of Jesus.

Jesus, I trust in you!

36

Fasting to Fight for Our Children

How did Jesus prepare for his public ministry? He went into the wilderness to fast and pray for forty days. Here, Our Lord gives us a powerful witness of how we should prepare ourselves to do God's will in our lives. As the *Catechism* tells us, fasting helps "us acquire mastery over our instincts and freedom of heart" (CCC 2043).

Throughout history, kings and rulers called on their people to fast for the good of their nations. Since Old Testament times, uniting prayer and fasting has been the way to overcome evil and unleash the power of God. It is only through fasting that we feel the personal sacrifice in our body, just as Jesus felt his passion.

Dr. Ralph Martin of Renewal Ministries mentions fasting in one of his talks, calling it "putting some skin in the game." Jesus, he said, offered the ultimate example by dying on the Cross for us. Fasting provides a way we can show our commitment to the cause as well.

Of course, fasting is hard. But that is exactly why it is so powerful. When adding fasting to our prayers, we pour ourselves out to God both physically and spiritually. It is important to note, in this chapter on fasting, that since some people have eating disorders, we are cautious about anyone fasting in a way that could harm their health. If you struggle with healthy eating, please consult a doctor and/or spiritual director before embarking on a fast for spiritual reasons.

CLEARING OBSTACLES

Archbishop William Goh of Singapore frequently writes and speaks on the power of fasting. "It calls for a personal commitment and sacrifice," he said in a recent homily. "Fasting is very important if we want to develop an authentic spiritual life. It will help us practice detachment and go back to the basics of life."[117]

In 2020, Archbishop Goh called for a day of prayer and fasting for God's divine intervention. Previously, in 2015, he encouraged all of his diocese's 200,000 Catholics to fast each Friday during Lent on bread and water to promote the New Evangelization. "For prayer to be effective, it must be accompanied by fasting," he says. "We learn this from Jesus, our model in evangelization, by looking at how he prepared his ministry, going into the wilderness where he fasted for forty days."[118]

Archbishop Goh emphasizes that adding fasting to "devout and fervent prayers" is the only way to defeat the "hostile secularism" that is undermining society. He also credits fasting with removing obstacles while cleansing us from sin. But for it to bear fruit, he says that fasting should be a source to open our hearts to God and show mercy and charity to others.

FASTING IS A POWERFUL WEAPON

In her book *A Family Guide to Spiritual Warfare: Strategies for Deliverance and Healing*, Kathleen Beckman explains that fasting increases the power of prayer, especially during spiritual warfare. She writes, "In the Old Testament, the Lord told Isaiah that a fast properly undertaken would 'loose the bonds of wickedness ... undo the thongs of the yoke ... let the oppressed go free' (Isaiah 58:6)."[119]

In her twelve years in deliverance ministry doing prayer support and sometimes being present at exorcisms, Beckman says, "I've discovered the efficacy of even a small fast. God appreciates our efforts no matter how small ... When spiritual combat is intense and prolonged, we must employ the weapon of fasting." She notes that when the disciples failed to cast a demon out of a boy, Jesus told them, "This kind cannot be driven out by anything but prayer and fasting" (Mark 9:29). "If you combine prayer and fasting for your family, you will supercharge your intercessory power for the protection and holiness of loved ones," Beckman says.

SCRIPTURE DIRECTIVES

The Bible is filled with stories that show the power of fasting. Here are a few:

- "Yet even now—oracle of the Lord—return to me with your whole heart, with fasting, weeping and mourning. Rend your hearts, not your garments, and return to the Lord, your God" (Joel 2:12–14).

- "Prayer is good with fasting and alms, more than to store up treasures of gold" (Tobit 12:8).

- "Know ye that the Lord will hear your prayers, if you continue with perseverance in fasting and prayers in the sight of the Lord" (Judith 4:11).

- "The days will come when the bridegroom is taken away from them, and then they will fast" (Matthew 9:15).

- "When you fast, do not look somber as the hypocrites do, for they disfigure their faces to show others they are fasting. Truly I tell you, they have received their reward in full" (Matthew 6:16).

Some of the saints are reported to have existed solely on the Eucharist or on just bread and water. Only certain privileged souls can undertake such extreme fasting. For the rest of us who have to take care of our bodies in order to fulfill our daily responsibilities, we must navigate a fast that is sacrificial but still allows us to function.

PATTI: During a Lenten retreat I attended several years ago, a priest addressed the topic of fasting. He explained that it is good to make sacrifices and give things up, but whenever fasting is mentioned in the Bible, it always refers to going without food. It was assumed that we would fast because it said *when* you fast, not *if* you fast. "There is something unique in sacrificing through fasting," he said. "It is a way to deprive ourselves physically to become stronger spiritually."

There is more than one way to fast. Here are some options:

- Have only one meal a day.

- Skip a meal.

- Abstain from a particular food at each meal. For example, do not put mustard on your sandwich, do not order the french fries, have no bread with your dinner, etc. St. Francis de Sales advises us never to leave the table without having refused ourselves something.

- Pick a day, or a meal, where you fast on bread and water.

- Keep meals "plain," such as a hard-boiled egg, dry toast, and a banana. This was St. Teresa of Calcutta's daily breakfast.

- Do not eat between meals.

It is important not to make fasting about dieting. One way to do that is that whatever you eat, make it simple and about survival and health rather than about enjoyment. For example, if you have decided to make your breakfast an egg, toast, and a banana, have just dry toast and a hard-boiled egg without salt, eaten alone and not on the toast like a sandwich. In this way, you are denying yourself enjoyment and offering it as a sacrifice. And when we actually experience hunger pains, offer them to God along with your prayers for your intentions.

STANDING IN THE BREACH

On day 221 of *The Bible in a Year* podcast, Fr. Mike notes how the prophet Ezekiel points out the false prophets of the day and tells the people they are committing robbery, oppressing the poor and needy, and extorting the sojourner without redress (see Ezekiel 22:29). Then, in verse 30, he speaks for the Lord: "I sought for a man among them who should build up the wall and stand in the breach before me for the land, that I should not destroy it, *but I found none*."

Recalling men like Abraham, Moses, and, in the future, Jesus—all of whom have stood in the breach for others—Fr. Mike says, "All these sins are happening in Israel, and the Lord seems to be saying, 'If someone were willing to stand in the breach, I would not allow this disaster to fall upon them.'"

He asks, how often do we go before the Lord and intercede on behalf of others? If you are a parent or grandparent, or someone else in a position of authority, you can stand in the breach for those in your care who do not yet see the dangers ahead. "It might even be an older sister or brother who says, 'OK, God, I see what is going on in their lives, and I'm going to stand in the breach.'" But along with offering a prayer, Fr. Mike suggests something even more serious. "What about fasting with prayer, knowing that maybe this prayer is the only thing between this person you love and judgment upon them?" he says. "We can fast on their behalf, and with that, pray that the Lord gives them mercy, changes their hearts, and brings them home."

It is certainly worth a shot.

37

Divine Mercy

As the lector proclaimed the second Scripture reading that Sunday after Easter in 2011, the words entered Ramona Trevino's ears and darted straight to her soul, reaching a place that had been dormant for far too long.

"Blessed be the God and Father of our Lord Jesus Christ, *who in his great mercy* gave us a new birth to a living hope through the resurrection of Jesus Christ from the dead," the reading from 1 Peter 1:3–9 began.

It was the word "mercy" that grabbed hold of her heart, banishing the hold the abortion industry had had on her soul for the past several years.

The desire to flee from her job as a manager at a Planned Parenthood abortion-referral clinic in Sherman, Texas, had been growing lately to the point of overwhelm. And yet something had held Ramona back from doing what she knew she ought: fear. The fear of how her family would survive. The fear of what her friends would say. The fear of her identity being lost.

"In this you rejoice," the lector continued, "although now for a little while you may have to suffer through various trials, so that the genuineness of your faith, more precious than gold that is perishable even though tested in fire, may prove to be for the praise, glory, and honor at the revelation of Jesus Christ."

No matter how hard things might become, Ramona was beginning to sense she and her family would be OK. The worry that had been weighing her down for so long was being replaced by an even stronger feeling of serenity and peace.

Then, the hymn for the Eucharist began; her favorite: "Pescador de Hombres." But it was as if Ramona were hearing the words for the first time. "Lord, when you came to the seashore, you weren't seeking the wise or the wealthy, but only asking that I might follow." *Could it really be that simple?* she thought. *That's me, isn't it, Lord?*

At that, Ramona resolved to accept the gift being offered. On Monday, she would put in her notice. She was done with Planned Parenthood, forever.

For weary parents, the peace and promises of Divine Mercy can be something to hold onto as we wait and pray, repeating as often as needed: "Jesus, I trust in you."

LEARNING TO TRUST IN HIM

Looking back on that transforming day, as described in her conversion story *Redeemed by Grace: A Catholic Woman's Journey to Planned Parenthood and Back*, Ramona says that as a baptized Catholic who had not been living devoutly, she had no idea what Divine Mercy Sunday was at the time. Later, she would learn that at the very moment she was singing at Mass, St. John Paul II, who shared her love of that song, was being beatified. And further, that he had been the one to declare the first Sunday after Easter to be Divine Mercy Sunday, promoting St. Faustina Kowalska's promulgation of Jesus' unfathomable font of mercy.

Later, understanding more fully the profundity of the message, Ramona would claim the words from St. Faustina as an everyday utterance, especially in moments of anxiety: "Jesus, I trust in you." With that as a foundation, Satan could no longer whisper his lies into her ear.

Referring to Ezekiel 46:9, in *The Bible in a Year* podcast (day 236), Fr. Mike noted, "When you come into the Lord's presence and give him the worship he deserves, you can't just go back the same way that you came. You can't remain the same as you were before you offered him worship. It has to change you."

After years of wandering away from God, Ramona was leaving that life behind. And she was not going to go out the way she came in. Despite her past choices, the woman who, as a little girl, had sensed God's presence in a lighting flash one frightful summer night, returned to her loving Father.

Jesus' Divine Mercy had provided that grace.

WHAT IS THE DIVINE MERCY DEVOTION?

Most Catholics know of the Divine Mercy image, meant to draw us into the abundant and ever-flowing mercy of God. The image was transmitted by Jesus to a young Polish nun, Sister Maria Faustina, born Helen Kowalska, on August 25, 1905. She died October 5, 1938, in a convent of the Congregation of Sisters of Our Lady of Mercy in Cracow, Poland, and was buried October 7 of that same year.

Sister Faustina, who later became St. Faustina, had come from a very poor family that had struggled mightily on their little farm during World War I. With only three years of very simple education, she was given the humblest of tasks in the convent, usually in the kitchen or the vegetable garden, or as a porter. On February 22, 1931, Jesus appeared to this simple nun, bringing with him a wonderful message of mercy for all mankind.

> In the evening, when I was in my cell, I became aware of the Lord Jesus clothed in a white garment. One hand was raised in blessing, the other was touching the garment at the breast. From the opening of the garment at the breast there came forth two large rays, one red and the other pale. In silence I gazed intently at the Lord; my soul was overwhelmed with fear, but also with great joy. After a while Jesus said to me, "paint an image according to the pattern you see, with the inscription: Jesus, I trust in You."[120]

Sometime later, Our Lord again spoke to her:

> The pale ray stands for the Water which makes souls righteous; the red ray stands for the Blood which is the life of souls. These two rays issued forth from the depths of My most tender Mercy at that time when My agonizing Heart was opened by a lance on the Cross ... Fortunate is the one who will dwell in their shelter, for the just hand of God shall not lay hold of him.[121]

In St. Faustina's day, the heresy of Jansenism had a hold on the hearts of many. In essence, Jansenism is the belief that one must be perfect in order to approach God. But since *no one* is perfect, this false belief caused many to avoid coming to God and seeking his forgiveness. The message of Divine Mercy challenges this skewed idea of what our relationship with God should be. Though mostly eradicated, Jansenist attitudes have a way of sneaking back into our fallen world, convincing many that we are too wounded, broken, and sinful to approach our Lord. This is why the Church has embraced the Divine Mercy so eagerly.

ANOTHER DIVINE MERCY STORY

In this story, Dave shares the power of praying the Divine Mercy Chaplet prayer for his dying mother.

"Your mom fell and hit her head and is in a coma now," my Dad informed me over the phone. She had been fighting bone cancer, but this sudden fall and coma was a shock. I lived halfway across the country from my parents.

I had no idea when Mom last went to confession, but I felt it was important for her to see a priest. It seemed that opportunity might be gone now. I was just not at peace with her time being over without that sacrament.

My wife and I began praying the Chaplet of Divine Mercy for my mom. We knew it was a powerful devotion from Jesus through St. Faustina that could help convert even hardened sinners. It is especially encouraged to recite it for the dying where the last struggle between God and the devil takes place. I was informed that Mom was not expected to recover consciousness.

I flew in to be at our mom's bedside and also comfort our father.

"She's out of the coma!" my dad announced upon my arrival. A priest-friend of my parents had also arrived to be with them. My other two brothers (both ex-Catholics) and I, my dad, and the priest gathered in a room outside Mom's hospital room, and Father led us in praying the Chaplet of Divine Mercy. Then he went in to give Mom Last Rites, complete with confession, Holy Communion, and an anointing. They were in the room together for a very long time.

Later, when no one else was around, Mom told me where her journals were and asked me to burn them. "I no longer feel that way," she explained. For Mom, who was not one to admit mistakes or take anything back, it was unusual. Our family had a week together before she died peacefully.

Two years later, my Dad shared with me that many years earlier, in an army hospital in another country where we lived at the time, Mom had an abortion. The Army doctor had recommended it, saying that due to complications, the baby would not be normal if allowed to continue. Mom and Dad agreed to it. Mom's vehement pro-abortion stance during her lifetime made sense now. What an infinite blessing that she awoke from her coma and had the opportunity for a final confession.

THE DIVINE MERCY CHAPLET

Jesus taught St. Faustina prayers to implore his Divine Mercy, which is referred to now as the Chaplet of Divine Mercy.

On a rosary, begin the Chaplet with an Our Father, Hail Mary, and the Apostle's Creed. Then on the "Our Father beads," pray the following: *Eternal Father, I offer you the Body and Blood, Soul and Divinity of your dearly beloved Son, our Lord Jesus Christ, in atonement for our sins and those of the whole world.*

Then, on the ten "Hail Mary beads," pray: *For the sake of his sorrowful passion, have mercy on us and on the whole world.*

Continue praying in this way for each of the five decades. Then, pray the following words three times: *Holy God, Holy Mighty One, Holy Immortal One, have mercy on us and on the whole world.*

As Jesus told Sister Faustina,

> Say unceasingly this chaplet that I have taught you. Anyone who says it will receive great Mercy at the hour of death. Priests will recommend it to sinners as the last hope. Even the most hardened sinner, if he recites this Chaplet even once, will receive grace from My Infinite Mercy. I want the whole world to know My Infinite Mercy. I want to give unimaginable graces to those who trust in My Mercy. ... When they say this Chaplet in the presence of the dying, I will stand between My Father and the dying person not as the just judge but as the Merciful Savior.[122]

THE HOLY HOUR

Jesus told St. Faustina that the hour he expired on the Cross is the hour in which to especially implore his Divine Mercy, because at that moment his saving mission was accomplished, and his blood and water were poured out on the Cross for the sins of the whole world. Because Jesus made the three o'clock hour sacred, whenever the clock strikes this hour, his mercy can be powerfully implored.

At three o'clock, implore My mercy, especially for sinners; and, if only for a brief moment, immerse yourself in My Passion, particularly in My abandonment at the moment of agony. This is the hour of great mercy ... In this hour I will refuse nothing to the soul that makes a request of Me in virtue of My Passion.[123]

As often as you hear the clock strike the third hour immerse yourself completely in My mercy, adoring and glorifying it, invoke its omnipotence for the whole world, and particularly for poor sinners, for at that moment mercy was opened wide for every soul. In this hour you can obtain everything for yourself and for others for the asking; it was the hour of grace for the whole world— mercy triumphed over justice.

Try your best to make the Stations of the Cross in this hour, provided that your duties permit it; and if you are not able to make the Stations of the Cross, then at least step into the chapel for a moment and adore, in the Most Blessed Sacrament, My Heart, which is full of mercy: and should you be unable to step into chapel, immerse yourself in prayer there where you happen to be, if only for a very brief instant.[124]

The message of the Divine Mercy can fill us with great hope. In the end, its message is simple: God loves us, and his mercy is greater than any of our sins. The promises given by Our Lord to St. Faustina are almost unbelievable—that is, the degree of mercy God will grant us by trusting and praying the Chaplet of Divine Mercy. Jesus wants us to call upon him for our loved ones, especially our children who are away from the Faith, trusting in the power of his infinite love and mercy.

38

Waiting and Praying
with Mary

Mary suffered. She suffered profoundly. She did not run away from the Cross but was with her Son every step of the way. As Our Lady of Sorrows, she persevered to the end—and she endured, joining her sufferings with those of her Son.

Remaining faithful to the end, Mary witnessed the greatest event in history. All generations call her "blessed." As our mother, she loves and intercedes for us, desiring we claim our place in heaven. She wants that also for our children.

At the Carmel of Mary Monastery in Wahpeton, North Dakota, a white statue of Our Lady of the Prairies "greets" visitors near the entrance of a winding road that leads to the cloister. Both of us have visited this monastery and spent time in prayer at the foot of this image. Like others through the years, we are moved by her serenity, calmness, and loving heart. Just a short time before he died, our Lord gave her to his beloved apostle, John, with the words, "Behold, your mother!" (John 19:27). In so doing, he gives his mother to us, ensuring that we would not be without her maternal assistance.

Every August, for sixty-five years, pilgrims have come to this small glimmer of heaven on earth that abuts the twisting Wild Rice River. Outside, these travelers pray with the sisters, who, in recent decades, have been able to "join" them through a sound system within the cloister walls. The pilgrimage to the monastery of this ancient order of Carmelites, whose origins date back to the time of Elijah, includes a Rosary walk, with stations moving from tree to tree; a presentation by a spiritual leader; an outdoor Mass; confession under tents; and finally, an offering by the people from the surrounding rich, rural farmland of their first fruits of the harvest. The people give what they have to the sisters, who have taken a vow of poverty and are, as it were, beggars, subsisting only on what God and his people provide.

At Mass here, everything slows down. Words are belabored but intentional, while the songs of the sisters are pure and divinely oriented. The joy that emanates on their faces from behind the iron grille speaks of a deep trust and hope—a gift they offer all who visit. And behind every smile of anticipation in someday meeting their maker lies a heart dedicated to Our Lady.

Back at her spot near the entrance, Our Lady of the Prairies gently clutches in her arms a sheaf of wheat. It represents the rural mindset of patiently waiting on the Lord. The farmers of the area know well what it means to wait. "The earth produces of itself, first the blade, then the ear, then the full grain in the ear. But when the grain is ripe, at once he puts the sickle, because the harvest has come" (Mark 4:28–29).

WE WAIT WITH MARY, TOO

As our children grow into adulthood, our instructive words to them become fewer and our prayers deeper than when they were smaller and nearer. In our increasing surrender, and in our soul's quieting to make room for God's plan, we see a parallel in our movements to that of Mary, who "kept all these things in her heart" (Luke 2:51).

Monica fled to the churches, in the places where she wept to bring her cares before the Lord, and in doing so, undoubtedly passed by statues of Our Blessed Mother. Weeping before God in the sanctuary, she likely rested at the foot of Our Lady, seeking solace in this feminine soul, one that Josef Ratzinger, later Pope Benedict XVI, described as "the holy soil of the Church."[125]

In the book he wrote with Hans Urs von Balthasar, *Mary: The Church at the Source*, Ratzinger says that "Mary makes herself entirely available as soil; she lets herself be used [*brauchen*] and used up, in order to be transformed into the One who needs [*braucht*] us in order to become the fruit of the earth."[126]

We, too, offer ourselves for our children, allowing ourselves to be used by God, and "used up," in a sense, in order that our children would seek heaven with us.

Even as Monica's tears were watering the soil beneath her, so was the earth being refreshed by her tears to bring new life, just as Mary's sorrows made way for the Resurrection. In a similar way, our grief at feeling the distance between our children and the Church can become an offering to God that, in time, can bear fruit.

GROWING IN A HIDDEN WAY

Author and spiritual director Elizabeth Kelly has said, in giving of ourselves to our children, especially as mothers, an element of being out of control enters as we "offer the nutrients of our body" to bring new life. "In Mary's maternity, she places her substance into the seed so that new life can grow," Kelly says. "As women ... the mystery of the gifts we bring might be more hidden and subtle, but this makes them all the more necessary."[127]

Like a seed planted, time must be given its rightful place. "Motherhood is all about waiting, allowing, surrendering," Kelly said. "This growing is going on in a hidden way, and we can't say on what day it will spring forth." Just like the farmer does not know for sure when the harvest will come. It depends on many things, mostly things out of our control or hidden away for a time. Likewise, with our children, there is "growing going on," yet we cannot say just when it will begin to blossom.

While we wait, we pray in hope. And prayer, properly understood, according to Ratzinger, is nothing other than "becoming a longing for God. ... In Mary this petition has been granted: she is, as it were, the open vessel of longing, in which life becomes prayer and prayer becomes life."[128]

"We're asked to pray without ceasing," Kelly said, "and to fan our prayers with a constant longing for God." This longing, she added, will never be completely satisfied in this life.

What if what we have gone through with our children, even as we have watched with great sorrow their departure from the Faith, ultimately brings us—and hopefully them in time—closer to God and heaven? Our patient waiting in this "vale of tears," as described in the "Hail, Holy Queen" prayer, can become a gift to us from God.

BECOMING INWARDLY COLLECTED

Ratzinger says our Western culture has increasingly separated Christ from his Mother. In doing so, we have forgotten how to wait. In our increased earthly abilities, we have treated the Church, he says, "almost like some technological device that we plan and make with enormous cleverness and expenditure of energy." But the Church is not a manufactured item; rather, "the living seed of God that must be allowed to grow and ripen."[129]

So, too, might we say that our children's hearts, and our relationships with them, are not manufactured, but living realities that need time and patience to flourish.

"We must retrieve the symbol of the fruitful soil," Ratzinger says. "We must once more become waiting, inwardly collected people who in the depth of prayer, longing and faith give the Word room to grow."[130]

We who have children who have been away from the sacraments can echo his words. They, too, need time to grow. And, for that matter, so do we.

THE WORD "RAINING" UPON OUR HEARTS

As parents, we want our children to be safe in times of confusion, too, and duly protected from the elements. So often, we have little control over those elements and whether our children will be caught in the storms. In all times of worry, we can place them confidently under the protection of Mary, who can be where we cannot, and draw on God's Word for solace.

"When we allow God's word to penetrate us," Kelly concludes, "it begins to penetrate the world." As we draw near God in his Word, and Mary through our prayers, these outpourings can rain upon the hearts of our children, as described in Isaiah 55:10–11: "For as the rain and the snow come down from heaven, and do not return there but water the earth, making it bring forth and sprout, giving seed to the sower and bread to the eater, so shall my word be that goes forth from my mouth; it shall not return to me empty, but it shall accomplish that which I intend, and prosper in the thing for which I sent it."

MARY CAN TAKE ON OUR STRESS

Even with Mary's powerful help, our lives will not become free of stress. Our Blessed Mother contemplated all things in her heart, but her life was surrounded by stressful situations. So whatever burdens we have from our family, we can hand them over to her.

Consider what the Blessed Mother was called to handle. She learned from an angel she was to be the mother of the Savior despite Joseph not knowing at first; rode a donkey while pregnant, looking for a place to have a baby; heard from Simeon, a prophet, that a sword would pierce her heart; fled Egypt in the middle of the night because Herod wanted her Jesus dead; and searched for three days for Jesus, knowing he was the Savior, yet was lost.

Before the unimaginable suffering of her Son's arrest, torture, and crucifixion were the murmurings of ill-intent among leaders. The Blessed Mother never lashed out: "He *is* God, you fools!" She had total faith in God and a complete union with whatever he was allowing in her life.

Perhaps most reassuring of all is that the very first miracle Jesus performed recorded in the Bible came about due to Mary's response to someone's stress. It was not a matter of life and death that the host of the wedding at Cana had run out of wine, but merely an embarrassing situation. After Mary told Jesus of it, he told her that it was not his time yet. However, his mother came to him for help, not for herself but to relieve someone's stress. Jesus responded by changing water into wine.

Mary was not given all the answers up front. It was through her great trust and desire to do God's will that she consented to become the mother of our Savior. She is our mother, too, and wants all her children in heaven. We can spiritually bring our own children to her, trusting that she will in turn bring them to her Son, Jesus.

Prayer of St. Augustine to the Blessed Mother

O Blessed Virgin Mary, who can worthily repay thee thy just dues of praise and thanksgiving, thou who by the wondrous assent of thy will didst rescue a fallen world? What songs of praise can our weak human nature recite in thy honor, since it is by thy intervention alone that it has found the way to restoration?

Accept, then, such poor thanks as we have here to offer, though they be unequal to thy merits; and, receiving our vows, obtain by thy prayers the remission of our offenses. Carry thou our prayers within the sanctuary of the heavenly audience, and bring forth from it the antidote of our reconciliation. May the sins we bring before Almighty God through thee, become pardonable through thee; may what we ask for with sure confidence, through thee be granted.

Take our offering, grant us our requests, obtain pardon for what we fear, for thou art the sole hope of sinners. Through thee we hope for the remission of our sins, and in thee, O blessed Lady, is our hope of reward. Holy Mary, succor the miserable, help the fainthearted, comfort the sorrowful, pray for thy people, plead for the clergy, intercede for all women consecrated to God; may all who keep thy holy commemoration feel now thy help and protection.

Be thou ever ready to assist us when we pray, and bring back to us the answers to our prayers. Make it thy continual care to pray for the people of God, thou who, blessed by God, didst merit to bear the Redeemer of the world, who liveth and reigneth, world without end. Amen.

39

A Prodigal's Plight

In *Good News About Prodigals*, Tom Bisset says that despite what it might seem, the Far Country—that place where the wandering child goes to escape the faith of his or her roots—may not live up to its lofty promises. The freedom our children think they are running toward, with visions of throwing off the shackles of their childhood faith, may be more elusive than they would wish.

While no one wants suffering for our children, keeping things in perspective helps us traverse the sorrows of living out these days of spiritual separation in hope. By becoming aware of how some children who left the Faith processed that departure after their return, we can direct our prayers away from our hurting and more to theirs, where the true suffering in living apart from God may be happening.

THE DRIFTER

Bisset shares the story of Dave, a man who abandoned his faith for a time, then returned fastidiously to it after a long period of drifting. Dave grew up in a home with fervent Christian parents and plenty of strong role models. His spiritual interests began to wane in high school, however, and in college, they diminished altogether. It was more of a "slow leak" than anything, Bisset shares. "Still, he left. In his heart of hearts, he was gone."[131]

His story includes four of the five reasons people who leave the Faith come back, as Bisset points out: 1) another Christian's influence, 2) an unsolvable problem, 3) a deep emotional and spiritual void, and 4) an unexpected, life-changing experience. "The fifth reason, concern about the spiritual future of his children, could not apply since he did not have children at the time."[132]

But everything else does. "In my view, the growing emptiness of Dave's life was key to his return," Bisset shares. "He wouldn't admit it, but deep in his soul, he understood the significance of the riches he had lost."[133]

In the end, it was the love and kindness that Dave's parents showed him that smoothed the way home. Bissett continues, "Whatever you do, don't miss the parent part of this prodigal homecoming ... [that is] the crown jewel of this story."[134]

In his interview with him, Dave gave Bisset the phrase to his chapter: "The Ache of the Soul." For that is what he experienced falling from his Christian underpinnings. "As soon as he said it, I knew it was the real-life description of void, the term I had been using to describe this particular reason for a prodigal's return," Bisset says. "Something immeasurably worse than a toothache or backache or headache. A soul ache."

No matter how smooth and comfortable our wandering children's lives may seem, Bissett sees a distinct pattern. "At the bottom of the bottom in every prodigal life there is an ever-deepening emptiness." It cannot be otherwise, "for wholeness and meaning cannot be found in life apart from an authentic relationship with Jesus Christ and a life lived in obedience to his commandments."[135]

Dave tells the story from there, explaining that his parents' involvement in their parish was "an integral part of our family's existence." He remembers their rules and regulations, but he did not feel overly rebellious. His strongest identity was being a star athlete, which ultimately led to his receiving a college baseball scholarship.

But when Dave ended up being cut from the team, he was dealt a crushing blow. He explains, "I had put all of my eggs in that basket, and all of a sudden, those eggs were all over the pavement."[136] From there, Dave began to experience a sort of existential crisis. He began to "eat, drink, and be merry," seeing nothing else to live for. He ended up dropping out of school and joining the military, where the ache began to become apparent. When he met and married a Christian of a different denomination, the two led very selfish lives, he said, focused mostly on themselves.

The couple had moved back to Dave's hometown and started going back to church, though not with zeal. Meeting a truly vibrant Christian man there helped reopen a door for Dave to Christ, but his life still reflected the world most of all. Around this time, he also became interested in flying planes.

It was a plane crash that ultimately jolted Dave awake. "When the plane finally stopped, I crawled out, stood on the runway, and stared at the wreckage," he recounts. Looking up to the sky in tears, Dave told God that something needed to change, and soon, both he and his wife were seeking repentance and turning back to their faith.[137]

Reflecting on his journey, Dave says his parents never panicked. "I always felt unconditional acceptance from them," calling them "the fragrant aroma of Christ to me."[138]

One evening during his drinking years, he had come home intoxicated and tried sneaking into his parents' home unnoticed. On the way to his room, he caught sight of his mother at the kitchen table praying. "She had a Bible open on the table and a handkerchief in her hand." That image, Dave says, never left him. "She prayed and prayed for me," he recalls, adding, "We need to remember the tremendous power of prayer."[139]

BERNADETTE'S STORY

Bernadette, a charismatic Catholic who left a vocation to religious life for marriage and family, raised five children with her husband, a farmer, and gave her life over to serving them, doing everything possible to see that their children would grow up to be strong Catholics.

She and her husband were taken aback, however, by their oldest daughter's choice of boyfriend. Being from a small town, they knew exactly what they were dealing with, and it worried them. For starters, he was four years older than their daughter, and she was still in high school. It was also clear that he was not an innocent.

"I went to a priest who was so loving and kind," Bernadette shares. "He told me to pray that God would put someone in their path who would show them the way. He told me to 'Just listen to her, and don't be critical.'"

Years later, she says, the same daughter told her that the best Christmas gift she got that year was her mother's listening ear. "She told me, 'You just listened to me, and you weren't critical.' It really is all about love."

But it was not easy, Bernadette says, waiting for that relationship to end. She remembers reading Scripture and getting the message, "I will heal what the locust has eaten." She began praying the Rosary more. "That's when I realized it was more for me than her," she says. "My husband wasn't quite there. I waited and prayed, but he was furious for a while, saying, 'Our family doesn't do this kind of stuff.' This was pride, but I could understand it to some degree. It hurts like the devil."

Bernadette shared with her husband some of her insights, and he agreed to try a different approach. "He decided to have supper with her and promised to tell her that he would always love her no matter what, but that if she didn't get her life together, he was going to take away her car and let someone else pay for her college education." He did it, and he meant it. And she finally broke. "She said, 'Daddy, I'm so sorry.' It was his love for her that changed her path." Holding his crying daughter, he told her that Jesus would forgive her, Bernadette says. "He ministered to her that the Lord wanted to make her new. She turned around that day and started over. This is how important it is for a man to be in authority regarding his family, with love."

THE POWER OF MEMORIES

Tom Bisset notes that in all the interviews he did with children who returned after being away from the Faith, two words continued to resound: *"I remembered."* He concluded that staying away from God is not as easy as it might seem. "If prodigals have contact with their families or friends in the Christian community, every visit becomes a reminder of their faith heritage even if nothing is said about spiritual matters," he says. Friends and family members trigger memories of a life in Christ once embraced. "It is a life gone, but not forgotten."[140]

Bisset says memories also play a critical role in the process by which wanderers come home. "You simply can't order your mind to forget those memories of faith and family ... no matter how hard you try." And few prodigals, while running, have a coherent view of what they are running toward. "They know what they don't want, but rarely know what they do want," he says. "Life is confused at best and senseless at worst." Even when some kind of order comes, he adds, their minds and spirits are rarely at rest because "it's not easy to walk away from God."[141]

According to Bissett, "Faith and family is the stuff of real life. These realities remain at the core of human experience, even though prodigals may seem to regard them with indifference, antagonism, or hostility."[142]

He encourages parents of children who have wandered from the Faith to take comfort by the fact that "the truth is embedded in their minds ... they feel something when you pray at the table, or hum a gospel song at the stove, or read the Bible, or even mention the Lord's name. Pray believing. Live trusting. Because coming back has a lot to do with remembering."[143]

THE HOPE OF THE PRODIGAL

While some readers might be bothered by the word "prodigal," here we are using it to mean "one who has returned after an absence," which is the second definition in the Merriam-Webster dictionary.

In other words, prodigals are never to be seen as hopeless cases. As we see in one of Jesus' most endearing parables, the Prodigal Son (see Luke 15:11–32), we should remain ever hopeful as we await and pray for our children's return.

In Baruch 5:5–6, we read the encouraging words: "Rise up, Jerusalem! Stand upon the heights; look to the east and see your children gathered from east to west at the word of the Holy One, rejoicing that *they are remembered by God*. Led away on foot by their enemies, they left you: but God will bring them back to you, carried high in glory as on royal thrones."

40

A Pathway Home

The turning back to God can begin in the most ordinary of moments for children who have walked away. For Emily, it happened one evening while catching sight of her reflection in the bathroom mirror. Who was that stranger staring back? She barely recognized herself.

"I just started crying. All of these questions were going through my mind," Emily recalls. "It was like I was just a shell of a person, walking around absolutely numb."

As a little girl, growing up in a non-practicing Catholic family, but drawn to the holiness she experienced in images and practices witnessed in Catholic school, she had had different imaginings of her future life. Now in college, and having turned squarely away from God, she asked, "Is this all life can offer? If so, is it even worth living?"

RUNNING FROM JESUS

Her parents' divorce changed everything. Despite positive experiences in elementary school, Emily says she did not have any immediate examples of living a vibrant faith. "In high school, I stopped receiving the Eucharist. I just didn't want anything to do with it," Emily says. "I still believed that it was Jesus' body and blood, but I didn't want him."

Her parents' split had worn her down. They had proven themselves to be unreliable. "There were many different facets from that one experience," she says, noting that one of the biggest was coming to believe in self-reliance, "that only I could make my own life happen."

At the end of high school and the beginning of college, Emily left the earlier image she had of Jesus behind. She began drinking, wearing immodest clothes, and allowing guys to take advantage of her. "My Dad didn't know how to love. So, as a daughter, I did not get what I needed, and I sought any kind of consolation I could."

With alcoholism an issue in her family, Emily followed the pattern one sometimes finds in such a home. She took on the role of overachiever by day, rebel by night. She made the dean's list every semester, but most evenings she would engage in risky behavior. "Nobody knew I was making these decisions in the dark. And no one really knew who I was—or cared," she says.

GIRL IN THE MIRROR

But then she saw it—the image in the mirror of a stranger; someone who looked like her, but with foreign, desolate eyes.

At the time, Emily did not know was that she was not alone. The God she had come to adore as a little girl at school, through mentors and religious symbols that brought her in contact with Jesus' unfathomable love, had never left her—not for a moment.

"I woke up the next morning, and it was Sunday. I still had the same feelings, but I remembered from Catholic school that people go to Mass on Sunday," Emily says. She was desperate enough to muster up the courage to attend Mass that evening at the campus Newman Center.

It was toward the end of Lent, Emily recalls, and the priest preached a powerful homily about how we were made for relationship with God, but that relationship has been broken by sin. "He said that if we keep living in a way that is outside of the Lord, looking for love in other places, we will never be satisfied." As she looked at the crucifix, she teared up, thinking, *This is what I have been looking for*.

FINDING FOCUS

After Mass that night, a Fellowship of Catholic University Students (FOCUS) missionary approached Emily and began speaking with her. "She was so sweet and kind, and she invited me on a retreat that was coming up," she says. Emily accepted this invitation.

The next week, Emily found herself "in the middle of nowhere Wisconsin at this retreat with a bunch of Catholic people," feeling very out of place. A portion of the retreat included Eucharistic Adoration and confession. She says, "I remember getting in line for confession, in disbelief at everything I had written down that I was going to confess," she says. "I remember not even being able to look at the priest. When I finished confessing my sin, though, I looked up, and I saw that he had tears in his eyes. He said, 'I am sorry for everything that has happened to you. Jesus wants to heal you.' In that moment, I truly encountered the person of Jesus in his mercy and gentleness, and it changed everything."

The priest, it turns out, was Fr. Mike Schmitz, renowned for his videos and podcasts on the Catholic Faith, though Emily had no clue about this at the time. "We had a good conversation afterward, and he could probably tell that I wasn't a regular," Emily continues. "I went back to Adoration and experienced such a profound moment of consolation, with Jesus just bestowing his love on me; love that I had been missing pretty much my whole life. I knew my life needed to change, and I wanted it to change at that moment."

DATING JESUS FIRST

Emily knew she needed time to heal and decided to put off dating for a while. "I needed to spend time with just Jesus," she says. Following the retreat, she became involved in activities at the Newman Center—which is where Matt came into her life.

"We had a really good friendship, and it was the first time I experienced beautiful masculinity—something I didn't even know was possible," she says. Since Matt was discerning the priesthood, they remained "just friends." But eventually, his spiritual director counseled him to date. Emily explains, "We dated a year, got engaged, and married nine months later during our senior year, on September 8, the Feast of the Nativity of the Blessed Virgin Mary."

"God is so good," Emily continues. "I seriously thank Jesus every day for Matt being in my life and my husband." The two have now added a third component to their union—a little daughter, Grace.

Even before their daughter was born, the couple wanted to serve the Church to repay God for his goodness. Matt had also left the Faith for a time before experiencing a reversion. "A FOCUS missionary asked us to apply to be missionaries, so we went through the application process," Emily says, noting that during the interview, it became clear: "Jesus was inviting us back into our poverty, to a time when we didn't know him, back to the college campus."

Now, they would get a chance to introduce students like themselves not long ago to Jesus and his Church, "and to receive love, maybe for the first time in their lives."

A MINISTRY'S MISSION

Eighty percent of those who fall away from the Church do so before they turn twenty-three, often in the middle of their college years. As Emily says, "College is such a confusing time in terms of identity. There are so many things pulling you to what you could be. And while it's good to focus on yourself, it's also a very selfish four years."

Missionaries like Emily and Matt journey with young people like our sons and daughters, asking them thought-provoking questions. "And since we're pretty close in age still, we can speak all of those good things into their lives."

The threefold mission of FOCUS, she says, includes authentic friendship, divine intimacy, and spiritual multiplication.

By inviting people into "the beauty of a Catholic's life," Emily says, they can help foster authentic, spirit-filled friendships, whether by a coffee date or an invitation to their home, "giving them another option besides partying and witnessing to the Christian life." Emily adds, "We're not out preaching in the campus square. It's more one-on-one. We get to introduce people back to the sacramental life; to the Catholic Christian life."

They also model to students what it is like to live in relationship with Jesus on a daily basis, praying a holy hour in front of the Blessed Sacrament as a team every day, and attending daily Mass. "Before we have anything to give, we need to be able to receive from the Lord."

Leading Bible studies, the missionaries equip others to do so as well, encouraging students to "actually open up their Bibles," Emily says, and initiating life-giving discussions. "We show them that the Word and Jesus are alive, and he's among us and wants to be part of our lives." Retreats, on campus and elsewhere, are another part of this component.

Even something as simple as teaching students how to pray can be a challenge, she says. "This generation growing up has a hard time sitting in silence for even just thirty minutes." Once they have tapped into that, she might encourage them to pray about their memories—both times when they felt Jesus' absence, and other times when they have felt his presence.

If she could convey only a few points to young people, she would let them know that God satisfies every desire of the human heart, and a relationship with Jesus is possible for everyone. "It's not about the rules. It's not about discipline, or feeling you have to do something to earn Jesus' love. It all boils down to a relationship with Jesus that makes life joyful," Emily says. "The gospel is so freeing, and we don't have to do it all by ourselves. Jesus already has an answer for our problems and has claimed us as his own. He died for us so that we might be back in relationship with him. Our job is simply to remain in that relationship through living a sacramental life, having a prayer life, and staying in a state of grace."

CONSECRATE YOUR CHILDREN TO MARY

Emily, though still a young mother, has already pondered the grief parents must experience when their children leave the Faith. "I think about the things that society says are normal, and it breaks my heart," she says. "I never want Grace to experience what I did. It is so twisted and so distorted."

Her advice to those struggling with straying children: appeal to Mama Mary. "Along with praying and fasting for your kids, I would turn to Our Lady. She's a good mother who knows the hearts of your kids. She takes such good care of her children," Emily says. "And consecrate your children to her."

Emily recalls an image she once saw of a vision of heaven. Jesus is looking around, asking, "How did this person get here?" And then, to the side, you can see Our Lady, bringing people in through the window. "She is not forgetful about any of her children. She loves them and wants them to be with her Son."

Stories like Emily's can give us an extraordinary amount of hope. They remind us again, as we have been learning along the way with Monica's help, that God often works in hidden ways in the hearts of our children.

He knows our desires for them before the words can be formed upon our lips. Even when they leave our nests and go far from home, and we can no longer see their every move, God is with them each second of their lives, accompanying them through life. And our prayers can only hasten our Lord and his mother's attentiveness to our heart's desires for them.

41

Where There Is Life, There Is Hope

ROXANE: When my father decided to return to the Church after a thirty-five-year absence, he did not tell my mother or his two daughters what he was planning. He simply made an appointment with a priest, went to Reconciliation, and came home, reporting that evening that he had come back to the Church. Perhaps he kept his decision to himself out of pride or embarrassment at how long he had been away—or perhaps it was due to a sudden prompting of the Holy Spirit. I never had a chance to ask him. Sometimes, we ourselves are unclear on our motives regarding spiritual matters, so we are unable to articulate the "why" to others. But I am eternally grateful Dad followed God's lead.

A similar scenario seemed to play out in the home of famous actor Vincent Price and his wife, Coral Browne, in the mid-1970s. Not long after they were married in a civil ceremony, Price, born and raised a Protestant, began leaving their home every Thursday night around the same time. (Coral herself was born Jewish but had converted to the Catholic Faith as an adult.)

Coral was concerned with what Vincent was up to. His explanations of where he was going every week were unconvincing. Eventually, he confessed to her that he had been sneaking out to pursue his new love—Jesus in the Catholic Church—and was receiving weekly religious instruction at a nearby parish.

To those who know Price's life story, the conversion of this master of horror films to the Catholic Faith might seem surprising. His mother was vehemently anti-Catholic, and she raised her son with a hatred toward the Church.

In the classic 1943 film *The Song of Bernadette*, Price plays the contemptuous imperial prosecutor Vital Dutour, who doubts the visions of the Immaculate Conception as experienced by young Bernadette Soubirous of Lourdes, France. After experiencing the miracle of being healed of throat cancer, he undergoes a transformation and begs forgiveness for his former ways, embracing the Faith he once so fervently resisted. In the end, this role turned out to be prophetic for the actor, a case of real life imitating art.

Price's unlikely conversion at age sixty-three offers insight for those who worry about the state of their loved one's soul. As noted, the journey toward God is, almost always, a deeply personal pursuit. Conversion stories such as Price's remind us that we simply do not know the secret movements of the soul. Indeed, the interior flutters, fruits of the invisible exchanges between God and individual, may never be fully seen in this life.

A SUPREME COURT JUSTICE'S BIGGEST WIN

US Supreme Court Justice Clarence Thomas offers an example of one who left the Faith in pursuit of the world but came back full throttle. For Thomas, the diversion claimed a quarter of his life. During a speech at Christendom College in 2018, Thomas called the Catholic Church "a guide, the way, the truth and the life ... I spent twenty-five years of my life in the wilderness away from the Church, and yet the clarion call of Sunday church bells never went away."[144]

For parents of children who have wandered from the Faith, twenty-five years can seem forever, but it is only a blip in God's timeline. Waiting with God requires patience and trust in the hidden movements of the divine.

In her book *Deathbed Conversions: Finding Faith at the Finish Line*, Karen Edmisten shares accounts of thirteen well-known individuals who returned to, or approached for the first time, the Catholic Faith on their deathbeds. Edmisten, a mother, wife, and convert from atheism, weaves words from Willa Cather's novel *The Professor's House* into her introduction: "The heart of another is a dark forest, always, no matter how close it has been to one's own."[145] Edmisten asserts the mystery of another's soul, which is why the Church refuses to make a pronouncement on who has been damned.

While we cannot know with certainty whether our loved ones are advancing toward God, we can and do know that God is merciful and believe in his ability to move hearts in his time.

CONVERTING AT THE LAST MINUTE

Writer Oscar Wilde had "a lifelong dalliance with the Catholic Church," having once concluded that Catholicism was "the only religion worth dying in." Wilde spent his entire life moving toward the Church, only to move away from it again. St. Augustine's famous utterance of hesitation, "Lord, make me chaste, but not yet," comes to mind. Though Wilde married a woman, he lusted after men throughout much of his marriage, eventually landing in prison on charges of gross indecency, sentenced to two years of hard labor.

Wilde's time in prison ended up becoming a grace, however, allowing him more time to read reflectively, including from St. Augustine, Dante, and the Gospels, bringing him to have and share keen insights, even before his conversion. "Those whom [Christ] saved from their sins are saved simply for beautiful moments in their lives," he once wrote. "All that Christ says to us by the way of a little warning is that every moment should be beautiful, that the soul should always be ready for the coming of the bridegroom."[146]

Wilde received the ultimate gift of Christ on his tongue as he lay dying. And yet, he did reach that point, thanks be to God. We can rejoice in Wilde's decision, however slow and painful it may have been.

An even more common utterance of Wilde's, "Every saint has a past, and every sinner has a future,"[147] reveals that life is a journey, and unlike most of us, God has enduring patience. Our own journeys likely have included many stops and starts. But if the Hound of Heaven could so tirelessly pursue and draw us to our current state—with hearts burning for our family's salvation—will not God be just as relentless in pursuit of our children's souls?

Edmisten assures that even late-in-life conversions are no less authentic than those that come earlier and demonstrate "the genuine acknowledgment that God is God."[148] If we ultimately desire our children to join us on our journey to heaven, even if that takes longer than we would like, will we not still be elated? Our love for our children and their ultimate good can help us let go and give God the timetable.

MERE CHILDREN BEFORE GOD

Another subject in Edmisten's collection includes Alexis Carrel, a brilliant French surgeon and biologist who won the Nobel Prize in 1912 for pioneering vascular suturing techniques. Carrel was baptized Catholic, but he soon abandoned the Faith. It was not until the last years of his life that the door to God that had remained so elusive began to open once again, particularly in meeting a monk who gently led him toward conversion.

Following a heart attack, Carrel remarked, just days before his death, that as the end of one's life comes near, "one grasps the nothingness of all things." He said that despite his great works and fame as a renowned scientist and scholar, "I am a mere child before God, and a poor child at that."[149]

The thought of hearing something so sublime from our own wandering children might seem far away, even impossible. And yet, remembering Cather's analogy, we recall that the dark forests within cannot be easily penetrated. God alone sees the forest through the trees, and every little branch of hope. The maker of forests himself will be the one to bring our children back. In the meantime, as we pray, fast, and continue drawing nearer to God's heart ourselves, we prepare for the day our children recognize and respond to God's beautiful beckoning, so that we might stand among those who warmly welcome them home.

42

Grab Your Mustard Seeds!

God gives us what we need to parent our children regardless of the stage we are at. Jesus promised so many times in Scripture to turn our sorrow into joy if we trust and follow him.

You might think, *But I am so lacking!* That is not a problem. Not for God. As St. Paul encourages us, "I can do all things in him who strengthens me" (Philippians 4:13).

The New Testament reveals that we can start with a faith the size of a mustard seed. Jesus gave his disciples this image because they sometimes struggled in their walk with him, as we can see from the following passages.

> The apostles said to the Lord, "Increase our faith!" And the Lord said, "If you had faith as a grain of mustard seed, you could say to this sycamine tree, 'Be rooted up, and be planted in the sea,' and it would obey you" (Luke 17:5–6).

Later, when the disciples asked Jesus why they could not drive out a demon, he said,

> "Because of your little faith. For truly, I say to you, if you have faith as a grain of mustard seed, you will say to this mountain, 'Move from here to there,' and it will move; and nothing will be impossible to you" (Matthew 17:20).

But maybe, sometimes, our faith isn't even as big as a mustard seed. In those times, we need to ask God for help. As Jesus tells us, if you can believe, all things *are* possible to those who believe (see Mark 9:23).

The conversion of our children may, at times, seem like an impossible dream. We have prayed and sacrificed for them, spoken with them many times, and maybe given them books and articles, yet they remain away from the Church. It might seem we have tried everything without any results—and we can grow impatient and start to doubt.

We want to see our children return to the Faith *today*, not tomorrow or next month or next year. But we need to remember Monica's story. Seventeen years into her struggle with Augustine, she still had not experienced the joy of her son's conversion. She did not know the wonderful gift that was coming. Would she have given up in year eighteen?

To be honest, there is no guarantee that our children's conversions are on the horizon. But we have faith in Jesus. We have trust that he is working in their lives. We must put our trust in him. When so many stopped following Jesus' teaching on the Eucharist, he asked his apostles if they too would leave him. Peter responds, "Lord, to whom shall we go? You have the words of eternal life" (John 6:68).

We know that giving up is not the answer. Like St. Monica and the widow who persisted with the unjust judge until finally having her request granted (see Luke 18:1–8), we have only one course of action: perseverance.

GOD'S PROMISES ARE RELIABLE

Jesus repeatedly tells us that he will bless us and answer our prayers—but we must persevere in the midst of our trials and struggles because nothing is impossible for God:

- "Ask, and it will be given you; seek, and you will find; knock, and it will be opened to you" (Matthew 7:7).

- "Therefore I tell you, whatever you ask in prayer, believe that you receive it, and you will" (Mark 11:24).

- "Jesus looked at them and said, 'With men it is impossible, but not with God; for all things are possible with God'" (Mark 10:27).

- "Come to me, all who labor and are heavy laden, and I will give you rest. Take my yoke upon you, and learn from me; for I am gentle and lowly in heart, and you will find rest for your souls. For my yoke is easy, and my burden is light" (Matthew 11:28–30).

- "But seek first his kingdom and his righteousness, and all these things shall be yours as well" (Matthew 6:33).

In order to embrace God's blessings, we are called to transcend our difficulties—to accept and offer them up, and we continue along the journey, just as the Blessed Mother did in the midst of her trials and difficulties. Embracing the Lord's promises demands that we do not let the mistakes of the past limit us.

A LIFE OF BLESSINGS

In his book *A Life of Blessings*, Michael H. Brown notes that it is up to us to embrace our blessings lest we lose out. Here is a summary of some of his insights:

- *The more you release, the more he sends*. Release all your anger. Release all your hurts. Do nothing you would not want to present to Jesus. Let his waters cleanse you.

- *Let go and let God.* Through this you will draw nutrients and bear fruit with him forever.

- *Be future focused.* You may not be able to undo the negatives from your past, but you can set out to have a positive future— with a positive attitude.

- *Seek God in everything.* When we pray, God grants us joy.

- *Call on the Holy Spirit to open your heart to all that God has for you and your family.* Ask him to cast out all fear: *Oh, Holy Spirit, come upon us. Come upon us with the richness of grace. Come upon us with healing. Come upon us to let us see with spiritual eyes. Come upon us in comfort and guidance. Oh come, Holy Spirit, and let us know how to tackle the issues in our lives.*

- *The natural is taken over by the supernatural.* Think big and God will act big—in the right way.

- **Become disciplined in prayer.** Become consumed by his Word instead of the whisperings of evil. Being negative stops the flow while the positive taps into a stream of miracles.

- **The secret weapon: humility.** Humility drives away evil spirits and shields us from the wounds that come from other human beings. When we are wronged, humility allows us to admonish with love.

- **Do not be caught up in worldliness.** "For where your treasure is, there will your heart be also" (Matthew 6:21). To be worldly is to chase the wind; no matter what we collect in life, it vanishes like vapor at the end of life.

- **Adore God through the day.** Do this from the heart. Love God. Praise him repeatedly throughout your day. *Praise you, Jesus, praise you, Jesus.* This will bring you joy because the Lord is joy personified.[150]

As we journey through the challenges and disappointments of life, we need to remember all the blessings God has given us, especially those we are experiencing right now. Regardless of what we are going through, we can remember God's promises and bask in his love for us. Being grateful for his blessings not only fills our hearts with joy, but it opens up channels of grace to increase our faith.

43

The Story Is Not Finished Yet

If I only knew then what I know now ... but wait ... no. We are not psychics but works in progress. We are in a better place now than before, moving forward and growing; healing and hoping; feeling sorry for and wanting to correct our mistakes; and reaching out to God, the Blessed Mother, and all the saints—and each other. So let's do this together!

Do not ever feel alone. Do not ever feel "less than." Remember, God loves the lowly and wants to draw near to those worn down in spirit. Keep in mind that other amazing Catholics are in your same situation and also praying hard for their family members who have left the Faith.

Consider the following real-life situations:

- A vibrant young Dominican sister and mother superior of a new branch of her order prays for her sister in a supposed same-sex marriage.

- Parents of a newly ordained priest this summer attended his first Mass with their other son, who showed no interest in the Mass and did not receive Communion.

- A vocation director knows his mother and sister attend a Protestant church and were sad when he became a priest a few years ago.

We could keep going. Instead, let's change the subject. What about happy-ending stories? Initially, we were surprised to find that some parents whose children returned to the Faith did not want to go public about it. A great story from a tight-lipped subject can be a journalist's worst nightmare. But in the case of this book, it gave us pause, and then understanding. Having a child walk away from the Church changed everything for them, so while we expected they would want to shout their stories from the rooftops, we found, instead, that they had been humbled. Permanently.

PATTI: I once asked a prominent Catholic influencer if he would have ever believed two of his children would leave the Faith. "No," he said. "I thought if we raised them right, that would never happen." Now, he stands in grateful awe at their return, given the extent of their departure. But he has no desire to go public, nor did most others with whom we spoke.

The caution of these parents shows they understand now that the story is not yet finished. We have not reached the end of the race as described in 2 Timothy 4:7: "I have competed well; I have finished the race; I have kept the faith." That is our goal. But the endings here on earth will not happen until "the" end. Parents whose children have returned (thanks be to God) know that if the unthinkable and impossible could happen once, it could happen again. From a humble and grateful posture, they thank God for their children's return and neither judge others nor presume the story is over.

Knowing the story is not yet finished—neither ours nor our children's—also means we still have time to get it right with God. Here, we find motivation to keep running the race in earnest. We have work to do—lessons to learn, prayers to pray, and a more certain ascent to God's will to attain. Our unfinished story means that as long as we have life, we have time. The past can teach and shape us. The same with our children. The fact that their story is not finished brings great hope to our hearts and helps us be patient, trusting that God works in their souls, day by day.

RULES FOR HOLINESS

One of the certainties when you set out to grow in holiness: Expect to be challenged. *Sure, pick up your cross and follow me. We get it.* No one really gets it, however, until we feel the weight of our cross, until it seems to be crushing us. No amount of biblical warning prepares us for such a weight. Feelings of betrayal often arise. Just as gold is purified in fire, the fire purifies us, if we so choose. If we agree to God's will, he can purify us during difficulties.

Even now, as we near the end of this book, thinking about growing deeper in our faith may spark a bit of reluctance or fear. Will we put a target on our back if we become *too* holy?

A friend once shared a story of her father praying a novena to St. Jude, the patron saint of impossible causes, for her brother who was a handful to raise. At the end of the novena, he burned down the family shed. Her father responded, "Boy, good thing I prayed that novena. Just imagine what would have happened if I had not."

Sometimes we have prayed hard, and it seems like all hell has still broken loose. Perhaps it has. Perhaps our prayers have loosened the grip of hell on a situation. Consider that closets do not get cleaned without first making a bigger mess. But that bigger mess can mean progress. It may not seem like it to the neighbor who stops in and sees the mess on the floor. Yet you know what is happening.

We have to trust God with our messes. If your prayers and pursuits of holiness stir up messes in your family, remember that you have tools to handle it. Keeping the dirt covered up is not progress. Even if it hurts and it is hard, it is better for truth to come to light. Our prayers will increase and grow more fervent when we face the messes we are handing over to God. It is a good and holy direction.

Many inspiring stories can be found in the book *Amazing Grace for Survivors*. At the beginning of each tale of catastrophe or hardship, though, most report feelings of anger or betrayal, or at least confusion. While never easy, pointing our feet in the direction of God and taking a step at a time brings us to a better place. Peace and happiness blossom where the seeds of faith were planted and watered, while bitterness and fatigue tempt us to give up. That is where fellow Christians can step in to help. We are called to uplift one another. We can find courage from saints like Monica, who never gave up. Whenever we are tempted to give up, we can ask ourselves, "What would Monica do? Better yet, ask her: "Monica, what *did* you do? How did you manage to keep the faith and keep going? Please pray for me that I will have that same faith and determination."

IN IT FOR THE LONG HAUL

Sometimes, it is just a matter of shifting our perspective. For that reason, let this be a resounding message: *We are in it for the long haul.* As Dr. David

Anders shared earlier, we are not running a sprint but a marathon, and we may need to adjust our thinking of time, with a perspective opened up to the eternal.

ROXANE: While on a walk discussing our chapters one afternoon, Patti uttered something that made me pause and take note. We were discussing some of the silent heartbreaks we had been experiencing in family life, and how hard it is not knowing how it will end, yet recognizing we must continue on in hope. "We keep going even as our hearts are breaking," Patti commented. Her words hit me in the heart. In that one line, the truth of this journey seemed to be summarized, in all of its sorrow and all of its hope. We have two choices: we can put one foot in front of the other, drawing on God's mercy, or give up. We choose the former, and hope you will, too.

Think of the scene during Jesus' carrying of his cross to Calvary, where Mary is following her son along his harrowing journey, at a distance. As his bloodied face meets her gaze, we recognize her pain. But we do not see her stopping or running away. She continues on, bolstered deep within by the Spirit of God, who has a plan. She must persist, keep walking, and even as her heart breaks, believe a happy ending will come. We have reason to hope for this, too, even if it seems against the odds. After all, the resurrection of Jesus was "against the odds," from a human perspective.

In Scripture, we read about the widow who keeps pestering the judge for a just decision. After a while, he grows tired of her requests, and finally relinquishes his position: "Though I neither fear God nor regard man, yet because this widow bothers me, I will vindicate her, or she will wear me out by her continual coming" (Luke 18:4–5). While we might giggle at this powerful man's fear of this humble, persistent woman, we can also identify with her great desire for things to be right. God is a just judge, and he does not need our pestering to turn the world right side up. But in this parable, he encourages us, like Mary, to continue onward and never give up, no matter what.

44

Mingling with Monica
and Her Son

Msgr. Jeffrey Steenson never fell *away* from the Church as a young adult. He did not have parents who prayed he would *remain* Catholic—after all, they were Protestant, as they had raised him to be. But something began stirring in his heart as a young boy that roused his curiosity and sparked something deep within him. In time, his heart's desire came to be to fall *into* the Catholic Church. Despite numerous obstacles, this dream finally became a reality—and both St. Augustine and St. Monica proved an integral part of this quest.

Raised in an evangelical church in the 1960s, in the farm country of Hillsboro, North Dakota, little Jeffrey loved Jesus from an early age. But something about his Catholic peers—the way they talked, their sacramentals, and the traditions they held—captivated him. After attending Trinity College, an evangelical institution in Chicago, believing he was destined to become a career sports journalist, he had an opportunity after graduation to study patristics at a nearby Catholic university that changed the course of his life. "Enrolling in the local seminary, I became completely smitten by the Fathers of the Church," he says.

Now married, the right denomination for him seemed to be the Episcopal Church. Steenson eventually was ordained a priest, and then a bishop, in that tradition. But his study of the early Church Fathers left him with a thirst that was not yet fully quenched.

"Growing up as a Protestant, I remember being taught that the Golden Age was the age of the apostles, and then you get blips of holiness, but nothing good until we come to the Reformation," he says. "I always wanted to fill in the gaps."

Some of his favorites were St. Justin Martyr, St. Basil, and yes, St. Augustine, with his mother, St. Monica, trailing behind. "St. Augustine was really the first Father to open up my life and draw me toward the Church, with his *Confessions*," Steenson says, noting that that work really was the first memoir—a self-reflective account of a life's journey—ever written.

The stories of these saints who had such great fidelity, despite their humanity, ignited Steenson's soul. Eventually, he was welcomed—along with his wife—into the Catholic Church as a priest. Having met and been influenced by all three recent popes, in January 2012, Steenson was appointed by Pope Francis as first Ordinary of the Personal Ordinariate of the Chair of Saint Peter to help other Anglicans cross the Tiber.

TOUCHING THE LIVES OF THE SAINTS

Through his travels, Msgr. Steenson has discovered the value of not only having read about the saints but also, as often as possible, "meeting" them in the places where they trod.

For example, while teaching at the University of Dallas one year, Steenson took students to Rome for a semester and, for an afternoon, to the Roman Forum. "I had them sit down on those old rocks, and we read a part of Justin Martyr's *Apology*, about the Eucharist, as it was celebrated in Ancient Rome. It was one of the most moving things, looking at these young people crying. They were making the connection between the Eucharist they attended and the way it was celebrated by the Fathers."

Though traveling to Hippo in these days would prove nearly impossible, Msgr. Steenson says, during travels to Italy, he had the chance to mingle, in a sense, with our hero and heroine, in some of the very spots where they held invigorating discourse about the Faith and, also, where ordinary life was lived.

In Augustine's *De Ordine* ("On Order"), Steenson first confronted the "toilet scene" and found it not only amusing but helpful in showing that, despite their hallowed status, Saints Monica and Augustine were still very much like the rest of us.

"I once spent a week on retreat in that very spot," Steenson says, describing the area "where the debate at Cassiciacum (in Italy) took place, about whether it is appropriate to sing psalms on the toilet. Monica initially thought it was disrespectful." He adds, "They had excavated part of the villa, and one of the places they excavated was the bathhouse."

Augustine, Monica, and friends would meet every morning for a time, discussing the finer points of Christianity. "They got into this funny debate because one of Augustine's students, Licentius, would sing this psalm on the toilet, and Monica got upset about it."

The next morning, a long discourse ensued over whether it was a proper place to sing songs. "By the end, they'd convinced Monica that there was no better place on earth more appropriate to praise the Lord."

ON TO MILAN

He also visited Milan, where Augustine and his friends ultimately became Christian. "He was disappointed with his academic work and his rhetoric—he was just kind of bored with it all." Then, in 386, the year before he was baptized, Steenson says, Augustine heard the words, "Take up and read," prompting his conversion. "We don't know exactly where the villa is where that happened, but that seems to be the place where he first turned back to Christ, while on summer vacation."

From *Confessions*, we know Augustine was beneath a fig tree with his friend Alypius when he heard what seemed to be a child's voice calling him to read. Sensing it as a command from God to open the Scriptures, Augustine found a Bible and read the first passage he saw, from the letter of Paul to the Romans: "Let us conduct ourselves becomingly as in the day, not in reveling and drunkenness, not in debauchery and licentiousness, not in quarreling and jealousy. But put on the Lord Jesus Christ, and make no provision for the flesh, to gratify its desires" (Romans 13:13–14). Suddenly, his heart flooded with light, as he later described, and he resolved then and there to dedicate his entire life to God, with Alypius agreeing to the same.

At that illumination, Steenson says, Augustine immediately resigned his teaching post. And the rest, as they say, is history.

A VISIT TO OSTIA

By the end of 386, Augustine had enrolled as a catechumen in Ambrose's class, and on Easter of 387, he was baptized in what today is the Duomo di Milano. "That's the big cathedral there today, and if you visit, you will see the actual baptistry where Augustine was baptized," Steenson says.

Another especially moving experience, he says, was visiting Ostia, Italy, where Monica's life ended, as described in *Confessions*, after her prayers for Augustine had been answered. The group had decided to go back to Africa, getting as far as Ostia on the seacoast. "They couldn't get a ship, partly because there was a war going on," Steenson notes. "They had to rent an apartment for the winter. There, Monica got sick and died."

Steenson continues, "It is fascinating to learn how Monica's tomb was found, around 1944, at the end of World War II, when some Italian teenagers, playing basketball, tripped over her gravestone—which had been buried for centuries. When the Vatican archaeologist saw it, he recognized it as Monica's tomb."

The area is now very accessible, he says. "You can walk right through the ancient city. It's been excavated, and is probably the most complete view of what an ancient city looks like. It's wonderful to see." Though historians don't know the exact spot of Augustine's apartment, or *insula*, he says, "you can get a good enough idea."

A VISION OF HEAVEN

In *Confessions*, Augustine tells of the vision of heaven he and his mother shared together in Ostia, looking out a window overlooking the sea. "That has to be one of the most beautiful pieces of lyrical writing, of spiritual writing, that we have from the Church Fathers," Steenson says. "They describe the road ahead, and moving beyond this creation to heaven itself."[151]

As Forbes describes in *The Life of Saint Monica*, their shared vision happened one evening during their journey, as Monica and Augustine sat together at a window overlooking the garden and sea, talking of heaven. "As their two souls stretched out together toward the infinite Love and Wisdom, it seemed to them that for one moment, with one beat of the heart, they touched It, and the joy of that moment was a foreshadowing of eternity."

Soon after, Monica passed into eternity. One of Steenson's favorite lines in *Confessions* occurs after Augustine describes her death, he says, when he speaks of his mother's new home in heaven: "For this city, your pilgrim people yearn, from there leaving it to their return."

ST. MONICA'S RESTING PLACE

After being transferred from several other spots, Monica's remains lie in final repose at the Basilica di Sant 'Agostino in Rome. Her epitaph, from her original resting place in Ostia—which, Steenson comments, seems to praise Augustine even more than his mother—reads: *"Here the most virtuous mother of a young man set her ashes, a second light to your merits, Augustine. As a priest, serving the heavenly laws of peace, you taught the people entrusted to you with your character. A glory greater than praise of your accomplishments crowns you both—Mother of the Virtues, more fortunate because of her offspring."*

While she is officially named the patron saint of abuse victims, wives, alcoholics, and widows, Steenson says that Monica ought also to be the saint of parents worried about their children. Certainly, many have claimed her as such. "With all of her life, and all of her heart, she devoted herself to seeing her son come to Christ. *That was the chief end of her life.*" In that sense, whether or not her epitaph reflects it accurately, he calls St. Monica "a tremendous inspiration" to forlorn parents everywhere, someone who can bring us great hope.

45

As We Prepare to Travel Onward

"What would Monica do?"

The title of our book makes plain what we sought to answer in our journey together. It has been a joy walking through Monica's life with you, discovering the many ways this beautiful saint drew closer to God as she sought her heart's desire: to know that her children were nestled in the bosom of our one, holy, Catholic, and apostolic Church. The achievement of that quest became a major victory in Monica's life—one that allowed her to face her early death peacefully.

How wonderful it is to know that another, now in heaven, has traveled this earthly road ahead of us and, despite the obstructions and sleepless nights, now holds forever in her soul the firm assurance that love and truth have won.

We trusted this experience would be richer with two of us seeking answers to this question together. Because the chapters of our lives are being written, with God, distinctly, we come away with unique takeaways, but always with the same goal: greater union with God and our families.

Perhaps someday we can meet you and hear your stories as well. Before we leave you for now, we want to end as we began: by sharing our stories. This time, stories of what we have learned while seeking answers to our driving question, *"What would Monica do?"*

ROXANE'S TAKEAWAYS

Just before we began putting pen to paper for this book, I learned that a traveling relics tour would be stopping at our city's cathedral. With my son's high school graduation nearing, I would be too tied up with preparations to go. But at the end of that busy day, I found myself needing the Eucharistic presence. So, I fled to the Adoration chapel downtown— the only one open at that late hour. Reaching for the door handle of the chapel, however, I realized I had forgotten the night combination for entry. My hasty text to the Adoration coordinator received a quick response, with an addition: "The relics are still on display in the basement!" she wrote. "We just left, but they'll be there for about another half an hour."

That's right! I had forgotten. Quickly, I ran around the corner of the building, trying to access the basement door from the outside. From the lower windows, I could see people milling about inside, and the hundreds of relics laid out on tables. *It's locked!* After waiting a bit, someone finally came out, and I was able to enter.

"Only fifteen minutes left, folks," the tour director announced. I was now on a mission and asked him, "Is there a guide to finding specific relics?" "They're not really in order," he said. "You'll just have to wander around a bit." Time was really of the essence, but my mind and heart were fixed. Spotting a friend, I asked, "Any idea where I might find St. Monica?" "I believe over in that direction," she said, pointing eastward. "Thanks!"

"Five minutes and I'll be shutting 'er down!" The summons came just before I spotted the golden vessels. Noting the name, "St. Monica," and nearby, "St. Augustine," I fell to my knees, gazing closely. It had been a long day, but thankfully, I had found these blessed, tangible pieces of my heavenly friends. Peering at the tiny piece of cloth once worn by the woman who was about to become a cherished companion for the next few months, I whispered, "Please help us, Monica. Pray for Patti and me as we walk with you. We need your assistance." After pressing a holy card to the relic, I did the same with the one next to it. "Dear Augustine, pray with us that God would help bring our children back to him, however long it takes, and in whatever manner necessary." Then, after a quick moment before the wood of the holy cross and a relic of Our Blessed Lady, I rushed away, into the Adoration chapel, to thank God for that unexpected grace.

Now, months later, we have reached the end of the road we set out to traverse. To help bring forward the best insights, I have found a welcomed harbor at two different religious communities not far from my home, where I have been able to research, write, and spend countless hours in prayer. My prayer now is that you will receive our insights as a gift of consolation, and that in contemplating them with God, your faith, like ours has, will increase more than you could have imagined.

And that, dear readers, has been my biggest takeaway. I started out with the thought that Monica could show us how to lead our children closer to God, as she seemed to have done for her son. But in the end, I realized that she was leading me closer to God. I discovered that, as Patti and I sought ways to help strengthen the souls of our children, our souls were being transformed, challenged, and changed for the better.

"Even in the midst of our woundedness ... our brokenness ... you still call us back to yourself, Lord," Fr. Mike Schmitz prayed in Ascension's *Bible in a Year* podcast (day 234). "May our hearts be the kind of hearts that can love you the way you deserve to be loved."

It's more about us, isn't it, Lord? Yes, God seeks our families, but he is not finished with us yet, either. We still have our own soul's work left to do—in fact, plenty more than I thought possible before starting down this path. He is after our children's souls but also every bit as much after ours. We are not off the hook quite yet!

"There is severe discipline for him who forsakes the way; he who hates reproof will die" (Proverbs 15:10). Hearing these words read by Fr. Mike, I paused to pray: "Lord, help me be docile to you. Help me to be open to your teaching, even now. I am but a child before you, still." Reflecting further, I begged the Lord: "Do not let me fall into foolishness, forgetting that you are still molding my heart, too."

In that same podcast, Fr. Mike draws from Jeremiah 12:5, which asks, "If you have raced with men on foot, and they have wearied you, how will you compete with horses?" It's a reminder, he says, that we are limited in our own efforts, and will need God to finish the race well, because things will become harder before they get easier.

And yet God makes it clear that, despite the hardships ahead, he has a plan, and it is good. He is going to "pluck them up from the land," those who have forsaken him, and after he has done so, he will "again have compassion on them" and "bring them again each to his heritage, and each to his land." And when he does, "They will diligently learn the ways of my people, to swear by my name."

"In the midst of this chaos, there's this drop of hope," Fr. Mike says. "There's that sense of the Lord saying, 'Come back while there's still time.'" Maybe that's meant for our kids, but maybe it is meant more for us. "Is there any place in my life right now where God is asking me, at this moment, 'Hey, come back to me?'" Fr. Mike asks. "Maybe an area where you've grown cold?"

Fr. Mike seems to be saying that we need to check our own hearts first, asking, "Where in my life is God asking me to surrender my heart? To say, 'Okay, I am yours, now, always, and forever?'" If we take care of our part, the rest will follow, Fr. Mike suggests. But we have to do that, sincerely.

I think once more of St. Monica. In a way, it is too bad that her epitaph was written more with a nod to her son, for while her son's conversion was indeed a victory, for her and many, if Monica had not given her assent to God first, nor been docile to the leading of St. Ambrose, the rest might not have fallen into place.

No matter, I see now what I did not see before; that Augustine's was not the only heart that was deeply changed. Monica, through loving God above all and singing his praises despite her tears, was given a gift by God because of her faith. May that gift be ours to hold, too, whether on earth or in heaven, forever. Amen.

PATTI'S TAKEAWAYS

Writing this book has been transformative for Roxane and me. I hope reading it has been for you, as well. It forced us to go deeper in our own faith, often in ways not of our choosing. Most importantly, as spiritual dust was stirred up, sometimes creating discomfort and challenges, I reached for tools that were understood in deeper measures now. For instance, during irritations and challenges, I immediately started praising and thanking God while simultaneously offering up any negative feelings. I now more easily step back from the temptation of anger and muster feelings of love while turning my prayers on the source. These behaviors have become new habits and are reinforced by writing about them here. I step away with increased determination.

My most recent book, *Holy Hacks: Everyday Ways to Get to Heaven*, was about increasing our capacity to live holier lives and walk closer with our Lord with hundreds of ideas. This book continues that theme, but in a deeper way, targeting our children specifically to grow in personal holiness that will shine a light that will include them.

Initially, I had other plans for this book—that is, not writing it at all. I was waiting for that great happy ending where I would give hope to everyone based on the return of those who have strayed. Instead, thanks to Roxane's inspiration and persistence, I am walking alongside you, journeying closer to God, and pulling our children along with our heartstrings and the forces of heaven.

In the midst of working on this book, I visited my dad in Michigan. While there, I also visited my friend Fr. Joseph Marquis, pastor of Sacred Heart Byzantine Church in Livonia. He was excited to show me his latest first-class relic—an ankle bone of St. Augustine. As I looked at it, it took me a moment to absorb what was actually before me. The ankle of Augustine! With it, he fled from his mother to Rome. He used it in all his journeys as a priest and then as a bishop evangelizing the world. Now I was gazing upon it. I prayed: *St. Augustine, pray for us as we write this book, that it will help lead others to the Faith as you were once led.*

As we approached the submission deadline, August 31, the Novena to St. Monica was on tap for my email prayer group. Her feast is August 27, while St. Augustine's is on August 28. We had originally planned on completing the book in the spring but moved it back to accommodate our hectic schedules. In the end, it felt like St. Monica and St. Augustine were holding our hands all along.

Roxane and I are humbled to have written this book. So often along the way, we felt directed from above. Information we sometimes did not even know we needed would find us. At times, as I thought about this book, I have reflected: *You picked us, Lord? Lil' ol' Roxane and me?* I know it is not because we have impressive resumes for sainthood, but just the opposite.

One of my favorite saint stories is that of St. Margaret Mary Alacoque, the saint of the Sacred Heart Devotion. Jesus appeared at her convent in Paray le Monial, France, and revealed the burning love of his Sacred Heart. He wanted her to make this devotion known to the world. When Margaret questioned Jesus for choosing such a lowly person as herself for such an ambitious task, he responded that if he could have found someone lowlier, he would have.

Earlier, we heard from Fr. John Burns about the power of healing—something we hope we all have come closer to in learning about St. Monica's life. As we take leave, let us draw on the prayer this good priest's grandmother used to say to him each time they parted:

"Pray for me as I will for thee, that we may merrily meet in heaven."

Acknowledgments

After a series of intense and creative brainstorming sessions for *What Would Monica Do?*, Ascension set us free to write. At the word "Go!" we looked at our busy calendars and rearranged itineraries to meet the goal of a tight summer deadline. We rolled up our sleeves and got to work on this labor of love.

Along with our husbands, children, and grandchildren, who helped fill in the gaps left behind during our months-long obsession with everything Monica and Augustine, others came alongside in spurts to help us reach the finish line.

Firstly, a heartfelt nod to Ascension for their vigorous conversations and openness to our ideas, and for providing a wonderful title that doubles as a question—*What Would Monica Do?*—offering a beacon to us as we walked with Monica. Thank you for believing in our ability to pull off this incredibly timely and important endeavor. We owe a debt of gratitude to Joanne McHugh, who accompanied us and Monica steadfastly from beginning to end, along with our developmental editor, Mike Flickinger, who expertly trimmed our manuscript tome to a more manageable size.

We also would like to thank Matthew Pinto, our first Ascension contact and early collaborator. Given Patti's previous work with Matthew on the Amazing Grace series, it was a blessing and even a historic transition as he brainstormed and guided us just before turning the reins of Ascension over to the next president.

Additionally, half this book might not exist if not for the Carmel of Mary Monastery and Sisters of the Presentation Maryvale Convent, two North Dakota religious communities that offered hushed harbor for Roxane. The peaceful settings allowed her to attune her ears as St. Monica lovingly spoke into her heart.

Notably as well, this book would not be complete without the many personal stories shared with us; stories born through heartache and the quest for holiness, including accounts that did not make it into the final version but, nevertheless, contributed to the gain. The quiet prayers of friends also deserve a mention: thank you!

We'd also like to acknowledge our parents, those still on earth and those with God, who brought us the Catholic Faith and have instilled in us a desire to stay near Jesus through the sacraments. A special thanks to Patti's father, Frank, and Roxane's mother, Jane, who continue to pray for their children as we journey through life.

Finally, we wish to thank our heavenly helpers, beginning with the Holy Spirit, who kept us on course, along with our Blessed Mother, and, it goes without saying, St. Monica and her formidable son, St. Augustine, whose lives have inspired us and countless others. We hope, through this work, that their sacrifices find new life in the souls of many waiting for the turn of a loved one's heart toward our heavenly Father and his one, holy, Catholic, and apostolic Church.

Notes

1. George Barna, "New Insights into the Generation of Growing Influence: Millennials in America," *Cultural Research Center at Arizona Christian University* (October 2021), 41, available at foundationsoffreedom.com/.

2. "Day 98: Israel Asks for a King," in *The Bible in a Year (with Fr. Mike Schmitz)*™ podcast, produced by Ascension, available at ascensionpress.com and all podcast platforms.

3. Barna, "Millennials in America," 56.

4. George Barna, "The Seismic Generational Shift in Worldview: Millennials Seek a Nation Without God, Bible, and Churches," *Cultural Research Center at Arizona Christian University* (May 12, 2021), 5, available at arizonachristian.edu/.

5. Barna, 1.

6. Barna, 4.

7. Augustine of Hippo, *Confessions* (New York: Vintage Books, 1998), 183.

8. Jacques Philippe, *Time for God* (New York: Scepter, 2008), 15–16.

9. Giovanni Falbo, *St. Monica: The Power of a Mother's Love* (Boston: Pauline, 2007), 2.

10. Falbo.

11. Order of St. Augustine, "*Life of Augustine*: 1023 Augustine's childhood," augnet.org/.

12. Mike Aquilina and Mark Sullivan, *St. Monica and the Power of Persistent Prayer* (Huntington, IN: Our Sunday Visitor, 2013), 28.

13. Augustine, *Confessions*, xxxv.

14. Falbo, 35.

15. Francis, *Lumen fidei* (June 29, 2013), 57.

16. Falbo, 35.

17. Caitlin and Kent Lasnoski, *Thirty Days with Married Saints: A Catholic Couples' Devotional* (Boston: Pauline, 2021), 5.

18. Lasnoski, 5.

19. Falbo, 14.

20. Falbo, 18.

21. Tyler Rowley, *Because of Our Fathers: Twenty-Three Catholics Tell How Their Fathers Led Them to Christ* (San Francisco: Ignatius, 2020). Content shared in *Ave Maria Radio* interview, May 15, 2021, available at avemariaradio.net/.

22. Patti Armstrong, "Fierce Defender: St. Joseph Is 'Terror of Demons,'" *National Catholic Register*, March 19, 2021, ncregister.com/.

23. Interview with Emily Stimpson Chapman on the radio program *Real Presence Live*, air date July 12, 2021, *Real Presence Radio*, available at yourcatholicradiostation.com/node/55186.

24. Armstrong, "Fierce Defender."

25. Armstrong.

26. Jess Echeverry, *Dazzled: Finding the Key to Perfect Forgiveness* (Bloomington, IN: Balboa, 2020).

27. Fathers of the Church, "The Protoevangelium of James," newadvent.com/.

28. "St. Anne," ewtn.com/.

29. Anne Catherine Emmerich, *The Life of the Blessed Virgin Mary* (Charlotte, NC: TAN Books, 2011), 45.

30. Thomas Richter, "Our Treasured Place," talk presented as part of the 2018 Catholic Credence lecture series in Bismarck, ND.

31. Bartholomew J. O'Brien, *The Curé of Ars: Patron Saint of Parish Priests* (Charlotte, NC: TAN Books, 1987), 81, 83.

32. Falbo, 21–22.

33. Falbo, 22.

34. Gabriel Amorth with Marcello Stanzione, *The Devil Is Afraid of Me: The Life and Work of the World's Most Famous Exorcist* (Manchester, NH: Sophia Institute Press, 2020), 57.

35. These quotations of Fr. John Burns are from the EWTN *Women Made New* radio program, episode 20210626, June 26, 2021.

36. Quotations throughout this chapter are from the EWTN radio program *Called to Communion*, episode air date April 17, 2018, "How Do I Discuss Catholicism with Non-Catholics?"

37. Pew Research Center, "Majority of Public Favors Same-Sex Marriage, but Divisions Persist," May 14, 2019, pewresearch.org/.

38. Falbo, 37.

39. Falbo, 41.

40. Patti Armstrong, "How to Recognize Demonic Activity in the Church Scandals, According to an Exorcist," *National Catholic Register*, September 5, 2018, ncregister.com/.

41. Patti Armstrong, "Victimized Family Finds Healing in the Church," *Our Sunday Visitor*, November 30, 2018.

42. Patti Armstrong, "Clerical Abuse Survivor: Faith Is a 'Powerful Tool to Heal,'" *National Catholic Register*, November 21, 2020, ncregister.com/.

43. Armstrong.

44. Christopher Wells, "Pope Reflects on Holy Family at Sunday Angelus," *Vatican News*, December 27, 2020, vaticannews.va/.

45. F.A. Forbes, "How Augustine Went to Carthage, and How Patricius Died a Christian Death," chap. 5 in *The Life of Saint Monica*, 2nd ed. (London: R. & T. Washbourne, 1928).

46. Forbes.

47. Forbes.

48.   Forbes, "How St. Monica's Heart Was Well Nigh Broken by the News That Her Son Had Abjured the Christian Faith," chap. 7 in *The Life of Saint Monica*.

49.   Eve Tushnet, "My View: Catholic, Lesbian, Celibate, and the Journey to Self-Acceptance," *Deseret News*, September 21, 2016, deseret.com/.

50.   Grand View Research, "U.S. Sex Reassignment Surgery Market Size, Share & Trends Analysis Report By Gender Transition (Male To Female, Female To Male), And Segment Forecasts, 2020–2027," December 2020, grandviewresearch.com/.

51.   Catholic News Agency, "Vatican Says 'No' to Transsexual Godparents amid Spain Controversy," *CNA*, September 2, 2015, catholicnewsagency.com/.

52.   Francis, *Amoris laetitia* (March 19, 2016), 285, 304.

53.   Francis, Address to the General Assembly of the Pontifical Academy for Life, October 5, 2017.

54.   Tom Nash, "The Church's Position on 'Transgenderism,'" *Catholic Answers*, catholic.com/.

55.   Stephen Rossetti, *Diary of an American Exorcist: Demons, Possession, and the Modern-Day Battle Against Ancient Evil* (Manchester, NH: Sophia Institute Press, 2021), 157–158.

56.   Kathleen Beckman, *A Family Guide to Spiritual Warfare: Strategies for Deliverance and Healing* (Manchester, NH: Sophia Institute Press, 2020), 7.

57.   Beckman, 9.

58.   All quotes in this section are from Ray Guarendi, *The Doctor Is In*, air date August 6, 2021, *Ave Maria Radio*, avemariaradio.net/.

59.   Falbo, 41.

60.   Falbo.

61.   Forbes, "How St. Monica Lived in the Pagan Household of Her Husband Patricius," chap. 2 in *The Life of Saint Monica*.

62.   Forbes.

63.   Jean Paul de Caussade, *Self-Abandonment to Divine Providence* (Charlotte, NC: TAN Books, 1993), 113.

64.   Caussade.

65. Caussade.

66. Peter Kreeft, *Summa of the Summa* (San Francisco: Ignatius, 1990), 108.

67. Caussade, 193.

68. Walter J. Ciszek, *He Leadeth Me: An Extraordinary Testament of Faith* (New York: Image, 1973), 20.

69. Ciszek, 47–48.

70. Ciszek, 50.

71. Ciszek, 57, 59.

72. Ciszek, 58, 61.

73. Ciszek, 75.

74. Ciszek, 82, 83.

75. Ciszek, 114.

76. Ciszek, 125.

77. Ciszek, 127.

78. Jeff Cavins, *When You Suffer: Biblical Keys for Hope and Understanding* (Cincinnati, OH: Servant, 2015), 5.

79. Cavins, 31.

80. Tom Bissett, *Good News About Prodigals* (Grand Rapids, MI: Discovery House, 1998), 21.

81. Bisset, 22.

82. Bisset, 21.

83. See Jeff Cavins, Matthew Pinto, and Patti Maguire Armstrong, ed., *Amazing Grace for the Catholic Heart: 101 Stories of Faith, Inspiration, Hope, and Humor* (West Chester, PA: Ascension, 2004); and Emily Cavins et al., ed., *Amazing Grace for Catholic Mothers: 101 Stories of Faith, Inspiration, Hope, and Humor* (West Chester, PA: Ascension, 2004), available at ascensionpress.com.

84. All quotations in this section are from Falbo, 45.

85. Jim Keating, "Giving God Your Worries," talk at Kenrick–Glennon Seminary, St. Louis, January 21, 2021, available at youtube.com/.

86. Keating.

87. Forbes, "How St. Monica Lived in the Days of Her Widowhood, and How She Put All Her Trust in God," chap. 6 in *The Life of Saint Monica*.

88. Forbes.

89. Bissett, 31.

90. Bissett, 32.

91. Alyssa Bormes, *Catholic Kaleidoscope*, May 31, 2015, *Radio Maria*, radiomaria.us/.

92. Bissett, 20.

93. Bissett.

94. Bissett, 44–45.

95. Jacques Philippe, *Interior Freedom* (New York: Scepter, 2007), 9.

96. Philippe, 15.

97. Philippe, 16.

98. Philippe, 20.

99. Philippe.

100. Philippe, 21.

101. Philippe, 30.

102. Philippe, 31.

103. Philippe.

104. Forbes, chap. 7.

105. Forbes.

106. Jeff Cavins, *Praise God and Thank Him: Biblical Keys for a Joyful Life* (Cincinnati: Servant, 2014), xiv.

107. Cavins.

108. Cavins, xv–xvii.

109. Cavins, 6.

110. Cavins.

111. Cavins, 28.

112. Cavins, 100.

113. Author interview, August 11, 2021.

114. Maria Faustina Kowalska, *Diary: Divine Mercy in My Soul* (Stockbridge, MA: Marian Press, 1979), 529.

115. Kowalska, 139.

116. Kowalska, 811.

117. William Goh, homily on voluntary fasting, February 19, 2021.

118. Goh.

119. Beckman, 146.

120. Kowalska, 47.

121. Kowalska, 299.

122. Kowalska, 1541.

123. Kowalska, 1320.

124. Kowalska, 1572.

125. Hans Urs von Balthasar and Josef Ratzinger, *Mary: The Church at the Source* (San Francisco: Ignatius, 2005), 14.

126. von Balthasar and Ratzinger, 15.

127. Content quoted in this section is from an online prayer practicum participated in by author, July 6, 2021.

128. von Balthasar and Ratzinger, 15.

129. von Balthasar and Ratzinger.

130. von Balthasar and Ratzinger, 16.

131. Bissett, 70.

132. Bissett.

133. Bissett, 70–71.

134. Bissett, 71.

135. Bissett, 72.

136. Bissett, 73.

137. Bissett, 76.

138. Bissett, 77.

139. Bissett.

140. Bissett, 38.

141. Bissett, 38–39.

142. Bissett, 38.

143. Bissett, 39.

144. Clarence Thomas, Address to the students of Christendom College, May 14, 2018.

145. Karen Edmisten, *Deathbed Conversions: Finding Faith at the Finish Line* (Huntington, IN: Our Sunday Visitor, 2013), 12.

146. Edmisten, 36.

147. Edmisten, 37.

148. Edmisten, 14.

149. Edmisten, 59.

150. Michael H. Brown, *A Life of Blessings* (Palm Coast, FL: Spirit Daily, 2012).

151. See Augustine, *Confessions*, 10.24.

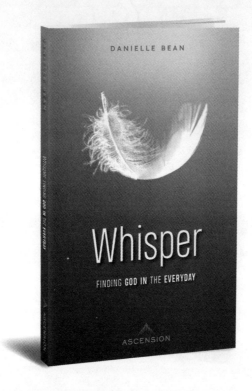

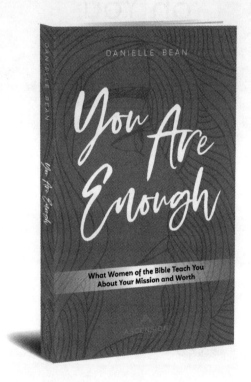